STORMING THE TOWER

STORMING
◄ THE ►
TOWER

WOMEN IN THE ACADEMIC WORLD

**Edited by SUZANNE STIVER LIE
and VIRGINIA E O'LEARY**

Kogan Page, London/Nichols/G P Publishing, New York

First published in Great Britain in 1990 by Kogan Page Ltd
120 Pentonville Road, London N1 9JN

Typeset in 11/13pt Cheltenham by The Castlefield Press
of Wellingborough, Northants, and printed and bound
in Great Britain by Biddles Ltd, Guildford.

British Library Cataloguing in Publication Data

A CIP catalogue record for this book is available from the British Library.
ISBN 1 85091 872 4

First published in the United States of America in 1990 by Nichols Publishing, an imprint of GP Publishing, 11 Harts Lane, East Brunswick, New Jersey 08816

Library of Congress Cataloging-in-Publication Data

Storming the tower: women in the academic world/edited by Suzanne Lie and Virginia O'Leary.
    p.cm.
   Includes bibliographical references.
   ISBN 0-89397-404-8
   1. Women college teachers. 2. Sex discrimination in education.
I. Lie, Suzanne Stiver. II. O'Leary, Virginia E., 1943– .
LB2332.3.S85 1990
378.1'2082--dc20

90-46012
CIP

Contents

Acknowledgements

There are many people whose support was invaluable in the preparation of this volume. Ailbhe Smyth helped to formulate the original conception. Margherita Rendel provided early insights. Marian Chamberlain's encouragement was continuous. Betty Nicolaisen retyped many manuscript pages in the final days of editing. Steen-Olsen patiently converted and reconverted discs. Dolores Black at Kogan Page waited quietly when it became clear that we needed more time.

Thanks are due to the Institute for Educational Research at the University of Oslo and the Henry A Murray Research Center for the Study of Lives at Radcliffe College, Harvard University, for the use of their facilities and resources.

A final word of thanks is due to our families. Kisa and Kristina Lie did for themselves for extended periods so that Suzanne was free to work uninterrupted. Herb Eisenberg and Sean O'Leary cheered us on.

Foreword

Like so many feminist projects, the route to this volume's completion was beset with obstacles and detours. The idea was conceived in 1983 when Suzanne learned that her husband was to be assigned to the Norwegian Embassy in London. The prospect of moving the family to the United Kingdom for an extended period raised the question of how best to continue her own scholarly work in educational sociology. In her view, the opportunity to engage in a comparative study of the status of women in academe was appealing, given the promise of access to a Kyvik's recent study of sex differences in productivity among Norwegian faculty. She applied for the funds to conduct a study comparing female and male academics in Norway, the United Kingdom and the United States. Securing the funds was to take five years.

In the interim, she went to London where she read and was impressed by Ailbhe Smyth's work, as well as that of Margherita Rendel. If she could not obtain the funds for a comparative empirical study, why not put together a volume of comparative case studies focusing on the academic experience of women? She contacted Smyth at University College in Dublin and asked her to co-edit such a book. Smyth agreed and together they drew up a list of potential contributors and found a publisher. In the summer of 1987 Suzanne attended the Third International Congress on Women in Dublin where she learned that Ailbhe Smyth's health and family commitments had forced her withdrawal from the project. That same week she met Virginia and invited her to co-edit the volume.

In March 1988 Suzanne spent a week in Boston where Virginia was a Visiting Scholar at Radcliffe and the two finalized the list of contributors and completed the book prospectus. The original publisher had by this time completed the series of which the book was intended to be part, so another round of inquiries began. A contract with Kogan Page was signed that autumn and the 'real work' began.

Suzanne's spouse Kia accepted a Fellowship at the Centre for International Affairs at Harvard in 1988, and in January Suzanne and their daughter Kristina joined him for the semester. Suzanne was a Visiting Scholar at the Henry A Murray Research Center for the Study of Lives at Radcliffe College, Harvard University and affiliated with the Graduate School of Education at Harvard. Many of the chapters in this volume were completed at that time. Access to a facsimile machine was invaluable during this period, especially for communication with colleagues in the UK and Turkey.

The final editing of the manuscript was done at Suzanne's home in Oslo, where Kisa and Kristina took over the household chores to free Suzanne and Virginia to work uninterrupted. The final weeks of the project were fraught with small crises – such as incompatible discs that defied all attempts at conversion – and filled with laughter. In the end more was accomplished than time allowed, testifying again to the value of feminist commitment and perseverance.

The funds for the comparative study have finally come through and Suzanne will be meeting with a small group of researchers in Paris this summer to begin designing a study to examine the status of academic women around the world. Anyone interested in contributing to this project should contact her directly at the Institute for Educational Research at the University of Oslo.

Suzanne Stiver Lie
Virginia E O'Leary
Oslo
June 1990

Notes on the Contributors

Feride Acar is an Associate Professor at the Department of Public Administration, Middle East Technical University, Ankara. She has written widely on women's issues. Her publications include, 'Turkish Women in Academia; Roles and Careers', in *METU Studies in Development*, and 'Women in the Ideology of Islamic Revivalism in Turkey: Three Islamic Women's Journals', in Richard Tapper (ed), *Islam in Turkey* (forthcoming).

Adrienne M Aziz is Assistant General Secretary to the Association of University Teachers in the UK. She is responsible for the equal opportunities area of work in the Association and has given written evidence to numerous government and public bodies. She also holds public appointments on a regional health authority and on an industrial tribunal panel.

Helen S Astin is Professor of Higher Education and Associate Director of the Higher Education Research Institute at UCLA. She has been President of the Division of the Psychology of Women of the American Psychological Association. Her major books include: *The Woman Doctorate in America* and *The Higher Education of Women*.

Evelyn Torten Beck was born in Vienna and emigrated to the United States in 1940. She has won fellowships from the American Council of Learned Societies and the National Endowment for the Humanities. She is currently Professor and Director of Women's Studies at the University of Maryland-College Park. Her major published works include *The Prism of Sex*, and *Nice Jewish Girls*.

Diane E Davis is currently Assistant Professor of Sociology at the New School for Social Research. She is co-author of several publications on gender and productivity, including 'Reputational Standing in Academe', in the *Journal of Higher Education* and 'Research Productivity Across the Life and Career Cycles: Barriers and Facilitators for Women', in Mary Frank Fox (ed), *Scholarly Writing and Publishing: Issues, Problems and Solutions*.

Jennie Farley is Professor of Industrial and Labor Relations at Cornell University. She has authored or edited five books on women workers in academic life and in industry. She served as a co-founder of Cornell's Women's Studies Program and as its first director.

Veena Gill is Lecturer in Political Science, St Stephen's College, University of Delhi and is presently an Assistant Professor at the University of Bergen. She was the recipient of a Ford Foundation Scholarship at the Australian National University. Gill is a doctoral candidate at the University of Oslo and has written extensively on military aspects of the politics of developing nations.

Anne Hawkins hails from England, but her career has spanned three continents. She is a formal Director of the UNESCO Experimental Program, Educational Technology in Asia. She is also a former Senior Lecturer in the Department of Research and Development at the University of Utrecht, and Webster University, Leiden. She is presently Educational Consultant with the International College of Business Administration in Zeist.

Celia Kitzinger is Senior Lecturer in Social Psychology at the Polytechnic of East London. She is the author of *The Social Construction of Lesbianism*, recipient of a Distinguished Publication Award from the Association for Women in Psychology and co-author (with Sheila Kitzinger) of *Talking with Children About Things that Matter*.

Suzanne Lie is Associate Professor in Educational Sociology, Institute for Educational Research, University of Oslo. She is author of *Immigrant Women in Norway*; she has edited several volumes on immigrant women and has published widely on women in higher education. She has been a Visiting Scholar at the University of London, Institute of Education and at Murray Center, Radcliffe College, Harvard University. Currently she is Director of Women's Studies for the Social Science Faculty at the University of Oslo.

Judith Mitchell is a recent PhD in Counseling/Educational Psychology from the University of California, Los Angeles. She is Staff Research Associate in Public Health, University of California, Los Angeles where she specializes in statistical analysis in AIDS and family planning research.

Virginia E O'Leary is the author of *Toward Understanding Women,* co-editor of *Women, Gender and Social Psychology,* and has written numerous articles on women and work. Twice recipient of the Association for Women in Psychology's Distinguished Publication Award, O'Leary is currently Professor and Chair of the Department of Psychology at Indiana State University.

Pamela Trotman Reid is Professor and Head of the Department of Psychology at the University of Tennessee at Chattanooga. She is a former Director of the Office of Social and Ethical Responsibility of the American Psychological Association. She is currently an associate editor of *The Psychology of Women Quarterly* and is editing a special issue of *Sex Roles* on 'Gender and Ethnicity'.

Dagmar Schultz is publisher of the Orlanda Frauenverlag (women's publishing house), editor of an anthology of texts by Audre Lorde and Adrienne Rich, and co-editor of *German Feminism: Readings in Politics and Literature.* Her study on the work situation of female and male professors at West German universities will be published this year.

Nina Toren is Senior Lecturer in Organizational Theory and Behavior at the School of Business Administration, The Hebrew University in Jerusalem. Among her numerous publications are *Social Work: The Case of a Semi-Profession,* and *Science and Cultural Context: Soviet Scientists in Comparative Perspective.*

Berit Ås is Associate Professor at the Institute of Psychology, University of Oslo. She has been a Visiting Professor at US and Canadian universities. She has published widely in traffic safety, consumer research, adult education, peace and women's studies. Her major English works include: *Women in All Countries: Handbook for Liberation,* and *Sisterhood is Global.* She is the founder of the Feminist University of Norway.

Part I
Introduction

Chapter 1

In the Same Boat? Academic Women Around the World

Suzanne Stiver Lie and *Virginia E O'Leary*

Storming the tower is a lonely business, as any academic woman who has tried can tell you. Even with the support of other feminists in one's own institution or country the sense of isolation can be overwhelming. This volume is dedicated to reducing the sense of isolation among women engaged in the worldwide struggle to break down the walls of the ivory tower.

The book contains a collection of papers dealing with various aspects of the careers of women in academic life from an international, comparative perspective. Information detailing the status of academic women in nine countries – India, Israel, Jordan, Norway, The Federal Republic of Germany, The Netherlands, The United Kingdom, the United States and Turkey – is included along with analyses of these women's experiences in socio-historical context. The authors were selected to parallel the experience of women in academic settings: some have well-deserved international reputations in their respective fields, while others are virtually unknown, not because their work lacks merit but because the patriarchal system has prevented them from receiving the recognition they deserve. Thus, both the authors and the topics included in this volume represent the reality of academic women around the world in the decade before the millennium.

As gatekeepers, academic women have the potential to play a critical role in shaping tomorrow's woman today. It is, therefore, important to understand their 'herstory' and their ideological commitment to improving the status of women in the academy. This volume attempts to do just that.

Women have struggled for centuries to gain access to higher education, both as students and as scholars. The rationale for their exclusion from the educational arena has traditionally centred on their inferior intellectual ability. For example, Aristotle contended that in comparison to men, women were biologically defective, rendering them morally and spiritually inferior. In his view, women were not creative, and their souls were incapable of reaching the last stage of reason. Given their underdeveloped brains, women could not be educated. History is replete with more recent versions of this Aristotelian argument.

The French philosopher Rousseau, writing in the late 1700s, expressed a view on the education of women that typifies the attitude of many men of letters even today.

The whole education of women ought to be relative to men. To please them, to be useful to them, to make themselves loved and honoured by them, to educate them when young, to care for them when grown, to counsel them, to console them and to make life sweet and agreeable to them – these are the duties of women at all times, and should be taught them from their infancy. (In Martin 1984, p 34)

During the late 1800s women's intellect was defined in the range between that of animals and men. Educated women were regarded as 'asexual and grotesque' (McDonagh 1989). It was widely feared that educating women would incapacitate them for their biological tasks. In England, Herbert Spence, who was initially positive about women's education, expressed caution for fear that the development of women's intellect would diminish their reproductive powers, and threaten 'the welfare of posterity' (Bryant 1979). Edward H Clarke, author of the sensational bestseller *Sex and Education* published in 1873, argued that the brain required excessive blood when in active use, and that women could ill afford to use their brains for fear blood would 'be drawn away from the nervous system and reproductive organs' (Frankfort 1977, quoted in McDonagh 1989, p 46). The medical faculty in Norway used this same argument in 1884 in trying to deny women admittance to medical school.

As Oakley (1981) so aptly observes, the scientific evidence for the arguments against women's education coincided precisely with periods of feminist activism or the threat thereof. For example, concern about women's fragile constitutions occurred in conjunction with the Industrial Revolution and the concomitant increase in women with enough leisure time to pursue intellectual interests. Until recently the backlash has been sufficient to stem the tide of women entering higher education and the professions.

The admission of women (and Blacks) to institutions of higher education began in the USA in 1833 with the establishment of Oberlin College. The first Bachelor's degree was awarded to a woman there in 1841. The admission of women to Oberlin was predicated in part on the requirement that all students work while attending school – household tasks were 'women's work', so women students were welcomed to do them.

The dates when women were first granted admission to institutions of higher education and the dates when the first degrees were granted to women in each of the nine countries represented in this volume are presented in Table 1.1. Although the dates of admission and matriculation appear to coincide, the story is more complex than it appears. For example, although women were allowed to study for degree examinations at Cambridge University as early as 1869, they were not allowed to attend university lectures. Indeed, it was not until 1947 that they were formally admitted to the university on the same terms as men (see Chapter 2). The University of Durham's College of Science in Newcastle began admitting women to all scientific courses in 1871, and women were allowed to take degrees at the University of London beginning in 1878 (Rendel 1980). Clearly the situation varied greatly from institution to institution within the same country.

In the USA women's enthusiastic response to the opportunity to obtain advanced degrees was a cause for alarm. The enrolment of women in higher education between 1870 and 1900 multiplied almost eightfold. There was real fear that women would take over the colleges, as their enrolment rose from 21 to 34 per cent during this period. At the University of Chicago the percentage of women students rose from 24 to 52 per cent in the first decade of its existence (1892 to 1902). During this period women received a majority (56.3 per cent) of the Phi Beta Kappa awards. To stem the tide of women students, Chicago instituted sex-segregated classes. Responding to a similar problem, the University of California established junior colleges all over the state (Solomon 1985). Bryant (1979) describes the growth of women in higher education in England during this time as 'the unexpected revolution'. The revolution was no more welcome than it was expected.

Of course there were examples of educated women in early history, but they were always the exception to the rule. For example there were female scholars in India during the Vendic period (1500 to 600 BC) (see Chapter 11). In ancient Egypt there was a tradition of women practising medicine. Nuns did scientific work in cloisters from 700 to 1400 AD, and there were a few women professors of philosophy in Bologna in the 1200s. The first woman in the world to be granted a PhD was Elena Lucrezia Cornaro Piscopia, who stood for her orals in Padua at her father's insistence in 1687.

In the course of the hundred years or so which have passed since the doors of the university were opened to them, the proportion of women students has increased steadily. Today women represent roughly half of all undergraduate students enrolled in higher education in Israel, Norway, and the USA (see Table 1.2 on p 22).

Paralleling the increase in women undergraduates has been a dramatic, albeit much slower, increase in the number of women

Table 1.1 *Year women first admitted to institutions of higher education and degree programmes in the countries under study.**

Events (Year of first occurrence)	India	Israel	Jordan	Netherlands	Norway	Turkey	United Kingdom	US	West Germany
Right to study at university	1877	1925	1964 (Jordan univ. est.)	1871	1882	1915	1871	1833	1908
Right to take an academic degree	1883	1925	N/I	1878	1884	1917	1878	1841	1908

Sources

*Countries are listed in alphabetical order.

Information was supplied by the contributors of this volume as well as Margherita Rendel, School of Education, University of London and Marilyn Safir, University of Haifa.

N/I = No information available.
United Kingdom includes England, Wales, Scotland and Northern Ireland.

engaged in graduate study. Despite the adequacy of the current pool of potential women faculty, the history of their entry into faculty ranks continues to be disheartening. At Cornell the first woman to be named to an assistant professorship in nature study (now known as botany) was quickly demoted back to lecturer by the board of trustees (see Farley in this volume). Later, when it was proposed that women teaching in the College of Home Economics be promoted to faculty rank, a male professor protested, 'Cooks on the Cornell faculty? Never!' By 1921, there were 8516 assistant, associate and full professors at US universities and colleges. Of these, only 627 (7 per cent) were women (Kasper 1989). In 1989, women constituted 25 per cent of the faculty in US institutions of higher education, but they were unequally distributed at the lower ranks and among the least prestigious centres for learning. And the future is not very encouraging. According to Farley's analysis of the faculty at Cornell University (see Chapter 12), it will take until the year 3000 before women are as well represented on the faculty there as they currently are among students. Even women who have managed to enter academe have not fared very well once inside.

As can be seen in Table 1.3, the higher the position in the academic hierarchy, the fewer the women represented there, regardless of the country under scrutiny. The much-touted progress of women in the world of work has been restricted primarily to entry-level positions in both education and in industry.

Ironically, of all the countries represented in this volume, only Turkey, a Muslim nation, has a substantial percentage of women (20 per cent; see Chapter 8) represented at the rank of full professor. According to Acar (in this volume) the explanation for this phenomenon lies at least in part in the unique role assigned to elite women in the process of westernizing Turkey. Perhaps even more importantly, the total pool of highly educated individuals in Turkey is so small that restrictions based on sex are of relatively little concern. Historically, women's talents have been more readily recognized when talents in general are in short supply, such as times of war.

Despite the variations across the cultures represented in this volume, the fact that women lag significantly behind their male counterparts in promotion to positions of power and prestige in the academic marketplace in each of the countries represented is all too clear. As we shall see, the communalities of experience among academic women far exceed their differences at either the individual or institutional level.

The book is divided into four sections. The first section focuses on defining the problems faced by women in academe, who are treated as the 'other' because of their sex and whose additional status characteristics such as age, marital status and ethnic-minority representation often result in added stigmatization. Adrienne Aziz, a British educator,

Table 1.2 *Enrolment of women in higher education in the countries under study.**

	India (1984/85)	Israel (1986/87)	Jordan (1979–82)	Netherlands 1986–88	Norway (1985)	Turkey (1989)	US (1984–86)	United Kingdom (1987/88)	West Germany (1985)
Education at the third level* %	1975 '80 23 26	1975 '85 46 46	1975 '84 33 44	1975 '84 33 41	1975 '85 38 47	1975 '84 16 31	1975 '85 45 52	1975 '84 36 45	1975 '85 39 42
% of female enrol. at university level (undergraduate)	28.5	50 (total enrol.)	39.2 (1982)	41.3 (1986)	52	37.0	51.0 (1984/85)	43.4	37.7 (total enrol.)
% of female enrol. at postgraduate level	29.9	N/I	14.8 (1979/80)	39.0 (1986)	33	34.0	N/I	39.0	N/I
Master's level or equival.	N/I	43	9.9 (1979)	N/I	N/I	36.0	50.0 (1984/85)	33.3	N/I
Doctorate level or equival.	N/I	31	5.3 (1979)	25.4 (1988)	20	38.1	35.5 (1986)	25.2	N/I

*Countries are listed in alphabetical order.

N/I = No information available.

Sources

*Education at the third level, which requires a minimum condition of admission, the successful completion of education at the second level (eg at middle school, secondary school, high school, teacher-training school at this level, schools of a vocational or technical nature) or evidence of the attainment of an equivalent level of knowledge (eg at university, teachers' college, higher professional school). *Unesco Statistical Digest* 1987.

India: Postgraduate level includes degrees similar to US master's and doctorate levels. Compiled from University Grants Commission Report, 1984–85.

Israel: Recipients of second-level degrees similar to US master's degree. Recipients of third-level degree similar to US doctorate level (see Toren this volume).

Jordan: Haj-Ismail, Hanan (1987), *The Participation of Women in the Government Sector in Jordan*, Unpublished MS thesis, Department of Public Administration, Middle East Technical University, Ankara. Barcaive, Abeer Adnan (1986), The role of Jordanian women in development, paper prepared for the conference, 'Arab Women's Roles in Development', Tunisia.

Netherlands: Enrolment of women in Dutch universities in the Netherlands in 1986, HOOP (Hoger Onderwijs en Onderzoek Plan) (Higher Education and Research Plan) Volume 2 Feiten en Cijfers (Facts and Figures) Ministerie van Onderwijs en Wetenschappen (Ministry of Education and Science) Den Haag (The Hague) 1987. From Table 345, 3rd Version 'Hoop' Facts and Figures (Courtesy Ministry of Education and Science).

Norway: 52 per cent new students, 33 per cent recipients of higher degrees, 20 per cent recipients of doctor degrees in 1985. St meld nr 28 (1988–89), om forskning, pp 14–15.

Turkey: *The 1988–89 Academic Year Higher Education Statistics*, Student Selection and Placement Center, Ankara, 1989.

United Kingdom: Includes England, Wales, Scotland and Northern Ireland. At undergraduate level: Central Statistical Office, Tables 3.18 & 3.17, 1987/88. Women students domiciled in UK. *University Statistics 1987–88* vol 1 Students and Staff, 1988. At postgraduate level: Universities Statistical Record/University Grants Committee. Cheltenham, extracted from Table 1. These figures include students from abroad. Special thanks to Margherita Rendel, School of Education, University of London for gathering these figures.

US: (Recipients of BAs and MAs) US Department of Education, National Center for Educational Statistics, 1986 in Fox, Mary Frank (1989), Women and higher education: gender differences in the status of students and scholars, in *Women: A Feminist Perspective*, edited by J Freeman, Mountain view, Calif: Mayfield. (Recipients of PhDs) Camberlain, M (ed) (1989): *Women in Academe: Progress and Prospects*, New York: Russell Sage Foundation.

West Germany: Statistisches Jahrbuch der BAD, quoted in Zentraleinrichtung zur Forderung von Frauenstudien und Frauenforschung an der Freien Universitat Berlin, Frauen in Schule und Hochschule im Bundesgebiet und Berlin (W), Fraueninformationsblatt, Freie Universitat Berlin 1988. p 18.

Table 1.3 *Women's share of faculty positions in higher education (per cent)*

Status group**	India (1979/80)	Israel (1983)	Jordan (1989)	Netherlands (1988)	Norway (1987)	Turkey (1989)	USA (1986)	United Kingdom (1987/88)	West Germany (1986)
Full professor	N/I	10.0	2	2.1	6	20.0	12.3	3.0	5.1
Assoc. prof.	N/I	15.0	6	4.6	18	22.7	24.6	6.0	
Assis. prof.	N/I	42.0	10	15.1		26.8	38.4	14.0 (Lecturer) 32.0 (Contract Researcher)	12.7
Instructor	N/I	33.0	72	26.5		30.3	53.3	N/A	19.7
Lecturer	N/I		23		31	N/A	49.5	N/A	25.5
Women's share of faculty jobs All ranks	22 (Colleges of gen. ed.) 10 (Univ.) 14 (Prof. sch.)	12.5	15	18.0	19	32.2	26.9 (1982/83)	18.8	15.0

*Countries are listed in alphabetical order.   **Exact comparisons between the countries are not possible because the categories and definitions vary. Only general conclusions and broad parallels can be made.   N/I = No information available.

Sources

India: No information available for the academic staff by gender. See Chapter 11.

Israel: See Chapter 5.

Jordan (1989): *The University of Jordan Statistical Yearbook 1988–89.* Planning and Statistical Dept p 165. Figures pertain to women academics at the University of Jordan only and not Jordanian women academics. Statistics for the latter are not available. The above figures do not include part-time faculty members.

Netherlands: Reader and senior lecturer are similar to US associate professor. Lecturer is similar to US assistant professor. Third version 'HOOP' Facts and Figures, December 1988 (courtesy Ministry of Education and Science), Table 345.

Norway: Norges allmennvitenskpelige forskningsråd (NAVF) (1989): *NAVFs sekretariat for kvinne forskning- en evaluering. rapport.* In Norway the junior staff is similar to US research assistants and those on scholarships are regarded as lecturers (see Chapter 7).

Turkey: Acar, F. (1991): Women in academic science careers in Turkey in *From Token Women to Gender Equity in Science,* V Stolte-Heiskanen et al (eds). UNESCO and International Social Science Council Publication, forthcoming.

United Kingdom: Includes England, Wales, Scotland and Northern Ireland. Readers and senior lecturers are similar to US associate professor. Lecturer and contract researcher are similar to US assistant professor. Contract research staff are appointed on salary points on the lecturer pay scale. They are always appointed on the lowest salary points on that scale, and generally reappointed on the same low points when their contract is renewed. Statistics taken from *University Statistical Record,* Volume 3, 1987/88.

US: Fox, Mary Frank (1989). Women and higher education: gender differences in the status of students and scholars, in *Women: A Feminist Perspective,* edited by J Freeman, Mountain view, Calif. Mayfield.

West Germany: Full professor (tenured) includes associate professors; assistant professors (non-tenured, usually limited to 6 years); teaching assistants are similar to US instructors, lecturers or persons with special tasks. Wissenschaftliches und Kunstlerisches Personal (1986): Bundesgebiet und Berlin, Tabell 38. Hauptberufliches wissenschaftliches und kunstlerisches Personal an den Hochschulen im Bundesgebiet und Berlin (W) 1980, 1982, 1984 und 1986.

examines the proportion of women academicians promoted in the context of the number available by area of specialization in recent years and finds little reason for optimism. In the UK, as in other countries, women are disproportionately numerous in the lower grades and in the lower salary points of those grades. Further, the current trend to make short-term appointments at academic and related levels has escalated the rate at which women are squeezed out of the competition for permanent academic posts. The result of this trend is the increased 'casualization' of women in academic employment settings. The prospects for the future centre on change from within, with a determined effort to monitor the situation toward the end of initiating effective strategies to recruit, retain, train, retrain and develop women academics, recognizing them for the great national resource they represent.

Ann Hawkins, an educator, and Dagmar Schultz, a political scientist, explore sex discrimination in higher education in the Netherlands and the Federal Republic of Germany, respectively. Although the data clearly attest to the existence of sex discrimination in West Germany, women professors deny that they have been its victims. A cultural reconstructionist explanation is offered for women's patterns of denial, in contrast to the more overt strategies used by men to deal with the harsh realities of the academic world. An analysis of the recruitment and retention data in both countries reveals that women are less likely than men to be hired, and also less likely to be promoted.

During the last 15 years increased attention has focused on mentoring and networking as underutilized resources for women who have difficulty gaining access to the information and contacts they need to advance in their academic careers. Networking among peers does seem to provide a level of emotional support for many women, but it is less useful in establishing contacts necessary to enhance their professional careers. In contrast, relationships with mentors are an ideal way to gain the sponsorship of senior colleagues, but when the relationship is cross-sex there is the risk that it will be perceived as sexually motivated. Same-sex mentoring relationships can also be problematic because they are often viewed as burdensome by senior women who, when they are reluctant to meet the demands of their proteges for emotional as well as professional support, risk being labelled 'Queen Bees'. Virginia O'Leary and Judith Mitchell, both US psychologists, suggest that the combination of networking at the peer level and finding a mentor upon whom one is careful to place realistic demands is a creative, practical solution to women's need to acquire the wisdom of superiors and the emotional support of those in similar positions simultaneously.

The final chapter in the section on defining the problem is by Israeli sociologist Nina Toren. Her piece focuses on the structural impact of the inequitable distribution of women and men in academic departments. The results of her study reveal that the smaller the percentage of women in a given academic department, the more hierarchical (traditionally male) its structure. In Israel as in other countries, women's representation in the sciences is disproportionately low compared to the humanities and social sciences. Interestingly, however, women's status is lower in those settings where the male-to-female ratio approaches equality, suggesting that under some conditions increased numbers render women less salient and neutralize their potential power.

The second section of the book is devoted to an exploration of barriers to productivity. One of the most controversial subjects in the study of higher education is academic productivity. Are academic women as productive as men? Do the strains of marriage, household or family impinge upon women's ability to compete and produce in the academic world? If academic women are able to prove themselves competent, are they rewarded equally in terms of rank, salary, and reputation? Diane Davis, a sociologist, and Helen Astin, a psychologist, explore these questions, focusing on women in the United States. They conclude that women's productivity patterns are governed by their own individual motives, commitments and values, as well as by larger social and institutional pressures and constraints. The implications of this perspective are addressed with the aim of breaking myths and exposing truths about the productivity patterns of academic women.

Suzanne Stiver Lie, an educational sociologist, examines the rewards and costs of combining the multiple demands of career and family. Because recent empirical studies on sex differences in productivity find that married women are more productive than single women there has been a tendency to dismiss family as an explanation for the lower rates of productivity in comparison to men. Lie's investigation of Norwegian female academics' productivity suggests that family demands do make a difference when life-course analyses are used. Married women with children under the age of ten do show a dip in their productivity during this period. This dip contributes to their cumulative disadvantage in comparison to men and results in an average promotional lag of five years' duration. Importantly, older married women are as productive on the average as their male counterparts.

Little is known in the West about the lives of academic women in the Muslim world. Feride Acar, a Turkish political scientist, recently conducted a cross-cultural study of Turkish and Jordanian university teachers, their role priorities and career patterns. Academic women's own perceptions of their various roles and relationships in society are examined. Dramatic differences in role behaviour and self-esteem of academic women in these two countries help to expose as a myth the notion that the Muslim world is one world.

In the section entitled, 'Special Cases', Pamela Reid, a developmental psychologist, discusses the complex role of Black women in academe in the USA. These women, who are highly visible because of both their race and their sex, are saddled with a double burden. As a consequence, their struggle to attain positions of status and power in the academy have been particularly difficult, and their personal needs have often remained unmet. As Black women have made strides in attaining academic positions they have been able to establish networks with one another and to provide models for other women of ethnic-minority backgrounds, again at some cost to themselves.

Celia Kitzinger, a social psychologist from the United Kingdom, focuses on lesbian women, who represent a minority able to determine for themselves whether or not their status is known to others. This poses a dilemma given the history of intimidation and oppression of lesbian students and teachers and the patriarchal controls of the establishment that threatens to co-opt them. Kitzinger uses qualitative illustrations from her own experience and that of other open, self-identified lesbian women to explore the oppression and privilege of their status in the academic world.

The academic profession in India is highly respected. A significant number of women from a variety of socioeconomic backgrounds are employed as university teachers. These women enjoy the status of a 'privileged elite'. The cultural values that allow women to be employed in academic fields have their roots in traditional Indian philosophies about respect and veneration accorded teachers over the centuries. At the same time, the status of women academics in India is not as great as that of their male colleagues. Veena Gill, a political scientist, explores the experience in India with an eye towards understanding their unique situation in a world where they are simultaneously revered and derogated.

Jennie Farley, a sociologist, asks the question, 'Where are all the women professors in the United States?' The answer, disappointingly, is not surprising. They tend to be in the least well known institutions, often as part-time employees. When they have fought their way into the best-known universities, they often find themselves doing professorial work – but off the professorial ladder. The road to equality in higher education has proved a long one and the struggle is far from over.

The final section of the volume is entitled, 'Finding Solutions and Creating Alternatives'. The question of whether the most appropriate strategy to advance the cause of feminist scholarship is integration or separation remains a matter of some controversy. Evelyn Torten Beck details the emergence of 'Women's Studies' from a loosely conceived interdisciplinary 'field of study' into an academic discipline at the centre of a significant revolution whose aim it is to transform the university. Beck, whose field is comparative literature and who is Director of the Women's Studies programme at the University of Maryland, charts the course of this revolution, with its emphasis on curricular transformation, as a vehicle for producing fundamental changes in the structure and function of the academy.

Berit Ås, a psychologist and Norwegian politician, tells of her ten-year struggle to found the Feminist University in Norway. The premise on which the university is built is that women need to be provided with a 'room of their own' to which they can retreat to find themselves and to create new knowledge.

Social history attests to the predictable and cyclic nature of successful social movements, yet those involved in them rarely look to the experience of others as part of their strategic efforts to effect change. The final chapter in this volume will attempt to pull from its contents, lessons of value for those concerned about the future of women in academic settings. Co-option, confrontation and negotiation are some of the strategies women around the world have employed to try to attain status and power commensurate with their numbers and their abilities. Some of these strategies have been employed at the individual level, others at the institutional level, and still others at the level of government policy. The relative success of these strategies along with an assessment of the cause for that success will be presented in political–historical context, along with some prescriptions for the future of the movement to capture the tower.

This book is the first to consider the problems of academic women from a global perspective. Its primary purpose is to provide women who are engaged in or contemplating an academic career with information about the problems academic women face and some models of how others have coped with those problems. By profiling the experience of women in many nations an attempt has been made to provide the reader with insight into the structural nature of the struggle women face in academe that may be of value to them as they seek both individual and collective solutions.

References

Bryant, M (1979), *The Unexpected Revolution: A Study in the History of Education of Women and Girls in the Nineteenth Century*, University of London Institute of Education, Studies in Education (new series) 10.

Kasper, H (1989), High education goals: low salary increases: the annual report on the economic status of the profession, 1988–89, *Academe*, Bulletin of the American Association of University Professors.

Martin, J R (1984), Philosophy, gender and education, in S Acker et al (eds), *World Yearbook of Education, 1984: Women and Education*, London: Kogan Page.

McDonagh, E L (1989), An oppressed elite: educational patterns of notable American women, in D Kaufman (ed), *Public Private Spheres: Women Past and Present*, Boston: Northeastern University.

Oakley, A (1981), *Subject Women*, London: Fontana Press.

Rendel, Margherita (1980), How many women academics?, in *Schooling for Women's Work*, Rosemary Deem (ed), London: RKP.

Solomon, B M (1985), *In the Company of Educated Women*, New Haven: Yale University Press.

Part II
The Problem Defined

Chapter 2

Women in UK Universities – the Road to Casualization?

Adrienne Aziz

Setting the scene

Alas, for women academics in the United Kingdom, the imagery of battle is still prevalent in accounts of progress towards what is perceived as 'equality' in the university world, and it accurately reflects the erratic pattern of exhortation, achievement and setback which characterizes the changes of the last century-and-a-half.

The Victorian scene typified the male view of women's dependence on their spouse, and the assumption that women should not earn their own living. The notion of an 'academic' education for girls was therefore alien, and schools in the early and mid-nineteenth-century generally prepared their largely middle-class pupils for lady-like accomplishments, but certainly not for study at college or university level. As Carol Dyhouse (1984) points out, the subsequent pressure for change was subtly based, not on a desire to reject these Victorian concepts of femininity but on the need to redefine them. Like many other reforms, the initial steps were taken within the limits of social rigidity and therefore, instinctively, or perforce, on the basis of compromise. Arguably, this position of negotiation and compromise has not substantially altered today, despite the changes which have taken place: the aim remains the same, but someone keeps moving the goalposts.

As girls schools mushroomed in the late nineteenth century, the role of men – businessmen, doctors, clergy – as necessary benefactors, simply reinforced the image of the 'superior' male provider. Not surprisingly, this image was perpetuated in the universities where women students held an almost reverent esteem for their male academics and where, in Oxford and Cambridge, for instance, they were not even allowed to call themselves 'undergraduates' because they were not formally admitted to university membership on the same terms as men until 1947 (unlike London University, which did so in 1878). They were not encouraged to view their university education as a form of self development and particularly not as the road to a career. As a result, those women who survived to enter university teaching in the early part of the twentieth century were rare indeed; were mocked for being 'unfeminine'; were constantly under public scrutiny (more so than their male counterparts); and were subject to unreasonable restrictions (for example at University College, London, Dr Margaret Murray has described how they were not allowed to use the men's common room to drink coffee or discuss research with their colleagues). Furthermore, many of them believed that marriage and especially family responsibilities were incompatible with academic work for women. The term 'blue stocking' as Joan Whitehead, an academic at Cambridge, has pointed out was never meant as a compliment.

A survey by Cambridge University Women's Action Group (1988) showed that 40 years after the admission of women to the university and 16 years after their first admission to some of the men's colleges, not only are women still a tiny minority among both academic and administrative staff, they are also under-represented at the most senior levels in all categories of staff and on some of the most important decision-making bodies (notably finance).

After the Second World War universities in the UK went through a period of rapid expansion, but the increased independence of women and the valuable contribution they made to the economy during the war years, was very soon eroded as the men returned to their jobs: the number of nurseries diminished almost overnight, and the 'old order' of things was restored virtually as before. Just as women were beginning to be accepted in a range of spheres of work, they began to receive the message that their value was short-lived and their talent dispensable, having served its temporary purpose. The climate this created, and the consequent conflict in women's aspirations was to have a marked effect on the numbers of women entering higher education and subsequently entering the academic profession for the next two decades. It was not until the mid 1960s that there was an upsurge in the percentage of women undergraduates in the United Kingdom; in 1965 it had reached 27.7 per cent; in 1981 it was 39.8 per cent; and by 1988 it was 43.8 per cent with a correspondingly high out-turn of women postgraduates (39.8 per cent of the total in 1988) (DES). It is mainly from this pool of postgraduates that university staff are recruited. So why is it that today the distribution of women in the academic and related workforce remains so deferentially low, at barely 19 per cent in 1989, overall? And in the lower pay ranges?

Discriminatory environment?

There are a number of factors in play which may serve to throw some light on this position. After all, the academic work environment is only one of many professions which represent what can be termed 'discriminatory environments' for women; environments in which their careers are shaped and channelled in particular ways, as a result of their gender rather than of their abilities.

Table 2.1 *Women at the top of their profession*

Women circuit judges	19%
Women heads of BBC TV regions	10%
Women publishing directors	22%
Women senior managers in industry	7%
Women headteachers	40%
Women civil service under secretaries	5
Women professors	3%
Women vice-chancellors/principals	2%

Source: AUT (Research Section), 1990.

First, it must be said that the confidence and achievement levels are undoubtedly undermined by male values in higher education. This was confirmed by recent research (Thomas, 1990) which concluded that: 'higher education, by making use of widely available ideas of gender undermines its own apparent egalitarianism'. In other words, although higher education does not overtly discriminate against women, it nevertheless makes it harder for them to succeed through 'an acceptance of particular values and beliefs' which marginalize them. It also concludes that because science is 'bound up with notions of masculine success' many women feel pressure to be better than the men as if men 'were innately better scientists'. Women students in the science disciplines, however much they may question the traditional feminine stereotypes, still find themselves having to conform to male rules in the lecture-theatre. It is consequently inevitable that their perception of equality is adjusted to offer a compromise with their ideal.

This same approach is carried through to the Senior Common Room where there is a perceptible awareness of lingering but real prejudices against women and therefore a reluctance by many women to strive for advancement. The areas of entry to the profession and promotion within it, are particularly telling. Despite the comparatively high out-turn of qualified graduates (44 per cent) and postgraduates (nearly 40 per cent), the percentage of women entering the academic profession is still less than half that. And once they are there, the abysmally low number who are promoted to a chair tells its own story.

Subject ghettos and failed expectations

The earlier influences in the lives of women academics, mainly during school years and particularly in relation to subjects studied, inevitably show that many of the expectations they might have had are not in the event, being met. Even in subjects such as education or nursing and pharmacology with which women are more readily associated, they are still in a minority, especially when it comes to promotion. An analysis of statistics, undertaken by the Association of University Teachers, highlights the low levels of recruitment of women into academic posts and their poor prospects of promotion (AUT Statistical Survey, 1987a and 1987b). In science, for example, women's prospects are dramatically worse than in medicine, arts or social sciences: in 1984 12.5 per cent of the lecturers were female, but only 3.5 per cent of those promoted were women. Although cultural assumptions and school subject bias may account in part for this discrepancy, the question of why it is that those who do enter the university world of science have such a noticeable lack of success in obtaining promotion, remains unanswered.

It is clear from the figures for the following year (1985) that there had been no overall change, and the same was true of the promotion picture for 1986 as well, when, for example, 536 people were promoted from lecturer to senior lecturer or reader. Of these, 483 were men and 53 (10 per cent) were women. That is exactly the same percentage as in 1985. The movement in individual disciplines (or cost centres as they are known) hardly varies at all during those three years, and not more than 2 per cent in any discipline. In one cost centre – architecture – there were no promotions for women at all in either 1985 or 1986, despite the fact that 10 per cent of the teachers in architecture departments at that time were women (see Figure 2.1).

What emerges is that the proportion of women promoted is consistently smaller than the proportion of women in the pool of lecturers from which the promotions are made. The irony of the situation is that to be 'in the frame' for promotion in the first place, a woman has to be on a permanent contract, not a short-term one, and preferably not in a subject that is perceived by the (male) majority as atypical for women.

Creeping casualization

In theory there is equal pay for women in academic and related grades because there is one scale applicable in each grade, but in practice this equality is relative to the salary point and grade on appointment. As in many other sectors of employment, the women are disproportionately numerous in the lower grades and on the lower salary points in those grades, with the result that in a male-dominated profession there is little

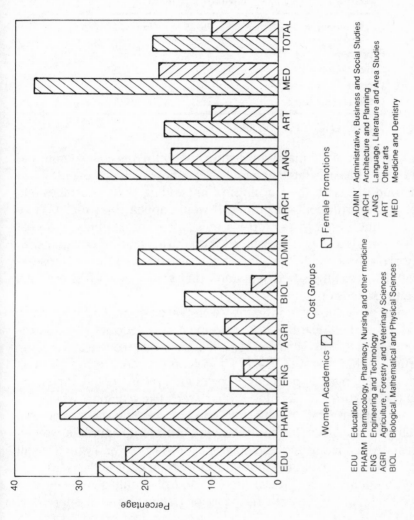

Figure 2.1 *Proportion of women, and percentage of promotions, by cost centre (1986 figures).*

enticement for the potential woman recruit when only 3 per cent of the professoriat is women. And this figure is unlikely to improve in the present economic climate as the number of staff on permanent contract gradually diminishes.

Table 2.2   *Women in academic grades*

Academic grade	%1987/8	Women 1980/1
Professor	3%	3%
Senior lecturer	6%	8%
Lecturer	14%	19%
Contract researcher	32%	N/A

Source: USR Vol 3, 1987/88.

The current trend to make short-term appointments at academic and related levels has escalated at a rate almost beyond belief over the last decade and belies all the warnings of impending skills shortages and forecasts of recruitment difficulties. It would appear that society here today is being urged to reinforce a message of profitability and cost effectiveness almost at all costs, as though this can be equated with quality of life. As a result, the number of university staff – mainly researchers, but increasingly, teaching and other staff – now on short term contracts exceeds one quarter.

No other profession in this country is in that position. And since more than 60 per cent of the total intake of women were recruited onto short-term contracts in both 1986 and 1987, it is clear that women are bearing the brunt of this pressure. By 1986, women on short-term contracts already formed over 30 per cent of the staff in research and analogous grades (see Figure 2.3), let alone other areas like teaching, where the trend to appoint staff on 'flexible' short-term contracts was also beginning to increase. This contrasts with the overall figure for women in university academic and related grades (see Figure 2.2) which is still barely 19 per cent, including those on short-term contracts.

When medium- to long-term funding and planning is reduced to a series of annual lurches as the basis of public financial support is changed, it is small wonder that universities are forced to take a cautious view and resort to increasing casualization as a 'safety measure', if nothing else. As might be expected, the majority of these short-term appointees are not only women but are also recently qualified and the wastage rate for university academics under the age of 30 now exceeds 20 per cent. Although by reason of its academic and intellectual base it is one of the top professions in the country, it is the only one where a doctorate is the norm, the average age of entry is 27, its expertise is unique and virtually irreplaceable, and its financial

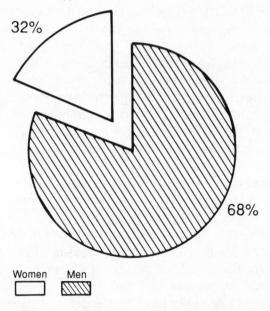

Figure 2.2 *Proportion of women in overall academic and related grades (1986 figures)*

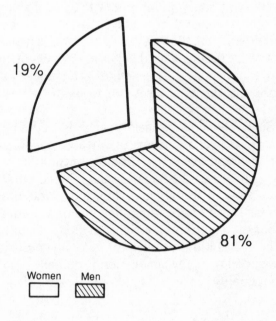

Figure 2.3 *Proportion of women in the research and analogous staff grades*

rewards (both salaries as well as working environment and equipment) are so limited as to act as a disincentive to all staff and consequently to reinforce those discriminatory practices which abound, whether conscious or unconscious.

Another notion which persists is that of the perception of the role of women in the department as being a 'caring and counselling' one, rather than doing hard research. This further serves to undermine the creation of helpful role models, especially as promotion depends largely on research output and male colleagues are past masters at avoiding extraneous duties.

Associated with this perception of women as carers, there has traditionally been an expectation by the male majority that women were less mobile when they married and that they would resign when they started a family, although the women themselves are now challenging these assumptions. There is increasing pressure for creche and other childcare facilities, but for reasons principally concerned with the taxation until recently of such facilities as 'perks', in addition to the restrictions on university funding, the price of these facilities is often out of reach of the younger women. One of the main reasons for this is that the level of exploitation of this section of the university workforce is comparatively high, with contract holders being offered renewal of contract at the same salary point, rather than on the next point on the incremental scale and therefore having little or no choice when they are staring unemployment in the face. To be fair, this is usually the result of industrial sponsors driving a hard bargain when negotiating a research project with a university. The senior academics who attract the research work onto campus have still to learn the art of thinking in terms of good employer practice and of pricing the projects realistically to include such elements as salary awards, incremental drift and maternity leave as well as other overheads, and of bargaining the provision of academic expertise up, not down. In any case, they are usually anxious to attract the business and reluctant to stand firm in the face of pressure from the sponsorship and competition from other establishments. These are pastures new for universities in the UK for whom the concept of entrepreneurial activities on campus and marketplace bargaining has hitherto been a totally alien concept and is still resisted or avoided by many academics. Profitability is the watchword nowadays, not quality of life.

The influence of public funding

A new twist in the tale is the 'bidding' scheme introduced in 1990 by the Universities Funding Council (UFC) (an organization which receives and distributes the funds voted by Parliament for the universities each year). The scheme is a complex kind of 'blind auction' for funded student places whereby universities have to submit 'bids' for their student numbers over the four-year period from October 1991, but within a maximum price (already viewed by some as non-viable) which varies between subjects. There is an overall national limit, so universities will be competing with each other and in turn, lower bids will drive the overall funding basis down for future years. Connoisseurs of the UK university scene will readily appreciate that this further financial pressure will provide yet another excuse for deferring spending on improvements in equal opportunities on campus.

In contrast to this, or at least apparently so, additional sums of money were made available for the appointment of a limited number of young lecturers. This 'New Academics Appointments Scheme' as it is called, has no formal age limits but it is significant that the funds for it have been adjusted in favour of institutions with a below-average number of staff aged under 35. When its forerunner, the New Blood Scheme (with an age limit) was put into operation four years earlier, a successful case was taken against the funding body through an Industrial Tribunal by a woman medical researcher who had been offered the post but for whom the University had not been granted the funds by the UFC on the grounds that she was two years over the age limit. The tribunal ruled that the scheme amounted to sex discrimination because the proportion of women who could comply with it was smaller than the proportion of men who could comply with it. Although the new Scheme has slightly revised wording, it is the funding adjustment on age basis which does the damage and advertisements have appeared stipulating an age limit for posts under this Scheme. It would appear that another tribunal test case would be needed to overcome this new problem. Such is the operation of the law that it can seem to put up barriers when, in theory, it should be helping.

Thus, ageism is yet another example of how women in UK universities are not only discriminated against on grounds of age but as a consequence, are pushed into the ever-expanding casual labour market on campus. They have no career path, no stability in terms of their personal life, marriage, mortgage commitments and so on. They suffer the frustrations of enforced job changes and their low salary levels lead to low morale. Who could doubt that pay is perceived as measuring work value? Added to this is the indignity of insufficient continuous service to entitle them to benefits. For example, two-thirds of the short-term contract staff and part-time staff in the UK are without the university maternity leave benefits. Women academics on short-term contracts writing in *AUT Woman* describe graphically their experiences and their frustration (Summer 1990) revealing, the extent of the unfairness of this type of contract. One of them, in a department of philosophy, lectured for six years on a series of 12-month contracts. When she was finally given a permanent contract in the same university, she found that it included the 'normal' three-year probation period so that, in effect, she was 'on probation' for a total of nine years. Another who describes herself as a theatre practitioner paints a picture of a business which is fickle and where human resources can be the most expendable changeable factor in the equation. Another explains the obvious contradiction in terms when she was appointed on a part-time temporary contract as a project officer to develop equal opportunities courses at her university; she quite justifiably views this irony as 'double think'.

There is no doubt that women academics are just one group among many in this country who are working in an environment which is tangibly negative – it is no longer completely hostile but it is certainly not supportive. Indeed, it has been estimated (*Independent*, 1990) that sex bias in the UK is robbing women of about £15 billion a year. It is said that this is the cost to women workers of the unfair and unfavourable treatment they receive at the hands of the labour market, and women academics are by no means an exception to this. The academic and related workforce, is after all, more than 80 per cent male.

Cautious optimism

On the other hand, the picture is not entirely one of doom and gloom, and some real progress has been made, albeit with measured steps which often seem to take women back a pace with every two or three taken forward.

Childcare provision is one area, for example, where demographic trends are forcing changes in the political climate, with the result that the attitude of the universities' funding body to the use of the grant allocation for childcare facilities on campus or for, perhaps, shared nearby facilities with a local authority, has now changed since the announcement by Government in April 1990 of budgetary changes in this area. Nevertheless, such provision is pointless if it continues to be financially out of reach of most of the women on campus.

Another area where cautious optimism can be admitted, is that of the numerical imbalance of women in the academic grades compared with men. The Universities (Committee of Vice Chancellors and Principals) together with the funding body (Universities Funding Council) and the staff union (Association of University Teachers) are committed to promoting equal opportunities on campus and, jointly, are currently exploring the problem of this imbalance and the reasons for it. To this end, statistics on entry to the profession, through returns being requested on applications for posts and types of posts, as well as statistics on promotion, are being collected for analysis and monitoring.

This should reveal among other things the extent to which the very slow increase in the overall numbers of women can be attributed to the marked increase in casualization. It will also reveal the proportion of women applying for posts, compared with the proportion appointed. This should go some way to clarifying the reasons for the discrepancy between the out-turn of graduates and postgraduates, mentioned earlier, and the numbers of women entering the profession, apart, that is, from the obvious reasons of pay and insecurity also discussed earlier.

Legislation – help or hindrance?

The situation in Canadian universities is almost identical with statistics showing a very similar picture, despite much earlier moves towards legislation and establishing a regulatory environment than in the UK. The Report (1988) by the Council of Ontario Universities' Committee on the status of women puts the recipe for progress very succinctly:

- The principles of employment equity are straightforward: practices, procedures and policies can be changed to provide equal access, equal opportunity and an equal chance of success;
- remedies need to be 'systemic' in order to respond to the systemic nature of discrimination;
- change must be structural to be permanent and effective;
- change must come from within the system; the university itself has to carry out the process of establishing employment equity.

The Canadian report goes on to observe that the law often has not offered, and in many cases still does not offer, adequate protection to women. Unfortunately, this can also be said of the United Kingdom and, one suspects, a number of other Western countries as well. The main framework of the protective legislation for women is to be found in the Equal Pay Act (1970, as amended) and the Sex Discrimination Act (1975). These have served gradually to improve the overall climate and to raise awareness of the issues. It is certainly true to say that legislation creates a lifeline; but it also puts up barriers. The figures published by the Equal Opportunities Commission speak for themselves; the number of sex discrimination industrial tribunal claims completed in 1988/89 increased by a third but the number of successful cases as a proportion of cases decided by tribunals declined from 29 per cent to 22 per cent in that period. Even when cases are successful, as in the ageism case cited earlier, their impact can be limited and shortlived especially if the outcome does not change the underlying attitudes, but simply prompts defensive or retaliatory action by the employer concerned. This kind of reaction has been aptly called 'professional mugging' and its incidence and relationship to gender is a concept which still has to be explored in depth. Suffice it to say that women have come to realize that their work will never be the same, even if, or especially if, they are courageous enough to take their case to a tribunal.

As an employer, a university is already bound by law not to discriminate against a person, directly or indirectly, on the grounds of sex, race, or marital status (or colour or nationality, for that matter). Unhappily, the relevant rights do not extend cover to part-time employees. Furthermore, although they cover all full-time employees, it still does not prevent the creeping casualization of the female academic labour force being experienced at the moment. Change – as the Canadian report so rightly emphasizes – must come from within the universities, and it needs to be based on goodwill.

Change from within

There are signs, nevertheless, that universities are beginning to take the issue of equal opportunities more seriously. For the first time, in 1990, the concept was recognized and written into a national salary award. The Committee of Vice Chancellors and Principals has also put its name to a statement on good employer practice in relation to the employment of short-term contract staff. In addition, a small minority of UK universities are beginning systematically to monitor their own practice on campus. It has been said (Thomas, 1990) that the worst vice of Higher Education is its complacency. All too few of the UK universities, though, are making an effort to counter that accusation. One university that is doing so, however, is the Open University. It set up an Equal Opportunities team which was asked to review the University's policies and practices in employment, student recruitment and support and the curriculum in relation to equal opportunities, and to present a five-year action plan in respect of students and staff from under-represented groups. The Team's report aimed to:

- present data on disadvantaged groups and their current profile in the university, and discuss the different needs of different groups;
- discuss why the university should have a comprehensive equal opportunities policy, both in ethical and pragmatic terms;
- look at institutional barriers to equality of opportunity;
- propose an action plan comprising a costed and prioritized series of recommendations for implementation over the next five years to improve the situation;
- establish the necessity for an on-going Equal Opportunities Unit and regular review of the issues at all levels within the university.

This report was completed and presented to the University's governing Council in May 1990, so that it is still being considered and has not yet been published, but the signals being communicated throughout the university system are basically clear and helpful. Once universities take on board the need to monitor and define an action plan for improvements on each and every campus, the climate of goodwill will have been considerably improved. Then it will be the effectiveness of the action taken that will underline the depth and strength of the goodwill needed to bring about change at a time when economic pressures are working against such changes. In practice, the implication for the last few years seems to have been that equal opportunities are a virtue when times are good, but should be kept at arms length for immediate temporary relegation when they are not.

In a report on women at the top of their profession, (1989) the Hansard Society Commission declared that it was wholly unacceptable that UK universities should remain 'bastions of male power and privilege'. But fine words, declarations and even policy statements do not advance the cause of equal opportunities without a framework for practical progress. In the main, industry is leading the way towards change in this country at the moment, with the public sector, and particularly universities, limping behind, despite the increasing number of good examples to follow. At each stage in the progress of equal opportunities for women in universities during the last hundred years, women have stopped to review their position, and revise their targets. Following each success, the targets have changed and moved while the practical improvements achieved have brought only a superficial equality so far, but comparatively little real attitudinal change towards the value of women in the academic workforce.

The way forward now has to be based on change from within, with a determined move towards monitoring in order to initiate effective strategies for recruiting, retaining, training, retraining, developing and lifting the morale of women academics in the UK.

References

Association of University Teachers (AUT) Statistical Survey (1987a), Equal opportunities for women academic and related staff.

AUT Statistical Survey (1987b), 'Distribution of women in the academic and related workforce in UK universities'.

AUT Woman (1990), issue No 20, summer.

Cambridge University Women's Action Group (CUWAG) (1988), 'Report on the numbers and status of academic women in the University of Cambridge'.

Council of Ontario Universities (1988), 'Report of the Committee on the Status of Women'.

Department of Education and Science (DES) Statistics of Education (published annually by HMSO).

Dyhouse, C (1984), 'Storming the citadel or storm in a teacup? The entry of women into higher education 1860–1920' in *Is Higher Education Fair to Women?* S Acker and D Warren-Piper (eds). Guildford: SRHE and NFER-Nelson.

The Hansard Society Commission (1989), Report entitled 'Women at the top' (Hansard Society for Parliamentary Government).

Independent newspaper report 1990, April 16th.

Thomas, Kim (1990), *Gender and Subject in Higher Education* Milton Keynes: SRHE and Open University Press.

Chapter 3

Women: The Academic Proletariat in West Germany and the Netherlands

Anne C Hawkins and *Dagmar Schultz*

A few minutes discussion with almost any academic woman in any college or university in the world reveals that despite the progress that women have made in the last 20 years, the underrepresentation of women in academic settings is still a universal phenomenon. For example, a British woman scientist agrees that although there are more women in her department now than there were 15 years ago, many of them are, like herself, wives of professors, employed part-time. An administrator from the USA points out that although the proportion of women in positions of power within her institution is relatively high, the institution is characterized by its low status and low pay. A Dutch woman from an Arts faculty that has been struggling to survive for years, has had her full time post reduced to half-time. She is relatively grateful, as many of her colleagues have been cut from the faculty entirely.

The case for the existence of sex discrimination in academe has been amply documented although there is little empirical knowledge about its nature and the mechanisms that serve to maintain it. The current chapter focuses on two empirical studies of discrimination in academic settings in the Federal Republic of Germany and the Netherlands. Both studies explore some of the causes of women's failure to achieve positions of status and power commensurate with their numbers in the academic world. In both countries, women in the universities report that discrimination exists but frequently deny that they have been its victims. An analysis of both the recruitment and retention data in The Netherlands reveals that women are less likely to be hired and promoted to permanent posts in Universities than men in times of retrenchment. While the government statistics bureau heralds the overall increase in the number of women employed in universities overall, they are more likely than ever before to be found in part-time, short-term, temporary posts.

The case of West Germany

West Germany might aptly be characterized as one of the least advanced countries of Europe with regard to the position of university women. Although women constitute about 40 per cent of the student population, less than five per cent of the faculty (full-time professors) are female, and this percentage is beginning to decline. Only in the lower positions of assistant and associate professors has there been even a slight increase in the number of women in the last several years. The cause of this pattern is, one suspects, discrimination based on sex, although those most likely to have been its victims, the academic women themselves, largely do not attribute their treatment to discriminatory practices (Sommerkorn 1969; Schindler 1962; Wetterer 1986; Schultz 1990).

This study focuses on the career patterns and working conditions of male and female professors, their attitudes toward women and Women's Studies, and the relationship between their private and professional lives. The analysis is based on interviews conducted with 21 female and 22 male professors in four academic fields (medicine, psychology, education, and languages) at three West German universities.

Universities in West Germany are essentially homosocial (Lipman-Blumen 1976); men are dominant and act to exclude women from participation. This is true, despite the fact that the universities are now coeducational and women have attained faculty status (Billotet-Hoffman 1982). Despite its claim that it is a meritocracy, the university values reputational status above all. Reputational status is, of course, heavily dependent upon integration into the formal and informal structures of the academic community, a community that remains closed to women, who are forced, by their token status (Kanter 1977) to remain outside.

In contrast to women, men are inducted into their professional worlds under the tutelage of male models and mentors; women have no such advantage (see O'Leary and Mitchell in this volume). At best, women must rely on a process of acculturation (Jensen 1982) as they don't have access to women models and mentors in the academic world; a world for which their socialization does not prepare them. In fact, the experience of academic women may best be understood in the context of their need to construct for themselves a world that lies in between the public male world, and the private female one. This conceptual analysis is drawn from the work of Hettlage-Varjas and Hettlage (1984) who used the notion of cultural reconstruction to explain the adaptation of migrants to their new surroundings.

According to this analysis, academic women are not caught in conflict between two competing roles (work and family) as it is so often argued (cf, Lie in this volume), nor do they struggle to maintain two separate identities like Acar's (Chapter 8) compartmentalizers. Instead, they actively construct for themselves a reality which allows them to merge their two 'worlds' into a single, stable, homogeneous one; an act of both creativity and courage.

Sex differences in career paths

The career patterns of academic women and men in West Germany are quite different. Men follow the lead of their (male) mentors, who play the role of father figures. Indeed, in West Germany the thesis advisor is actually called a 'doctoral father'. Women are not often successful in finding a mentor, and report relying instead, on mothers and aunts as role models and on peers for social support. Unlike women, who while recognizing their own ability, attribute their academic success to fate or luck, men see their success as the direct result of their achievements (cf, Chapter 6). These two factors taken together prevent women's ready assimilation into the academic environment.

Although women members of faculty are cognizant of discrimination against women in their institutions, they most often deny it has affected them themselves. Given their small numbers (five per cent), they are some distance from reaching the critical 15 per cent required to remove them from their marginal status (Kanter 1977) and thus, are unwilling to risk being identified as part of the female minority. Not surprisingly, such women hesitate to provide support to one another.

Private lives

For women, home life is an important part of the world they construct for themselves. They spend a great deal of time and energy deciding whether or not to become involved with partners and children. In contrast, men assume that families will be a natural adjunct to their careers and they do not waste much time considering how they will handle the competing demands of work and family. Even single women are not spared the burden of family responsibilites. For example, many care for sick and ageing parents.

Unlike women, who view family responsibilities as detracting from their work, men do not regard familial commitments as interfering with their careers. In the words of one male professor, 'It does not make a difference to me if my wife has a child, it does not affect my work.'

Perhaps even more important, when men find their university positions unsatisfactory, they are freer than women to retreat into their own research without criticism. Women are expected to nurture students, to serve on committees *and* to conduct research. Men are also freer to pursue interests outside the university, a strategy that may actually enhance their reputational standing. When women use this strategy they risk being accused of refusing to 'pull their weight'. The last strategy open to disillusioned men in the Academy is to assume the role of critique. The system is much more likely to tolerate men who adopt this role than women.

Male faculty's attitudes toward women

Unlike the West German men in Anger's study (1960), who believed that women were intellectually, physically, and psychologically unsuited to be faculty members, more than half of the men interviewed in this study thought it would be desirable to have more women in academic positions. However, when asked to evaluate those women who were already there, their attitudes were considerably less favourable.

When queried about the women's potential role as faculty members, the male responses fell into seven categories ranging from women being incapable of achieving academic prominence through women's presence would have a calming and integrating effect on the scientific community. Some of the men supported women's particpation in higher education because they thought it improved and eroticized the social climate. While the men generally acknowledged women's right to membership in the academic community, they were hard on women whom they saw as not living up to their standards for performance. This latter finding may be in part related to the increasing competition for academic positions in the marketplace, but it also suggests that support for affirmative action, especially among younger men can be expected to be unenthusiastic at best.

Academic women

The women interviewed in this study used four distinct strategies for reconstructing culture. Their choices were governed to some extent by the time at which they entered the profession. Not surprisingly, their personal dispositions were also important.

One group of academic women might best be labelled 'suffering critics'. These women, who entered the university during the 1950s, had long histories of discrimination. For many, the isolation that they suffered at work resulted in bitterness.Most had renounced family life altogether in order to pursue careers. Even so, they had not been accepted. These women long for women colleagues and give support to women students when they can. They are among the few women who openly acknowledge that discrimination against women is practised, although not all of them see themselves as having been its victim. They support quota systems as one means of increasing the number of women in the Academy. They have never really resolved the conflict between family and career demands in that even though they renounced the former they see themelves as the victims of the demand to choose.

A second group of academic women comprise the 'self-assured, strategy-conscious professor'. These women were all in the field of medicine and were among the oldest in the sample. Like their bitter sisters they were single although not always without children. They had struggled mightily to establish their careers. They were conscious of their marginality and acknowedged the presence of discrimination in their institutions. They favoured perserverance, rationality and a commitment to excellence as means of acculturation. At the time they entered the profession they accepted their token position and survived by being better than the men who judged them. Although they generally did not favour affirmative action they did support younger women. The culture they constructed for themselves is a stable one based on their acceptance of their situations and the premise that to succeed women have to be better than men.

The third group of women comprise a group of 'assimilated, achievement-oriented professors'. These women rely on diplomacy and seek cooperation with male colleagues rather than female ones. Interestingly, they are the youngest group in the sample. Most claim that they have never been victims of sex discrimination and argue against any form of preferential treatment for women. They do not even support providing women students with special mentoring opportunities. The stability of their cultural reconstruction depends directly on their relationship with the men in their departments and disciplines.

The final group of women in the sample are the 'aggressive critics'. These women expect to change their work environment and are actively involved in efforts to do so. They are primarily at the midpoint of their careers or a bit younger, and all report that they have experienced some form of discrimination. They share strong political consciousnesses. Those who have partners expect their partners to share home and family responsibilities with them. They also expect the university to change its attitude toward family obligations. They speak out on behalf of women in the Academy. These women have established stable cultural reconstructions based on their analysis of the social origins of sex discrimination and share a strong commitment not to accept unequal treatment. They are the most likely to support programmes aimed at providing additional support for women students and to back affirmative action as a means to equalize the treatment of women in the university. Not surprisingly they are also the most ardent supporters of Women's Studies.

Based on the interviews conducted it is clear that women adopt cultural reconstructive strategies that are consistent with their personal experiences as well as the socio-historical context in which those experiences occurred. The nature of these strategies is heavily dependent upon their willingness to acknowledge discrimination in their own lives and the lives of other women. Over the course of their careers most women in the study had managed to create for themselves a synthesis of the worlds dictated to them on the basis of their gender and society.

The case of the Netherlands

In the decade between 1970 and 1980 the representation of women in academe deteriorated rather than improved (Hawkins & Van Balen 1984). This was true despite the institutional policies aimed at improving women's status by favouring their recruitment. The absolute number of women did increase during this period but so did sex segregation by rank and discipline. Even though there were more women employed in the universities, they were concentrated at low ranks and in just a few subject areas. This was particularly true for young women in the Arts and Social Sciences (Hawkins and Van Balen 1984). Recent data indicate that in the eighties women failed to maintain the precarious hold they had on university positions with decision-making power during the 1970s. As shown in Table 3.1, not only have both the number and the percentage of full women professors declined but even more importantly, the number of women in the second rank has declined dramatically. It is from this rank that future professors will be recruited. The 14.7 per cent of UD (assistant professors) who are women comprise 85.7 per cent of all women in the Dutch academy.

Table 3.1 *Distribution of women by ranks equivalent to full, associate and assistant professor in 1970, 1980, and 1988*

Rank	1970		1980		1988	
Professor (Full)	65	2.7%	71	2.2%	50	2.1%
Associate (WHM;UHD)	312	9.4%	577	8.9%	105	4.6%
Assistant (WM:UD)	571	11.8%	769	15.0%	927	14.7%
Total	948	9.0%	1417	9.6%	1082	9.8%

Sources: Hawkins & Van Balen, 1984; HOOP, 1989.

A number of factors have contributed to the decline in the proportion of women in academic ranks in the Netherlands. Once known as the 'Land of the Eternal Student', the cost of producing a college graduate in the Netherlands was notoriously high. In an effort to reduce that cost a number of measures were introduced in the 1980s, most of which worked to the disadvantage of women. For example, small university departments were merged or eliminated resulting in fewer available positions in areas of women's traditional strengths such as modern languages. About 33 per cent of the positions affected in this manner were held by women. As women represent only 14 per cent of the overall university faculty the impact of this change was disproportionately great.

The redefinition of ranks was also disadvantageous for women. Academic ranks were redefined in two stages beginning in 1980. First, the position of *lektor* (assistant professor) was eliminated. New faculty were appointed at the *lektor* level of remuneration, but with the title of full professor. Second, the positions of *Hoofdmedewerker* and *Medewerker* (WHM and WM in Table 3.1) were redivided into *Universitair Hoofddocent* and *Docent* (UHD and UD in Table 3.1). As a result, assistant professors had to reapply for their own jobs. Only about one third of the *Hoofdmedewerkers* were reappointed as *Universitair Hoofddocents*. Of these, only a few were women.

Although a policy had been instituted to protect women at the level of recruitment and appointment, it has not been successful. The results of a study conducted at the University of Leiden indicated that appointment boards were either unaware of this policy or they ignored it (Deminent 1989). A second study reveals that although the policy, when followed, has resulted in an increase in the number of women in new posts, these women are concentrated in temporary positions only. Selection boards retain their reluctance to appoint women to permanent posts (Portegijs 1989). Thus, despite institutional efforts intended to eliminate sex discrimination, actuarial data indicate that it continues adversely to affect women. Given this reality, how do academic women and men perceive their work situations?

Perceived discrimination

As part of an extensive survey administered to 250 academic women drawn from six universities in the Netherlands (Hawkins & Noordenbos 1990) information about family background, education, employment history and current employment was collected. In order to obtain comparative information about male faculty, the women in the sample were asked, where possible, to nominate a male colleague who could be considered a 'match'. Fifty of them did so, and an adapted version of the questionnaire was sent to these men. Twenty men replied. The comparisons presented are therefore based on a subsample of 125 of the women surveyed in the original study and their male 'matches'.

The majority of women in the sample indicated that sex discrimination in academe existed, although, as in the West German sample, few characterized themselves as its victim. It should be noted that by definition, the survey was distributed only to survivors so it may be that none of them had ever encountered discrimination. However, a more plausible explanation is that they, like the West German women, had engaged in cultural reconstructions of their experience in order to cope. As Hempe (1985) so aptly observes:

Nobody likes to admit that something went wrong in their lives, especially if there are feelings of apprehension that damage might be expected when one gives information to strangers about one's frustrations. A further reason is the raising of the threshold of stimuli to recognize unequal treatment over time, and the resulting acquisition of a high limit of tolerance towards discriminating attitudes and practices.

Because the perception that sex discrimination no longer exists in academe is so widespread, albeit inaccurate, Goffman (1956) suggests that unfair treatment, when it is acknowledged, is likely to be treated as deserved. Of course these results suggest that it is not likely to be acknowledged. Only one of the men indicated that discrimination adversely affected women, whereas one third of the men (twice the proportion of women) indicated that women were *favoured* over men.

Career strategies

Comparisons of the career strategies of women and men in the Dutch sample indicated that unlike men who were particularly likely to report that they had been encouraged by a professor or teacher, women did not enjoy parallel support for their career aspirations.

This is especially distressing in light of the fact that as students women and men's career aspirations did not differ. Yet, when women did pursue academic careers they were four times as likely as men to do so at the behest of professors or other university contacts. Previous research has indicated the importance of mentors (see O'Leary & Mitchell in Chapter 4). These results suggest that although women may need more encouragement from their professors, they seem less likely than men to receive it.

Comparisons of the career values of academic women and men suggest that they are more alike than different. For example, men and women did not differ in the extent to which they valued the independence from authority, community prestige and salary commensurate with their academic positions. Interestingly, given the propensity of women academics to labour under the dual burdens of both career and family responsibilities, women were only slightly more likely than men to view the flexibility of their work schedules favourably. In comparison to men, women were less likely to endorse the chance to contribute to the field of knowledge or the freedom to carry out original ideas as positive aspects of their academic employment. The women in the sample were as productive as the men and as likely to hold advanced degrees, although the men were more likely than the women to obtain their doctorates within a relatively short time span. The greatest sex difference obtained was with regard to the application for, and receipt of, external funding for research. Women were much less likely than men to apply for, and be granted, research funds. Women were also less likely than men to be appointed to powerful committees at their universities.

Conclusion

According to Kanter (1977) the smaller a minority women find themselves to be in an organization, the greater their chances of being isolated and evaluated on the basis of role stereotypes. She dubs such women *ésolos* and suggests that the critical mass necessary to mitigate against the solo phenomenon lies between 15 and 20 per cent of the workforce. Given the veracity of the solo phenomeon it should logically follow that as the percentage of women increases their isolation should decrease rendering them more able to recognize and confront discrimination. This was not the case in the Netherlands, even in the Arts and Social Sciences where women comprise a greater percentage of the faculty. Institutional discrimation persists as indicated by the failure to appoint women to positions for which their background and experience qualifies them but for which they may be reticent to apply (Noordenbos 1990). Given the overwhelming evidence presented in this volume for the systemic nature of sex discrimination in academe, the solution required is surely an organizational, rather than individual one. In order to obtain an adequate organizational response women are going to have to keep pressuring the (male) system. The voluntary abdication of power is rare.

References

Anger, Hans (1960), *Probleme Der Deutschen Universität*, Tübingen.

Billotet-Hoffmann, Claudia et al (1982), Arbeidsplatz hochschule: frauen in forschung und lehre, *Politik und Zeitgeschichte*, Beilage zur Wochen-zeitschrift *Das Parlament*. 6, 3–12.

Deminent, M (1989), Arbeidsduur, organisatie en emancipatie; over de kwaliteit van deeltijdarbeid. (Duration of work, organization and emancipation; on the quality of part time work), PhD thesis, Rijskuniversiteit Leiden.

Goffman, Erwing, 1956, *The Presentation of Self in Everyday Life*, Edinburgh, University of Edinburgh, Social Sciences Research Centre.

Hawkins, C A & Van Balen (1984), De positie van vrouwen in het wetenschappelijk onderwijs van 1970–1980. (The Position of Women in Universities 1970–1980). *Universiteit en Hogeschool*, 30, (3) pp 194–209.

Hawkins, C A and G Noordenbos (1990), Blokkades in het doorstromen van vrouwen naar hogere functies aan de universiteit. (Obstacles to the progression of women to higher posts in universities). *Universiteit en Hogeschool*, 36 (5) pp 269–278.

Hawkins, C A et al. (1990), Back to the future? The deteriorating position of women academics in Dutch universities in the 1980s and beyond. (In preparation). VVAO (Dutch Association of University Women), Postbus 13226 LE Utrecht.

Hempe, Asta (1985), An unpublished empirical study, 1978–79 undertaken for the Deutsche Ahademesinpond.

Hettlage-Varjas, Andrea/Hettlage, Robert (1984), Kulturelle zwischenwelten, fremdarbeiter – eine ethnie, *Schweizerische Zeitschrift für Soziologie*, 2, pp 357–404.

Hicks, E H and G Noordenbos (eds) (1990), *Is Alma Mater Vrouw Vriendelijk?* (Is Alma Mater Sympathetic To Women?). Netherlands, Assen/Maastricht, Van Gorcum.

Jensen, Katherine (1982), Women's work and academic culture: adaptations and confrontations, *Higher Education*, 11, pp 67–83.

Kanter, Rosabeth Moss (1977), *Men and Women of the Corporations*, New York: Basic Books.

Lipman-Blumen, Jean (1976), Towards a homosocial theory of sex roles. An explanation of the sex-segregation of social institutions, *Signs*, 3, pp 15–32.

Ministerie van Onderwijs en Wetenschappen (Ministry of Education and Science) (1989), *Hoger Onderwijs en Onderzoek Plan* (Higher Education and Research Plan) (Hoop), Volume 2, Feiten en Cijfers (Facts and Figures), Netherlands, The Hague.

Noordenbos, G (1990), En vergelijkend onderzoek naar de loopbaanontwikkeling van mannelijke en vrouwelijke wetenschappers (A comparative study of the career development of male and female academics). In E H Hicks and G Noordenbos (eds) (1990) *Is Alma Mater Vrouw Vriendelijk?* (Is Alma Mater Sympathetic to Women?) Netherlands, Assen/Maastricht, Van Gorcum.

Portegijs, W (1989), In- en uitstroom van vrouwelijk en mannelijke wetenschappers aan de nederlandse universiteiten, 1986–1988 (Input and outflow of male and female university teachers and researchers in the universities in the Netherlands 1986–1988). In E H Hicks and G Noordenbos (eds) (1990) *Is Alma Mater Vrouw Vriendelijk?* (Is Alma Mater Sympathetic to Women?) Netherlands, Assen/Maastricht, Van Gorcum.

Schindler, P (1962), *Die Stellung der Dozentin an Wissenschaftlichen Hochschulen*, Ergebnisse einer Umfrage, Deutsche Universitätszeitung, 11, pp 11–27.

Schultz, Dagmar (1990), *Das Geschlecht Läuft immer mit . . .* Die Arbeitswelt von Professorinnen und Professoren.

Schultz, Dagmar (1989), Die Bedeutung von Beruf und Familie, von eigener und Partner/innenkarriere. In: Bathe, Sylvia et al (eds), *Frauen in der Hochschule*. Lehren und Lernen im Wissenschaftsbetrieb, Weinheim, pp 158–189.

Sommerkorn, Ingrid N (1969), *On the Position of Women in the University Teaching Profession in England:* An Interview Study of 100 University Teachers: PhD Diss, University of London.

Wetterer, Angelika (1986), 'Ja, geben tut's das, aber mir ist das nie passiert.' Was sagen subjektive Diskriminierungserfahrungen über die objektive situation von wissenschaftlerinnen aus? In: Clemens, Bärbel et al (eds), *Die Töchter der Alma Mater*. Überblick zum Forschungsstand Frauen in Hochschule und Beruf, Frankfurt/M/New York, pp 273–286.

Chapter 4

Women Connecting with Women: Networks and Mentors

Virginia E O'Leary and *Judith M Mitchell*

Women academics have been found repeatedly to be less well integrated into their academic departments and disciplines than men (cf, Lie in this volume). The most frequently offered explanation for this fact is that women do not have access to the same networks nor enjoy the same relationships with mentors as men. The purpose of this paper is to explore the empirical research on the effects of mentoring and networking on professional integration and productivity with a view toward better understanding the contribution of these factors to observed sex differences in the career patterns of academic women.

Networking

Networking has been considered a crucial ingredient of success in any professional career. Career networks usually involve contacts with a variety of colleagues for the purpose of mutual career benefits. In academia, networking has been defined as 'scientists and scholars that . . . collaborate with, encourage, inform, evaluate, reward, compete with, and befriend co-workers' (Reskin 1978). It is a relation between individuals of equal or higher status. It differs from a mentor–mentee relationship in that it involves contact with many colleagues. An important characteristic of networking and the 'old-boy' network is that it is dependent upon informal interactions involving favours, persuasion and connections to people who already have influence in the academic environment (Henning & Jardim 1977).

The benefits of networking to academics can be categorized into five types: information exchange, collaboration, career planning and strategizing, professional support/encouragement, and access to visibility and upward mobility (Green 1982; Stern 1980; Welch 1980). Networks provide essential information on office policies and the actual requirements of work situations not found in formal publications (Nieva & Gutek 1981). Colleagues provide information on grants and research funds as well as contacts leading to research resources. Collaboration on research projects and ideas can increase productivity as well as keep professionals up-to-date on the status of the field (White 1970). Networking with others already influential in academia can potentially benefit a new professional by providing her with opportunities to increase her visibility in the profession. Networking can provide researchers with a forum to discuss career stategies informally and consider the rewards and costs associated with specific career decisions. Because women are less well integrated into their home departments than men (Kyvik 1986) they may be particularly dependent upon networks outside their institutions to maintain a sense of professional identity and validity. In sum, networks benefit academic scientists by providing them access to new knowledge prior to publication, information on trade secrets and financial resources, professional information on department operations and career advancement opportunities (Reskin 1978).

The old-boy network surfaced as the buzzword of the late 70s and 80s and the 'skill for success.' However, in academia the origins of the concept date to the seventeenth century, where it was referred to as the 'invisible college'. The invisible college consisted of an 'in-group' of scholars who claimed to have access to everyone of significance in a particular area of research. The members of the 'college' functioned as gatekeepers, controlling finances, reputations, and the fate of new scientific ideas (Prize and Beaver 1966). The advantages of networking have been amply documented for men. They report that informal conversations with colleagues assisted them in acquiring 'scientific concepts and research of major . . . significance' (Glass & Norwood 1959). Medical researchers cite colleagues as their primary source of ideas and inspiration (Henner 1959). Menzel (1962) found that elaborate interpersonal networks linked scientists together so that crucial information was transmitted effectively among them.

Indeed, research productivity appears to be heavily dependent upon collaboration. Highly productive scientists spend more energy contacting other scientists and maintaining those contacts than do their less productive peers (Pelz 1956). Researchers who work alone or with just one collaborator publish only four papers or less every five years in contrast to those with more than 12 collaborators who published more than 14 papers in the same period (Prize & Beaver 1966). Highly productive scientists have efficient networks according to Finkelstein (1982) who found that they receive collegial benefits with minimal extra-departmental interactions, suggesting that when they need something they know exactly who to call.

Women's networks

Women's access to networks has improved considerably in the last 30 years. In the 1960s and early 70s women scientists had much less contact with other researchers than did men. Findings cited in Bernard (1964) on women zoologists indicate that these women were not routinely included on reprint mailing lists and rarely attended scientific meetings. Even those women who did attend meetings reported fewer productive conversations leading to collaboration compared to men (Zuckerman & Cole 1975).

Feelings of exclusion from the communication network are commonly reported among women in science. Simon, Clark and Galway (1972) found that women had difficulty locating colleagues with whom they could discuss ideas over lunch or with whom they could share research interests. One such woman observed that she had 'achieved less than full membership in the club and was left with a feeling that she was a member of a minority group that had not gained full acceptance' (Simon et al 1972).

Not only do the men fail to include women in their networks, but women hesitate to push their way in as well. For example, Epstein (1970) reports that women attorneys avoided joining their male colleagues for business lunches because they did not want to intrude. They based their reluctance on the receipt of sometimes verbal, but often nonverbal signals indicating they were not welcome.

When women do have friends among their colleagues, it is not clear that they benefit professionally. In a study of associational ties Kaufman (1978) found that 33 per cent of the women sampled reported that they had never received a professional benefit from their collegial relations with men. Although it was the women who had made the effort to cultivate these relations, the men did not collaborate with them. In Kaufman's view these women befriended men who either 'couldn't, wouldn't, or didn't know how to help them professionally.' Not surprisingly, married women held an advantage over unmarried ones, presumably because men were more comfortable with them.

Not every study has found women to be at a collegial disadvantage. Zuckerman and Cole (1975) examined authorship and co-authorship on published papers as an indicant of collaboration. They failed to find evidence for sex differences. The distribution of women and men as authors and co-authors was equal.

In spite of this contradictory finding, the available research pertinent to networking among academic women suggests that they are generally disadvantaged at least when the network is comprised of 'old boys.' Women do not participate in networking activities as often as men and men's efforts to exclude women from these networks frequently takes the form of subtle discrimination which is further exacerbated by women's reluctance to intrude.

Deviant, or token women may be treated as subordinate by men based on their ascribed status as women, rather than their achieved status as colleagues (Reskin 1978). Kanter's (1977a,b) research on tokenism indicates that tokens are very visible and function as symbolic, representative of their entire social category. As such, they are often stereotyped and assigned limited roles, reducing them to self-conscious isolates on the periphery of collegial interaction.

A recent study (Mitchell 1986) interviewed women assistant professors in the biological, physical and social sciences at a large university in California. These women were asked to indicate the extent to which they were connected to the collegial network in their home department on a five-point scale ranging from highly connected to un-connected. Highly connected women were found in all three fields. Not surprisingly, their publication rates were higher than their less connected peers. All of the highly connected women reported that they were sought out by their male colleagues for collaboration, and all were typically included in informal research discussions over lunch. All believed themselves to be well regarded within their departments and their disciplines, and the majority indicated that they had focused their research in specialized areas. This specialization was viewed as advan-tageous in attracting collaborators, establishing expertise, and providing professional visibility.

In contrast, low-connected women published less and reported that they were not often sought out for collaboration by male colleagues. Only half of them indicated that they were invited to research lunches. Only half of them felt they had received professional recognition for their work. Interestingly, none of these women had specialized in a particular area of research and 75 per cent of the low connected women characterized their work as outside the mainstream of their disciplines. The latter may explain why their male peers were less interested in col-laborating with them than the peers of the highly connected women.

There were no significant differences due to either scientific discipline or years in the field, suggesting that area of specialization is a key to integration in scientific networks. Consistent with this interpreta-tion, women who reported low connectedness with the old boy network saw themselves as operating on the periphery of their disciplines which resulted in difficulty in obtaining resources for their work, getting published, and earning recognition. In contrast, the highly connected women used their mainstream specialities to develop reputations for expertise and thereby gain introductions to other colleagues in related fields. Their specialities provided them with a springboard to establish visibility and contacts.

It has been suggested that marital status influences academic women's access to networks. Academic women tend to marry men in the same or similar fields (Astin 1969). Through their husbands these women may be introduced to other colleagues and expand their collegial network (Mitchell 1987) using a route to which unmarried women have limited access. Research results obtained by both Kaufman (1978) and Long (1989) support this interpretation. Male scientists may see married women as safer colleagues than unmarried ones. A survey of nine major universities by Mitchell (1987) found marital status, having a supportive academic spouse, and involvement in mainstream or 'hot' research topics were the major predictors of successful collegial relations with men.

Strategies

Like so many other behaviours the efficient constructive of effective networks is learned. All of the women in Mitchell's (1987) study recognized the importance of networking as a strategy for increasing visibility. They understood the importance of attending conferences, publishing, giving presentations, and organizing and participating in symposia in this regard. However, the highly connected women used other interpersonal tactics to build their networks as well. These tactics included

a) specializing in an area of research and offering to serve as a consultant in that area;
b) actively seeking out opportunities to display their abilities;
c) assertively soliciting introductions to colleagues;
d) investing time and energy in colleagues projects without reimbursement; and
e) utilizing their mentors networks for introductions.

These tactics are similar to those recommended by Scheele in her book, *Skills for Success* (1979). Scheele identified four interpersonal skills she deemed critical for career success: showing belonging, exhibiting specialization, magnifying accomplishments, and risking links with others. In addition to these tactics, men report utilizing telephone contacts, correspondence with major research facilities, and reliance on pre prints of publications (Parker, Linwood & Paisley 1968). Certainly, there is abundant anecdotal evidence that women are less assertive in advancing their own self interest than men. For example, male students seek out the professor to answer their questions, women students rely on teaching assistants; men praise one another's achievements and brag about their own, women are not as free in acknowledging one another, and they are often unduly modest about their own achievements.

Overall, the results of empirical studies of sex differences in access to and utilization of academic networks suggests that for women, one's selection of research area, the protection of marriage, (especially marriage to an academic spouse), and assertive efforts to be recognized by colleagues all help to advance women's academic standing.

The old girl network

Much of the literature on networking is really a literature of 'old boy' networks; networks that have traditionally excluded women. This suggests that women would be well served if they established their own networks to help themselves and each other. Several books have been published in the last decade that provide guidelines on how to go about establishing a woman's network. These books provide testimonials to the advantages of women using professional networks of other women. However, some of the academic women in Mitchell's (1986) study indicated that they were reluctant to participate in networks comprised exclusively of women for fear they would be labelled as 'feminists' or troublemakers by their male colleagues and regarded as unsuitable for their positions. Others had so few women colleagues that for them networking with women was not an option. Still others reported that their male colleagues' responses to women's networks were so derogatory that it made them self-conscious about associating with women. Nevertheless, the women in Mitchell's studies (1986, 1987) did indicate an increasing reliance on female colleagues for network contacts.

It is clear that the informal system of exchange among professional peers is essential to maintaining one's professional identity. What is less clear is the extent to which 'old girl' networks benefit women. For example, Brass (1985) found that men's and women's corporate networks were of approximately equal size, but that both sexes tended to interact within sex-segregated networks. Findings such as this one have led to the suggestion that women should *not* be encouraged to form their own networks as it isolates them from the integration that their careers require for advancement. However, women often have restricted access to informal networks and even when they are not restricted their avenues of access do not parallel those of men (Miller 1975; 1986).

Interestingly, at least one study examining the effects of female representation in the workplace found that when women represented a large minority, they were actually disadvantaged(South, Bonjean, Markum & Corder 1982). Contact with male co-workers decreased with the proportional representation of females. More importantly, the higher frequency of male contact generated by low proportions of female workers tended to increase the amount of social support they received from their male coworkers. In this study, one of the ways that large minority group representation negatively affected intergroup relations was by reducing intergroup contact. The greater the number of women in any given department, the less likely their male supervisors were to encourage any one of them to seek promotion.

The effect of female representation on relationships among females proved to be of two counterbalancing elements. On one hand, a large proportion of female workers promoted more frequent contact among females which lead to more mutual encouragement for advancement. On the other hand, female representation appeared to present competitive threats to female workers that impaired intragroup support. The net effect was for female representation in work groups to bear little relationship to the quality of relationships among women workers.

As South and his colleagues (1982) aptly observe, merely increasing the number of minority workers without altering the power relationships between dominants and subordinates is unlikey to improve the position of minorities. In fact, increases in minority group representation may lower the quality of dominant–submissive relations.

Toren (in Chapter 5) examines the relative efficacy of two contradictory predictions concerning the effects of proportions on the fate of minorities. Research in the race relation tradition (Blalock 1967) suggests that the smaller the minority, the less threatened the majority will feel and the less its members will discriminate against the minority. Kanter's (1977a) work suggests the opposite: that is that very small minorities (less than 15 per cent) will encounter greater discrimination, isolation and performance pressures than larger minorities. Toren obtained less evidence of discrimination among women in the physical sciences, whose numbers are actually fewer, than among women in the social sciences and humanities. She concludes that the greater discrimination against women in the social sciences and humanities is due not only to their proportional representation, but also to the differential salience of the sex role stereotypes that characterize women in the various disciplines.

If this is the case, increasing the proportion of women in positions of power and responsibility without a commensurate increase in the perception of their suitability for these positions is unlikely to have much effect on their ability to break into the old boy's network, or to ensure that the old girl's network advantages women to the same extent that the old boy's network advantages men.

In a recent survey (Hierick and Struggles 1986), less than half of the corporate women who responded indicated that they believed that networking had been a useful way to advance their careers. Instead, they ranked hard work, intelligence and leadership ability as the most important contributing factors to their career success. It may be that women are not as apt to recognize the importance of networking as are men, even though they may engage in the practice (O'Leary & Ickovics (1990), in press).

Queen Bees

A great deal has been written and assumed about the failure of women to support, even nurture, other women in the workplace. Staines and his colleagues (Staines, Travis, & Jayerante 1974) labelled such women 'Queen Bees.' Queen Bees are described by them as women who have achieved professional success and are anti-feminist. They are strongly individualistic and tend to deny the existence of discrimination based on sex (O'Leary 1988). Despite the fact that they hold positions of power and could help other women, they do not offer their support. It has been widely assumed that Queen Bees are not supportive because they fear that the success of other women would challenge their positions of power, positions maintained at the cost of other, lower status women (Kanter 1977b).

In 1977, Bardwick looked at the behaviours associated with queen beeism and suggested the possibility that their behaviour had been mis-interpreted. In her view, successful senior women rarely see themselves as powerful. Instead they focus on the increased responsibilites associated with their high status positions. Women without power, on the other hand, see its possession by one woman as a *de facto* obstacle to its attainment by others, including themselves. Thus, their relation-ships with successful women are ambivalent, at best. They ingratiate themselves to the more powerful woman in an attempt to secure her approval, while simultaneously resenting her.

Bardwick (1977) sees the disparity between the concept and experience of power among the powerful and the powerless as funda-mental to understanding the conflict so frequently observed between the two groups; a conflict rendered almost inevitable by the differential meaning assigned to power by those women who have it and those who do not. This alternative explanation for queen beeism is intriguing. It offers a rationale for powerful women's reluctance to support their weaker peers, anchored in a sensitivity to their positions as targets of ambivalence rather than to their personal ambition. To offer assistance to someone who demands your support – while at the same time resents you for being in a position to provide it – is difficult, at best.

Conceptually consistent with Bardwick's speculation, there is some suggestion in the literature relevant to women mentors' relationships with their proteges that breakdowns in these relationships occur when proteges' demands for attention exceed their mentors' expectations for reciprocity (O'Leary 1987). It may be that situations involving the violation of expectations that women hold for one another's behaviour result in the kind of (negative) affective intensity stereotypically associated with competitive relationships among women at work (O'Leary & Ickovics 1990).

In Ely's (1990) view, the notion of competition as being capable of taking on both constructive and destructive forms, centres on the processes of identification and differentiation in relationships between individuals. Identification involves experiential or psychological connectedness, and it occurs on the basis of perceived similarities. In contrast, differentiation is the expression of individuality based on differences in personality, skill, race, class, etc.

Ely (1990) suggests that the balance between identification and differentiation in interpersonal relationships at work is affected by the degree to which one's group memberships are represented in positions of organizational power. Over-identification and over-differentiation, which tend to result in dysfunctional competitiveness, are most likely to occur under conditions in which one's group membership is not adequately represented at senior levels within the organization. In one study, conducted in an almost exclusively woman operated institution, for instance, secretaries working for women directors reported healthy, productive relations – devoid of competition (O'Leary & Ickovics 1990).

Mentoring

Mentorship is not new. Odysseus had Mentor; King Arthur had Merlin. What is new is that women are now serving as mentors, and mentorship is recognized as a formal component of overall career and human resource development (Gerstein 1985). Derived from Greek mythology, 'mentoring' implies a relationship between a younger adult, and an older more experienced adult that helps the younger individual learn to navigate in the adult world and the world of work. A mentor supports, guides, and counsels the young adult as she or he accomplishes this important task.

Levinson and his colleagues (Levinson, Darrow, Klein, Levinson & McKee 1978), in their study of adult males, suggest that a mentor relationship is the most important relationship of young adulthood. They emphasize the importance of the mentor in the young adult's development:

In the usual course, a young man initially experiences himself as a novice or apprentice to a more advanced, expert, authoritative adult. As the relationship develops, he gains a fuller sense of his own authority and capability for autonomous and responsible action. The young man [sic] becomes more experienced in the "I am" of the adult, and the relationship becomes more mutual (Levinson et al 1978).

Relationships between younger and older adults that contribute to career development are alternatively referred to as mentor relationships (Levinson et al 1978), sponsor relationships (Kanter 1977a), patron relationships (Shapiro, Hazeltine, and Rowe 1987), godfather relationships (Kanter 1977a) or as a relationship between good friends. Each of these suggests a slightly different picture of the relationship. While there is some agreement about the potential value, there are different perceptions about the range of developmental functions provided, the intensity of the relationship, and the exclusivity of the relationship.

Kram (1985) suggests that there are a range of possible adult working relationships that support career development and that can be subsumed under the heading of mentoring. These functions can be divided into two broad categories; *career functions* to enhance learning the ropes and preparing for advancement and *psychosocial functions* to enhance a sense of competence, clarity of identity, and effectiveness in one's professional role. While career functions serve primarily to aid advancement, psychosocial functions affect each individual on a personal level by building self-worth.

The most critical element in successful mentor–mentee relationships is the recognition of reciprocal benefits. In one study, each of the benefits that accrued to the mentee also accrued to the mentor (Keele and La Mare-Schaefer 1984): opportunities to advance, increased control over the work environment, the creation of a support system, accessing more resources, developing reputations and personal satisfaction. Reciprocity seemed to underlie all aspects of developing proteges, leading the authors to conclude that even if women did not have mentors, they should be mentors.

Research results are equivocal on the question of whether or not women and minorities find fewer mentors than white men. However, there is some indication that mentor relationships are harder to manage and provide fewer benefits for women and minorities (Fagenson 1988; Herbert 1986; Kram 1985; Morrison and Von Glinow 1990).

Mentors and sponsors represent key relationships attributed to career success (Merriam 1983). However, a closer examination of the literature suggests that neither the enthusiasm about the mentors' value nor the protestations that everyone must have one (Collins & Scott 1978) are warranted (Speizer 1981). While having a mentor may be helpful there are also risks. As La France (1987) notes, if women get the mentoring they need, they may be seen as needing the mentoring they get. Others warn that mentoring relationships may be exploitive, over-protective, limiting, and damaging if the mentor of choice is a bad one (eg, Fury 1979; Levinson et al 1978). Despite these cautions, mentors still represent one efficient way of providing women access and even integration into the organization.

Although most advocates of mentoring recommend that mentor and protegé be of the same sex, there is some indication that women both prefer and attain the greatest benefits from male mentors. For example, Farylo and Paludi (1985) found that women indicated that sex was not a significant factor in their choice of role models, and they preferred men on the grounds that men were more 'professional'. Erkut and Mokros (1984) found that women with male mentors who attended women's colleges were academically most successful, felt most successful relative to male and female peers, and were significantly more likely to plan to attend graduate school than women whose mentors were women. Women preferred female mentors only when they had concerns about the sexism of the available male mentors (Paludi & Fahey 1986) and mentors who combined personal and professional roles (Paludi 1987).

It is important to note here the distinction between role models and mentors. Role models are individuals like whom one wants to be. It is not necessary to interact with a role model to be influenced by her or him. In contrast, the relationship between mentor and protegé requires interaction. One might select a woman as a role model and a man as a mentor, on the assumption that the man could provide more concrete career advice and rewards.

Gilbert, Gallesich and Evans (1983) obtained evidence that same sex role models were important to students' professional development. Women graduate students who identified women professors as role models viewed themselves as more career oriented, confident and instrumental than students identifying with male models. Tidball (1973) found that the number of career-successful women was directly proportional to the number of (successful) women available as role models in undergraduate institutions. Until women have as much power as men in the academic world, it is plausible to assume that women may prefer to look to them as visible experts on how to play professional roles, while looking to men to provide entry into those roles.

In one study (Dowdall & Boneparth 1979) found that junior women had different expectations of mentors than did junior men. Men expected more in terms of letters of recommendation and appointments to new positions (career functions) than did women. Further, women selected their mentors on the basis of personal knowledge, whereas men selected theirs on the basis of reputation. Consistent with this finding, Paludi and Fahey (1986) found that women chose women mentors when the senior women had children or appeared interpersonally warm.

There is some evidence (O'Leary 1988) that women's expecations for one another's performance in the workplace is high, often unrealistically so. When women actually have women mentors they may place demands upon them that are excessive; demands for both career and social emotional support. And women mentors may expect no less of themselves. One academic woman, when asked to describe her best mentoring experience related a story about assisting a young protegé when she went into labour in her office. She drove her to the hospital, stayed until the baby was born, and then helped to make a series of international telephone calls to inform her protegé's family of the birth. Her assistance at this time of need is not surprising. The fact that she categorized it as part of her mentoring functions is surprising. It may be that women have difficulty maintaining boundaries between professional and personal roles giving rise to unrealistic expectations and, invariably, to violations of these expectations that result in disappointment if not resentment (O'Leary 1987). To the extent that this is the case, it may explain some of the tension observed among junior and senior women at work.

Conclusion

To the extent that women in academe are isolated and even alienated, networking and mentorship provide them with potential avenues for integration. As career stategies they can and should be used singly, and in combination, to one's advantage, remembering that reciprocity is the key to both sucessful networking and mentoring relationships. One particularly appealing strategy involves restricting one's expectations for sponsorship to senior women and relying on peer support to satisfy one's socioemotional needs, thereby equalizing the demands placed on other women.

References

Astin, H (1969), *The woman doctorate in America*, New Russell: Sage.

Astin, H (1978), Women and work, In J Sherman and F Denmark (Eds), *Psychology of Women: Future Directions of Research*, New York: Psychological Dimensions.

Bardwick, J M (1977), Some notes about power relationships among women, In A G Sargent (Ed) *Beyond Sex Roles*, St. Paul, MN: West.

Bernard, J (1964), *Academic Women*, Pennsylvania: Penn State University Press.

Blalock, H M, Jr, (1967), *Toward a Theory of Minority Group Relations*, New York: Wiley.

Brass, D J (1985), Men's and women's networks: a study of interaction patterns and influence in an organization, *Academy of Management Journal* 28, pp 327–343.

Collins, E G & Scott, P (July–August, 1978) Everyone who makes it has a mentor, *Harvard Business Review* pp 89–101.

Dowdall, J A & Boneparth, E (August, 1979), Mentors in academia: The perceptions of proteges. Paper presented at the annual meeting of the American Sociological Association, Boston.

Ely, R (August, 1990), The dynamics of competitiveness and supportiveness in relationships among White professional women. Paper presented at the annual meeting of the Academy of Management, San Francisco.

Epstein, C (1970), Encountering the male establishment: sex-status limits on women's careers in the professions, *American Journal of Sociology*, 75 (6), pp 965–982.

Erkut, S & Mokross, J R (1984), Professors as models and mentors for college students. Working Paper No 65, Wellesley College Center for Research on Women.

Fagenson, E (1988), The power of a mentor, *Groups and Organization Studies*, **13**, pp 182–194.

Farylo, J & Paludi, M A (1985), Developmental discontinuities in mentor choice by male students, *Journal of Social Psychology*, **125**(4), pp 521–522.

Finkelstein, M (1982), Faculty colleagueship patterns and research. Paper presented at the annual meeting of the American Educational Research Association, New York. ERIC document Nos 216–633.

Fury, K (December 1979), Mentor mania, *Savvy* pp 42–47.

Gilbert, L A, Gallesich, J M & Evans, S L (1983), Sex of faculty role model and students' self-perceptions of competency, *Sex Roles* **9** (5), pp 597–607.

Gerstein, M (1985), *Journal of Counseling and Development*, Oct, Vol 64, pp 156–157.

Glass, M & Norwood, J (1959), How scientists actually learn of work important to them. Proceedings of the international conference on scientific information. Washington, DC: National Academy of Sciences.

Green, M (1982), A Washington perspective on women and networking: The power and the pitfalls, *Journal of NAWDAC* **46** pp 17–21.

Henner, S (1959), The information gathering habits of American medical scientists. Proceedings of the international conference on scientific information. Washington, DC: National Academy of Sciences, National Research Council.

Henning, M & Jardim, A (January 1977), Women executives in the corporate network, *Psychology Today*, pp 76–81.

Hierick and Struggles Consulting Firm (1986), *The Corporate Woman Officer*, Chicago, IL: Author.

Herbert, J I (1986), *The Adult Development of Black Male Entrepreneurs*. Unpublished doctoral dissertation, Yale University.

Kanter, R M (1977a), *Men and Women of the Corporation*, New York: Basic Books.

Kaufman, D (1978), Associational ties in academe: some male and female differences., *Sex Roles* **4**(1), pp 9–21.

Kanter, R M (1977b), Some effects of proportion on group life: skewed sex ratios and responses to token women, *American Journal of Sociology* **82**, pp 965–990.

Keele, R L, & La Mare-Schaefer, M (1984), So what do you do now that you don't have a mentor? *Journal of NAWDAC* **47**(3), pp 36–40.

Kram, K E (1985), Improving the mentoring process, *Training and Development Journal* **39**(4), pp 40–43.

Kyvik, S (1986), Postgraduate education in Norway, *European Journal of Education* **21**(3).

La France, M (July 1987), The politics of mentoring. Paper presented at the Third International Interdisciplinary Congress on Women, Dublin.

Levinson, D J, Darrow, C N, Klein, E B, Levinson, M H & McKee, B (1978), *The Seasons of a Man's Life*, New York: Knof.

Long, J S (1978), Productivity and the academic position, the scientific career, *American Sociology Review* **43**, pp 889–908.

Long, J S (1989) The origins of sex difference in science, paper prepared as GTE lecture at the Dept of Science and Technology Studies at Rennselaev Polytechnic Institute, Troy, NY.

Menzel, H (1962), Planned and unplanned scientific communication, in B Barber and W Hirsch (Eds), *The Sociology of Science*, New York: Free Press.

Merriam, S (Spring 1983), Mentors and proteges: A critical review of the litera-ture, *Adult Education Quarterly* **33** (3), pp 161–173.

Mitchell, J M (1986), Relation of structural career barriers to the productivity of academic women in the sciences. Unpublished manuscript, University of California, Los Angeles.

Mitchell, J M (1987), Association of the old boy network with productivity and career satisfaction of women academicians, and antecedents to the oldboy network. PhD dissertation. University of California, Los Angeles.

Miller, J (1986), *Pathways in the Workplace*, Cambridge: Cambridge University Press.

Miller, J, Labovitz, S, and Fry, L (1975), Inequities in the organizational experi-ences of women and men: resources, vested interests, and discrimination, *Social Forces* **54**, pp 365–81.

Morrison, A M & Von Glinow, M A (1990), Women and minorities in manage-ment, *American Psychologist* **45**, pp 200–208.

Nieva, V & Gutek, B A (1981), *Women and Work: A Psychological Perspective*, New York: Praeger.

O'Leary, V E (July 1987), When reciprocity fails: another look at queen bees. Paper presented at the Third International Interdisciplinary Congress on Women, Trinity College, Dublin.

O'Leary, V E (1988), Women's relationships with women in the workplace. In B Gutek, A H Stromberg, and L Larwood (Eds), *Women and Work: An Annual Review, Vol 3* Newbury Park, CA: Sage.

O'Leary, V E & Ickovics (1990), Women supporting women: secretaries and their bosses. In H Grossman and N Chester (Eds), *The Experience and Meaning of Work for Women* Hillsdale, NJ: Erlbaum.

O'Leary, V E, & Ickovics, J R (in press). Cracking the glass ceiling: overcoming isolation and alienation, in U Sekeran and F Leong (Eds), *Women: Managing for the Future*, San Francisco: Jossey-Bass.

Paludi, M A (July 1987), Women and the Mentor – Protégé relationship: a feminist critique of the inadequacy of old solutions. Paper presented at the Third International Interdisciplinary Congress on Women, Dublin.

Paludi, M A & Fahey, M (November 1986), Women and the mentor–protégé relationship: perceptions of competency, aspirations and self-worth. Paper presented at the Research on Women and Education Conference, Washington, DC.

Parker, E, Linwood, G & Paisley, W (1968), Research for psychologists at the interface of the scientist and his information system. *American Psychologist* **21**, pp 1061–1071.

Pelz, D (1956), Social factors related to performance in research organizations, *Administrative Science Quarterly* **1**, pp 310–325.

Prize, D & Beaver, D (1966), Collaboration in an invisible college, *American Psychologist*, **21**, pp 1011–1018.

Reskin, B (1978), Sex differentiation and the social organization of science, in J Glaston (Ed), *Sociology of Science*, San Francisco, CA: Jossey-Bass.

Scheele, A (1979), *Skills for Success*, New York: Ballentine Books.

Shapiro, E C, Hazeltine, F & Rowe, M (1978), Moving up: role models, mentors and the patron system, *Sloan Management Review* **19**, pp 33–39.

Simon, R, Clark, S & Galway, K (1972), The woman PhD: A recent profile, in J Bardwick (Ed) *Readings on the Psychology of Women*, New York: Harper & Row.

South, S J, Bonjean, C M, Markum, W T, & Corder, J (1982), Social structure and intergroup interaction, *American Sociological Review* **47**, pp 589–599.

Speizer, J J (1981), Role models, mentors, and sponsors: the elusive concepts, *Signs: Journal of Women in Culture and Society* **6** (4), pp 692–712.

Stern, B (1981), *Is Networking for you?* New Jersey: Prentice-Hall.

Tidball, M E (1980), Women's colleges and women achievers revisited, *Signs* **5**, pp 504–17.

Staines, G, Travis, C & Jayerante, T (1974), The Queen Bee Syndrome, *Psychology Today* **7** (8), pp 55–60.

Welch, M (1980), *Networking: The Great New Way for Women to Get Ahead*, New York: Harcourt, Brace, Jovanovich.

White, M (1970), Psychological barriers to women in the sciences. *Science* **170** pp 413–416.

Zuckerman, H & Cole, J (1975), Women in American science, *Minera* **13**, pp 82–102.

Chapter 5

Would More Women Make a Difference? Academic Women in Israel

Nina Toren

Developing theories based on numbers of people and their distribution among different social positions has considerable appeal for social scientists, who are often accused of dealing with qualitative and ill-defined variables. This concern with numerical composition of groups and other social collectivities is closely associated with the issues of minority–majority relations and the emergence of structural inequality.

Two contradictory predictions concerning the effects of proportions on the fate of minorities have been put forward in the literature. Research in the race-relations tradition suggests that the smaller the minority the less threatened the majority will feel, and the less its members will engage in discriminating behaviour against the minority (Blalock 1967).

On the other hand, Kanter (1977), in her research on a large corporation, predicts that very small minorities (constituting less than 15 per cent of a group) will encounter greater discrimination, isolation and performance pressures than larger minorities. These adverse conditions for 'tokens' are produced by their greater visibility, contrast with the majority and stereotyping.

Empirical studies testing Kanter's hypothesis, especially for minorities of women in various organizational and occupational settings, came up with contradictory results. A study by Spangler et al (1978) examining the effect of small proportions of women law students on their academic achievements, confirmed Kanter's theory by showing that small minority size had a negative effect on achievement scores. Similar conclusions were also drawn by Izraeli (1983) in a study on sex composition in union work committees. On the other hand, a study by South et al (1982) on the effects of skewed sex composition of work groups in the US federal bureaucracy, largely disproved Kanter's theory, supporting the opposite hypothesis that the larger the proportion of a minority the more its members will be discriminated against by the majority. In any event, it is now well established that the sex composition of a group, organization or occupation is an important factor which affects women's working careers.

The objective of this study is to examine the effects of women's minority size on their academic positions and careers in Israeli universities. Academia provides a particularly interesting setting for such an analysis because of its fundamentally egalitarian and collegial ethos. Inequities between the sexes in this area should be less pronounced than in other occupational spheres in which so-called 'masculine' characteristics, such as physical strength, technical skills or leadership and authority are involved.

Notwithstanding ideological and formal equality, the academic labour market is segregated and sex-typed. That is, most of its members are of one sex – 88 per cent are men and 12 per cent are women – and entering this profession is still perceived as somewhat 'inappropriate' for women. Furthermore, it is documented by research in various countries that gender-linked differences exist in the distribution of rewards in academia. Women receive on average fewer rewards than comparable men – they hold lower ranks, are paid lower salaries, are promoted at a slower pace, fewer of them have tenure and more of them are in non-tenure track positions. Even when women are matched with men on the major determinant of performance in academia – the rate of publication – they still receive less reward and move up the academic ladder at a slower pace (Bayer and Astin 1975; Reskin 1978; Rosenfeld 1981; Cole and Zuckerman 1984).

However, these discrepancies between the sexes in academia vary by scientific and scholarly discipline. Research findings show that women fare better in terms of promotion opportunities, rank, salary and tenure in the natural sciences than in the social sciences and the humanities (Cole 1979; Morlock 1973). At the same time it has also been noted that women in natural-science fields constitute very small minorities (eg, about 4 per cent in physics), while in sociology and psychology they comprise 15 to 20 per cent, and over 20 per cent in the humanities and the arts.

Various explanations have been proposed for the differential inequalities between the sexes by discipline. For instance, that women physicists are less likely to be married than women in sociology and the arts; that the former tend to publish more and work in a more hospitable environment; and that both women and men advance more rapidly in the physical sciences. These explanations are not supported by adequate empirical data which could account for the discrepancies between women and men on the one hand, and among women in different scientific fields on the other hand. There has been no systematic attempt to explain the status of faculty women in terms of their proportions in different scientific fields, although over 20 years ago it was already noted 'that in [scientific] fields in which women comprise a larger component of the total labour force, more discrimination in promotions may be experienced.' (Bayer and Astin, 1975, p 199). Coser (1981) has more recently presented findings from a number of studies in the United States, the Soviet Union and Western Europe which support the conclusion that there is a *negative* correlation between women's rate of participation and their rewards in academia: the higher the proportion of women in a scientific field the lower are their rewards in terms of salary, tenure and rank as compared to those of men. Moreover, these findings are in accord with studies on segregation in the general labour market which show that higher unemployment rates and more income and promotion discrimination exist in occupations in which women are more numerous (Semyonov 1980; Pfeffer 1977).

The purpose of the following analysis is to compare the achievements of faculty women and men in terms of academic ranking and to examine the effects of sex ratios in different scientific fields.

Background and population

The distribution of the female faculty in Israeli higher education is similar to that in the United States and Western countries. Their percentage is lowest in the natural sciences (8.4 per cent), somewhat higher in the social sciences (11.3 per cent), and highest in the humanities (18.6 per cent). The average proportion of women across scientific disciplines and universities is 12 per cent (see Table 5.1).

Table 5.1 *Faculty by sex and scientific field (numbers and percentages)*

Field	Men N	Women N	Total N	Per cent Women of Total Faculty	Per cent Women of Total Women
Total	2946	411	3357	12.2	100.0
Humanities	677	155	832	18.6	38.0
Social Sciences	486	62	548	11.3	15.0
Natural Sciences	1119	103	1222	8.4	25.0
Engineering & Architecture	400	14	414	3.4	3.4
Law & Criminology	56	10	66	15.2	2.4
Social Work	47	9	56	16.0	2.2
Education	90	41	131	31.3	10.0
Other and Not Known	71	17	88	19.3	4.0

A number of differences between the sexes in respect to working conditions which characterize the American academic sphere do not exist in Israel. The faculty population studied here is therefore much more homogeneous: all faculty personnel by definition have a PhD or an equivalent degree; salaries are equal for the same rank with only slight differences according to number of children and seniority; and teaching loads are the same for all faculty members varying slightly by rank (but not by sex). Furthermore, there are no differences in working conditions, salaries and academic ranks among universities. All the institutions of higher education studied here are four-year universities with undergraduate, graduate and doctoral programmes, and a strong emphasis on research.

The data of this study concern men and women who held tenure-track, full-time academic appointments in 1983 in three large universities in the faculties of the natural sciences and the humanities. The academic hierarchy in Israel comprises four ranks: lecturer, senior lecturer, associate professor and full professor. Faculty members in these ranks are called 'senior academic staff'; tenure is usually granted with the rank of senior lecturer.

Individuals in lower ranks, such as research assistants, or with non-career appointments in which a person cannot advance beyond the rank of senior lecturer or cannot obtain tenure were not included in the sample (Toren and Nvo-Ingber 1989).

Figure 5.1 portrays the rank distributions of men and women across all scientific disciplines in all institutions of higher education in Israel in 1983.

We have chosen a faculty as the unit of analysis rather than a department in order to have a reasonable number of men and women in each group. Two faculties are compared – the natural sciences, in which the proportion of women is lowest, and the humanities, in which it is highest. The main departments composing the natural-science faculties are; mathematics, computer sciences, physics, chemistry and life sciences. The humanities include Jewish studies, history, languages, literature and art.

The present study does not examine the dynamics of majority–minority interaction, such as frequency and quality of contacts, encouragement, co-operation, discrimination and the like. Rather the focus is on the end result or the consequences of such processes as represented by academic rank. Thus, the dependent variable is the distribution of women along the academic hierarchy as compared to that of their male colleagues. The independent variable is women's minority size. The following analyses pertain to six faculties, two in each of the three universities investigated.

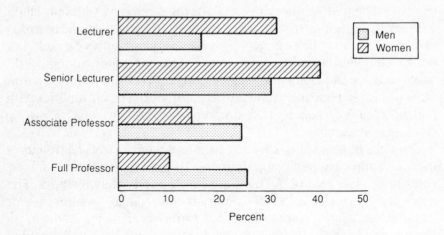

Figure 5.1 *Distribution of academic ranks by sex*

The effects of minority size

The effects of women's minority size on their academic status were analysed by using the aggregated distributions of men and women in each faculty on the four academic ranks. For measuring the dissimilarity between the sexes in respect to their position on the hierarchy, the Lieberson index of net-differences (Lieberson 1982) was employed.[1] The higher the value of this index the larger are the discrepancies between the rank distributions of men and women.

Table 5.2 shows the percentage of women in decreasing order, and the corresponding ND index, for each of the six faculties composing the sample. It can be seen that the higher the proportion of women in a faculty, the lower they are in terms of academic rank relative to their male colleagues. This conclusion is most clearly supported by the evidence from the three faculties of humanities. Figure 5.2 which is a graphic presentation of Table 5.2, shows a consistent decrease in women's relative ranking as their proportion increases. Two of the three natural-science faculties also fit this pattern; the exception being the natural-science faculty in Bar-Ilan University where women's position is

Table 5.2 *Faculty number, percent women, and net difference by scientific field and university*

Total number of faculty	Percent Women	ND*	Field and University
166	20.6	0.49	Humanities – Bar Ilan University
254	19.3	0.40	Humanities – Hebrew University
215	14.6	0.32	Humanities – Tel Aviv University
235	9.6	0.24	Natural Sciences – Tel Aviv University
358	8.3	0.14	Natural Sciences – Hebrew University
98	6.5	0.20	Natural Sciences – Bar-Ilan University

*The higher the ND index the greater the dissimilarity between men's and women's academic rank distributions.

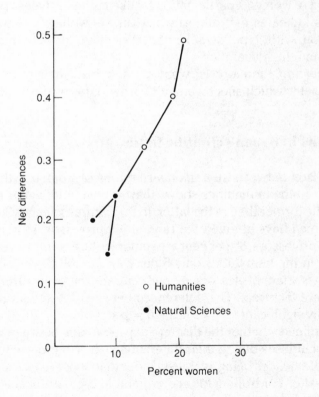

Figure 5.2 *Index of net differences by percent women and by faculty*

somewhat worse than could have been expected on the basis of their minority size.

These results are in accord with the studies mentioned above which show that the proportion of women in the general labour force is positively correlated with occupational and income discrimination against women. Our findings, however, do not support Kanter's theory which would predict women's position to be worse in natural-science faculties in which the sex composition is 'skewed' and women are 'tokens' (less than 15 per cent), than in the humanities where the composition is 'tilted' and women are a 'minority' (over 15 per cent), see Kanter 1977, p 209).

It is also apparent that minority size and type of faculty overlap; women comprise larger minorities in the humanities (over 14.6 per cent), and smaller minorities (less than 9.6 per cent) in the natural-science faculties. An analysis of variance shows that the interaction term between type of faculty and female participation, in regard to their relative ranking (ND) is statistically significant (at the .05 level). The main effect of women's participation by itself is nevertheless not significant. This indicates that minority size affects women's status only in conjunction with *type* of scientific discipline, namely the natural sciences and the humanities.

The question therefore is: what are the relevant factors of these scientific fields which affect women's career patterns differently?

Variations between scientific fields

A comparison between the rank distributions of *women* in the natural sciences and the humanities shows that women hold higher academic ranks in the former than in the latter. In the natural sciences 30 per cent of the women have attained the rank of full professor, 18 per cent are associate professors, 38 per cent are senior lecturers and 14 per cent are lecturers. In the humanities only 5 per cent are full professors, 16 per cent are associate professors, 42 per cent are senior lecturers, and 37 per cent are lecturers. The differences between these distributions is statistically significant ($X^2 = 25.23$; $df = p < .001$).

We examined whether the discrepancy in ranking between women in the two faculties is due to their different age distribution, with those in the natural sciences being averagely older than those in the humanities. However, after controlling for age, women in the natural sciences still fare better, in terms of rank, as compared to their sisters in the humanities.[2]

We can therefore conclude that the greater success of women in the natural sciences in respect to career mobility is not due to their age and/

or seniority, but is related to their minority size and the nature of the scientific field in which they are engaged.

As noted, sheer numbers do not account for differential status attainments of female faculty in the natural sciences as compared to the humanities. It is suggested that in addition to different sex composition there are important variations between scientific fields regarding the *salience* or *activation* of sex statuses and gender-based stereotypes, which should be considered when explaining women's academic positions.

According to expectation-states theory (Berger et al 1977) sex, like race and ethnic origin, functions as a diffuse status characteristic from which general assumptions about individuals are inferred. Expectations are higher for individuals whose diffuse external status is high (ie, men), while lower status incumbents (ie, women) are expected to perform less well; they are given fewer opportunities for interaction, their performance is evaluated less positively, and they have influence on group decisions. Irrespective of their relevance to task performance diffuse status characteristics, imported from the broader social environment, generate intragroup inequality.

Since science and scientists are generally perceived as masculine (Keller 1987), women possess the 'wrong' sex characteristic for the role of academic scientist or scholar. It seems, however, that the performance expectations directed at the small minority of women in the natural sciences are higher than those expected from women in other disciplines. They are expected to 'work like men' – spend long hours in the lab – and 'produce like men' in terms of publications. They are less afflicted by 'the haunting presence of functionally irrelevant statuses' (Merton as quoted in Zuckerman and Cole 1975, p 100). This imagery seems to be associated with the commonly held belief that if a woman holds a tenured and relatively high (professorial) rank, particularly in physics or mathematics, then 'she must be really good!' These perceptions and attitudes are adopted by women themselves as expressed by one respondent: 'To be successful in the natural sciences a woman has be "a real man"!' Furthermore, our data show that in natural-science faculties women usually do not stay away from work for the whole duration of the formal maternity leave (12 weeks) but return to their work much earlier. Commenting on women's work orientation in different scientific fields, a female natural scientist said:

The structure of the natural sciences demands absolute persistence. In the humanities and the social sciences you can intermit your career and come back again. In the natural sciences this is impossible. Women who choose these fields are more determined in their decision and therefore more successful.

And to quote another:

Women in the humanities have lower levels of aspirations, whereas in the natural sciences you have to make a serious commitment. There is no 'half and half' in these fields, no part-time jobs. Women have to devote themselves totally to their work. They need this kind of coercion.

In addition to differential expectations, inequality in social groups is also maintained by differential performance evaluations. Namely, achievements of individuals with lower status are not as highly evaluated and rewarded as those with superior status.

The evaluation of scientific output in the natural sciences is easier and more objective because these fields are characterized by greater clarity and consensus in judging the worth of a contribution. Under these conditions, gender effects are minimized or neutralized. When, however such criteria are ambiguous or lacking and it is difficult to assess the quality of performance, irrelevant extraneous attributes such as gender, become more salient and influence performance evaluations.[3]. To quote a respondent:

It is easy to measure and evaluate results in the natural sciences, therefore the worth of women's work and contribution cannot be disregarded. In the humanities and social sciences there are no clear criteria and evaluation involves a complex process of discretion.

By comparison, in the 'softer' scientific fields women enter academic careers in greater numbers and constitute larger minorities but are expected to be less talented and competent. Literature, languages, art, sociology and psychology, not to mention education and social work, are perceived as more appropriate for women. Work in these areas is more congruent with their traditionally cultural and nurturing roles. The female sex status is therefore more salient and both women and men find it difficult to disregard its concomitant stereotypes.

Conclusion

While academia is predominately the domain of men, there are some scientific fields that are more strongly sex-typed than others. Female minority per se cannot, however, account for the large disparities between the sexes in terms of ranking in the humanities and their greater resemblance in the natural sciences. If women fare less well in the former than in the latter it is not due to their different proportions alone but is associated with the different salience of sex stereotypes attached to women in these disciplines. In general, occupational sex segregation, sustained by gender stereotypes, is one of the most stable and stubborn characteristics of modern societies, and is one of the principal sources of differential status attainment by men and women, independent of their human capital.

This study suggests that increasing the proportion of women in university faculties without changing the prevalent perceptions of their sex-based attributes in relation to the academic–scientific role, is not likely to improve their position. Experimental research has shown that gender stereotypes can be challenged and changed by introducing valid information contrary to these images and expectations: namely, that the competence and commitment to achieve 'excellence in science and scholarship' is not sex-linked and is equally distributed among women and men.

Furthermore, when examining women's careers in academia (as well as in other occupational spheres) we should shift our attention away from individual dispositions and attributes. Women have been accused for too long of being less motivated, dedicated and involved in their work, and as investing less effort in their careers outside the home. These are untested assumptions which have not been unequivocally supported by empirical evidence but have served to justify women's inferior position and lesser attainments in the labour market. In any event, these beliefs do not apply to women in high-status professions, such as science and management, who are as committed to their work as men and who invest more, not less, effort in it (Bielby and Bielby 1988; Toren 1989). Rather, research should be focused on the structure of the occupational and institutional settings (eg, organizational barriers, sex segregation, sex composition) as important factors determining women's entrance, performance and achievement in academia and other work areas.

Notes

1. The ND index measures the difference and its direction between two distributions of inequality. The value of the index ranges from + 1.0 (if the lowest value of the academic rank in the male population exceeds the highest value of the academic rank in the female population) to –1.0 (if the lowest value in the female population is greater than the highest in the male population): it will be zero if the two distributions are the same.

2. The age-adjusted rank distribution shows that 18.3 per cent in the natural sciences as compared to 35.5 per cent in the humanities are in the lowest rank of lecturer. On the other hand, only 7.1 per cent in the humanities hold the highest rank of full professor, while 26.5 per cent in the natural sciences have achieved this rank.

3. Other studies have shown that in 'low consensus' fields (like political science) decisions concerning salary and promotion of faculty are more influenced by such factors as sex, age, prestige of PhD-granting institution, and personal relations. Whereas in 'high consensus' paradigmatic fields (like physics and chemistry) greater emphasis is given to performance criteria (Pfeffer et al 1977).

References

Bayer, Allan E, and Astin, Helen S (1975), Sex differentials in the academic reward system, *Science* 188, pp 796–802.

Berger, Joseph, Hamit Fisek, M, Norman, Robert, Z, and Zelditch, Morris Jr (1977), *Status Characteristics and Social Interaction*, New York: Elsevier.

Bielby, Denise D and William T (1988), She works hard for the money: household responsibilities and the allocation of work effort, *American Journal of Sociology* 93, pp 1031–59.

Blalock, Hubert M, Jr (1967), *Towards a Theory of Minority Group Relations*, New York: Wiley.

Cole, Jonathan R (1979), *Fair Science: Women in the Scientific Community*, New York: The Free Press.

Cole, Jonathan R, and Zuckerman, Harriet (1984), The productivity puzzle: persistence and change in patterns of publication of men and women scientists, pp 217–56 in *Advances in Motivation and Achievement*, P Maehr and M W Steinkamp (eds), Connecticut: JAI.

Coser, Rose Laub (1981), Where Have All the Women Gone? pp 16–33 in Cynthia Fuchs Epstein and Rose Laub Coser (eds), *Access to Power: Cross-National Studies of Women and Elites*, London: Allen & Unwin.

Izraeli, Dafna N (1983), Sex effects or structural effects? An empirical test of Kanter's theory of proportions, *Social Forces* 62, pp 153–65.

Kanter, Rosabeth Moss (1977), *Men and Women of the Corporation*, New York: Basic Books.

Keller, Evelyn F (1987), Women scientists and feminist critics of science, *Daedalus* 116, pp 77–91.

Lieberson, Stanley (1982), Rank-sum comparisons between groups, *Sociological Methodology: Annual Review*, San Francisco: Jossey-Bass, Behavioral Science Series.

Morlock, Laura L (1973), Discipline variation in the status of academic women, *Academic Women on the Move*, New York: Russell Sage Foundation.

Pfeffer, Jeffrey, Leong, A and Strehl, K (1977), Paradigm development and particularism: journal publication in three scientific fields, *Social Forces* 55, pp 938–51.

Reskin, Barbara F (1978), Scientific productivity, sex and location in the institution of science, *American Journal of Sociology* 83, pp 1235–43.

Rosenfeld, Rachel A (1981), Academic men and women's career mobility, *Social Science Research*, 10, pp 337–63.

Semyonov, Moshe (1980), The social context of women's labour force participation: a comparative analysis, *American Journal of Sociology* 86, pp 534–50.

South, Scott J, Bonjean, Charles M, Markham, William T and Corder, Judy (1982), Social structure and intergroup interaction: men and women of the federal bureaucracy, *American Sociological Review* 47, pp 587–99.

Spangler, Eve, Gordon, Marsha A and Pipkin, Ronald M (1978), Token women: an empirical test of Kanter's hypothesis, *American Journal of Sociology* 84, pp 160–70.

Toren, Nina and Nvo-Ingber, Judith, (1989), Organizational response to decline in the academic marketplace, *Higher Education* 18, no 4.

Toren, Nina (1989), *The Nexus Between Family and Work Roles of Academic Women: Reality and Representation*, (unpublished manuscript).

Zuckerman, Harriet and Cole, Jonathan R (1975), Women in American science, *Minerva* XIII: 82, p 102.

Part III
Barriers to Productivity

Chapter 6

Life Cycle, Career Patterns and Gender Stratification in Academe: Breaking Myths and Exposing Truths

Diane E Davis and *Helen S Astin*

New directions in gender stratification research

With the accumulation of close to two decades of research on gender, scholars are rapidly moving beyond their initial concerns with overall patterns of gender stratification across occupations, and analysing patterns of gender stratification within certain occupations or professions. Using theories of status attainment, much of the recent and innovative research on gender stratification explores the extent to which rewards like salary and promotion are equally distributed between men and women within certain professions

Among such studies, one professional domain that has captured increasing research attention is the academic. One reason for this is that academe offers relatively standardized and identifiable criteria for measurement of status attainment and its contributing factors.[1] What is probably most striking about the growing body of research on gender stratification in academe is that it has produced inconclusive results. There is widespread disagreement and controversy over the extent to which gender differences in status attainment in academe exist, as well as how and why.

In this chapter we attempt to place systematically the wide variety of published findings about gender stratification into a coherent framework that makes sense of the plethora of competing claims about gender and status attainment in academe. Are these competing claims due to problems in the formulation of the studies themselves? Or do these results reflect some version of reality?

In answering these questions, we have two objectives. The first is to demonstrate that women's ability to attain the same status levels as men is determined by factors and conditions beyond gender. In other words, it is not a woman's gender status, per se, but her age, marital status, and social relationships or position that determine productivity patterns and reputational standing in academe. Our second objective is to explain how and why life- and career-cycle expectations and constraints affect women in academe. Our goal is to construct a more empirically consistent and analytically sophisticated theory of status attainment, gender stratification, and of the role that social and psychological factors play in the process.

We begin with a discussion of the literature and the general findings on sex differentials in academe. We analyse findings from studies on gender and productivity as well as gender and reputational standing because they constitute two of the most critical aspects of status attainment in academe (Astin and Bayer 1979; Cole 1979; Long 1978). However, owing to the paucity of research on gender and reputational standing – as well as the fact that productivity patterns themselves play a principal role in determining reputational standing (Astin and Bayer 1979; Davis and Astin 1987) – we confine most of our discussion and analysis to studies of gender differences in productivity.

Data

To buttress our review and discussion of the body of published research on status attainment in academe, we also incorporate primary data and findings from two surveys we conducted over the last several years on women, productivity and reputational standing in academe (Davis and Astin 1987; Astin and Davis 1985; Jacobi and Astin 1985; Astin and Snyder 1982; Astin and Bayer 1979).[2] In the first study we surveyed 9500 academic personnel drawn from a representative sample of 98 higher-education institutions in 1980. A subsample of highly productive respondents (n = 299) to this survey was then selected for a second survey in 1982 which focused on highly productive scholars. The data presented here are for the social scientists only: N = 1410 and 51 respectively.

Together, these various sources of primary and secondary data are used both to break myths and expose truths about the extent to which gender – either directly or in conjunction with certain other conditions – facilitates or impedes status attainment in academe, how and why it does so, and with what theoretical implications and practical consequences for women and the academic worlds.

Sex differentials in academe: inconclusive findings

Research on the influence of gender on productivity has produced inconclusive results. Converse and Converse (1971), Cole and Cole (1973), and Astin and Bayer (1979) found that in the aggregate, academic women are less productive with respect to research and publication than their male colleagues. However, Robinson (1973) reported that gender accounted for no more than 1 per cent of the variance in productivity among faculty members in the fields of mathematics, political science, and chemistry. And Reskin's (1977) assessment of sex differences, using several measures of research productivity, suggests a small but statistically non-significant tendency for men to be more productive than women.

Studies of the influence of gender on reputational standing are also inconclusive, particularly if we compare our recent findings with the conclusions presented by Jonathon R Cole in an earlier study of women in American academe. Cole's controversial book, *Fair Science: Women in the Scientific Community* (1979), has provided one of the most thorough examinations of gender, productivity and reputational standing published in the United States. Cole concludes that in recent years the rewards of science have been distributed equally among its practioners, male and female, according to the universal criteria of quantity and quality of output.

Cole made his argument by first identifying the factors which were most influential in determining reputational standing for both men and women. They were: selectivity of current department, selectivity of PhD department, number of honorific awards received, and academic rank. After controlling for these factors, Cole identified gender as significantly affecting the prominence, esteem, and notoriety of scientists. He found that women had lower levels of reputational standing, which he attributed to lower levels of research performance, measured in terms of quantity and quality of work.

Cole's book stirred much debate among feminists and academic scholars, raising questions about the subtle biases and contextual factors that affect the scholarly enterprise for men and women. Precisely because his book ignored many of the personal and organizational factors that impose heavy burdens on women and that mediate the relationships between gender, productivity and status attainment in academe, we decided to analyse the impact of social, institutional, and personal factors on academic research and scholarship (Davis and Astin 1987).

In our subsample ($N = 51$) of highly productive academics in the social sciences, we found that there were no significant gender differences in reputational standing.[3] Women in this subsample did not have significantly lower research performance, either in terms of quantity or quality of work (see Table 6.1). Indeed, we found that women were *not* different from men in achieving both subjective and objective criteria of quality.[4] Moreover, the quantity of women's work was found to be equal to that of men in some respects (article publication) and higher in

Table 6.1 *Career productivity rates among highly productive social scientists, by publication type.* * N = 51 (means)*

	Total	Men	Women
Mean number of books	1.7	2.0	1.3
published	(1.9)**	(2.3)	(1.5)
Mean number of chapters	10.2	7.1	13.4
published	(10.5)	(6.2)	(13.0)
Mean number of articles	25.1	25.0	13.4
published	(12.2)	(13.4)	(12.7)

*Based on data from a sample of 26 female and 25 male highly productive social scientists, including psychologists.
**Standard deviation.
Source: Reputational standing in academe, Diane E Davis and Helen S Astin, *Journal of Higher Education*, vol 58, no 3, 1987.

others (chapter publications). And though women did trail behind with respect to book publication, they did so only negligibly.

Given these findings, one might conclude that biological sex alone is not a very good predictor of either productivity or reputational standing, since female status does not appear uniformly to influence either. Is there a gender dimension to status attainment? If so, what explains differences in productivity patterns and reputational standing? Might differences be greater among your average academic than among highly productive 'superstars' – and if so, why?

One possible response is that it is not biological sex difference per se, but subtle forms of discrimination and various gender-specific personal obligations and social responsibilities placed on women that negatively affect their professional life, up to the point of preventing them from reaching positions of high productivity and eminence.

Several studies have attempted to test this notion by investigating the effects of marriage on women's research productivity. Reskin (1977) found that neither marriage nor childbearing could explain the slightly lower productivity of women chemists. In fact, in our recent work (Astin and Davis 1985) we found that being married positively affects academic women's research productivity, at least in terms of the mean number of publications. At all academic ranks, married women published consistently more than single women.[5] Moreover, the patterns of publications for married women and married men were almost identical for all ranks, except for full professor where men tended to publish slightly more than women when productivity was measured cumulatively.[6] These findings have been corroborated by studies which found that married women's careers resemble those of men more closely than do the professional careers of single women, with respect to educational preparation, field of study and publication rates (Astin and Bayer 1979).

With the influence of marriage appearing negligible in explaining gender differences in productivity, researchers have now begun to consider that gender differences in productivity might be explained by mediating factors other than family obligations. It has been suggested that apparent differences in productivity might be attributable to gender differences in tenure status, since men tend more frequently to be tenured and they reach full professorial rank more easily than do academic women.[7]

Yet we found that both men and women continue to be productive following tenure; in fact, women's yearly productivity after tenure was higher (3.5) than that of men (3.0) (Astin and Davis 1985, p 152). However, women's article productivity rate before tenure (2.0) was significantly lower than men's (2.5) (Astin and Davis, 1985, p 152). In seeking an explanation for this tendency, we considered stages in the life cycle, and we found that low rates of productivity pre-tenure were not uniform among all women.

Rather, low pre-tenure rates may be the result of lower productivity among single compared to married women. Single women's productivity may be affecting women's overall post-tenure rates, as well, since after tenure single women's mean article-publication rate increases at a slower rate and continues to be lower than that of either married men or married women. This so-called life-cycle factor is a complex one: at the same time that they have lower pre-tenure article-publication rates than either married women or men, single women have higher post-tenure book-publication rates than either married women or men.

In short, there appear to be differences among women in the extent to which they reach parity with men in productivity rates, and these differences seem to correlate with stages in both the life and career cycles as well as with the type of publication preferred. The critical question, then, is why?

High productivity: institutional, personal, and organizational factors

In our preliminary review of the factors bearing on scholarly and research productivity among American academics some of the following findings emerged. Highly productive academics are more likely to be tenured (associate professor or above), regardless of sex (see Table 6.2). However, highly productive female academics tend to be distributed more evenly across the associate- and full-professor levels, while for men they are more concentrated among the full-professor level. Among the highly productive, there is also a higher proportion of women who were currently married (59.6 per cent

Table 6.2 *Characteristics of highly productive faculty compared to faculty in general, all fields, (percentages)*

Characteristics	Men		Women	
	Faculty in general (N = 7676)	Productive faculty (N = 176)	Faculty in general (N = 1684)	Productive faculty (N = 123)
Median age*	47.0	46,2	44.7	41.7
Maternal education				
College or higher	21.6	17.1	27.1	22.0
Marital status				
Married	88.3	86.6	51.6	59.6
Single, never married	4.6	3.7	30.5	22.0
Divorced/Separated/				
Widowed	7.1	9.7	17.9	18.4
Spouse's education				
Advanced degree	37.0	43.7	60.5	80.0
Spouse employed in academe	26.0	24.1	28.1	39.0
Rank				
Full professor	52.5	70.2	21.2	44.9
Associate professor	30.6	22.4	32.5	34.6
Assistant professor	10.6	5.6	28.9	17.8
Instructor or other	6.3	1.8	17.4	2.7
Median hours spent per week in:				
Administration	3.8	1.0	3.4	1.0
Scheduled teaching	7.3	3.5	9.1	3.5
Preparation for teaching	8.7	5.5	9.5	7.2
Advising and counselling	3.9	1.6	4.1	2.5
Research and writing	8.1	12.2	4.2	11.8
Committee work	3.0	0.7	3.3	0.7

*In actual age, not percentages.

Source: Survey of Academic Personnel, Higher Education Research Institute, UCLA, 1980.

compared to 51.6 per cent in the general sample). And among women in general, 40 per cent of the highly productive reported having academic spouses compared to 29 per cent of women in the larger sample. It is worth noting that there are many more single women than single men in academe.

Some additional differences between the productive group and faculty in general include age, maternal education and work activities.[8] For example, the median age of productive scholars was 41.7 years for women and 46.2 years for the men, compared to 44.7 and 47.0 years, respectively, among the sample of faculty in general. The younger age among productive scholars, particularly women, can be explained on two accounts: having more women assistant professors compared to men and the observed high productivity among young faculty prior to their achieving tenure. Also, we see differences in median hours spent in various activities for both men and women and between productive and non-productive faculty. The productive faculty indicate spending more time in research and writing and less in teaching and administrative work as compared to faculty in general.

In several of the activities there are also significant gender differences. As a whole, women spend less time on research and scholarly writing than men, and women faculty in general spend less than half the time male faculty do on these activities. Significantly, time spent on teaching preparation – which usually brings little kudos for professors and often impedes productivity, shows the opposite pattern: women as a whole spend more time preparing for teaching (see Table 6.2).

Our preliminary comparisons of highly productive versus faculty in general also highlighted the personal, organizational and institutional conditions that are associated with high productivity among men and women. The most productive faculty tend to be employed by the most selective academic institutions, tend to have received their degrees from selective institutions, and tend to be located at universities rather than colleges. Yet even within these institutional contexts, women exhibit slightly different patterns to men: highly productive women are much more likely than faculty women in general to be at highly selective institutions than are highly productive men (compared to faculty men in general). Also, highly productive women are more likely to have received their degrees from highly selective institutions (as compared to women in general) than are highly productive men (as compared to men in general). Nonetheless, women still tend to be more concentrated in less selective institutions and colleges (rather than universities), suggesting that the causal relationship between productivity and these institutional factors is still unclear. That is, women's lowered productivity may be as much the effect as the cause of their institutional 'ghettoization'.

Though structural factors like institutional location and training obviously affect productivity, we also found that personal and other organizational factors influenced (facilitated or impeded) productivity, at least from the point of view of the respondents.[9] Two factors – motivation and support from spouse and/or family – differentiate significantly between the sexes. One other variable – having student assistance – was also significant.

In order to assess differences based on cluster categories, we organized the 15 facilitators into two major clusters: personal characteristics and organizational characteristics. An examination of sex differences under the two major clusters indicates that women are more likely to attribute their research productivity to personal variables such as

Table 6.3 *Organizational and personal factors identified as facilitators to research productivity among highly productive faculty, all fields. N = 299 (percentages)*

	Men	Women	Total
Personal variables			
Hard work	10.6	15.5	12.7
Motivation	11.7	26.7**	17.8
Interest	17.9	20.7	18.8
Ambition/Need to be recognized	11.7	11.2	11.6
Curiosity	8.4	6.9	7.9
Creativity	11.2	11.2	11.0
Valuing scholarship	8.4	4.3	6.8
Skills	19.6	23.3	20.5
Organizational variables			
Available time	31.3	28.4	30.1
Resources	29.6	24.1	27.4
Colleagues	34.6	37.1	36.0
Environment	25.7	28.4	27.1
Students	25.7	17.2*	22.6
Funds	36.9	28.4	33.6
Spouse	2.8	10.3*	5.8
Need for career advancement	5.6	5.2	5.5

N = 176 males, 123 females.
* = significantly different to men (*p = .001) (**p = .08).
Source: Survey of Academic Personnel, Higher Education Research Institute, UCLA, 1980.

hard work, being motivated, being interested in the research topic, and possessing the necessary skills to do the work (see Table 6.3). On the other hand, men attribute their successful performance to having institutional resources such as time, student assistance and funds.

However, when we examine the organizational variables endorsed by women and the personal variables endorsed by men, we observe some interesting sex differences. Under the personal variables men attributed their success to curiosity, valuing scholarship, and greater ambition. On the other hand, women identified personal relationships in the social structure as being important facilitators of productivity: having good colleagues, an institutional environment that is supportive and a spouse or family who provide a structure that is facilitative.

To examine these differences further by gender we looked at the specific items included under the 'other' category. Opportunities and contacts reflected most of the responses. Of the ten individuals indicating opportunities and contacts as important facilitators, eight were men and two were women.

The most important observation that can be made from the analysis of facilitators presented above is that women are less likely to view the importance of organizational and/or structural variables as enhancing their research or scholarly productivity. As most studies of research productivity have identified the social organization as critical, one wonders whether women's lack of concern with institutional resources may be an important factor in their lower research productivity and visibility, though, of course, this underutilization may be more the result of institutionally imposed barriers than ignorance or personal choice on the part of women.

In order to explore these notions further, we turned to inhibitors in research productivity (see Table 6.4). Women differ significantly from men in their attribution of limited available time due to family responsibilities, greater time spent in teaching, and administrative demands. Men attributed most of their problems to lack of funds or institutional support or lack of student assistance. So, men again see limited resources as the primary inhibitors, while women identify limitations that are the result of their participation in the time-consuming activities expected of them, such as family, teaching, and committee work. What is interesting here is that a man identifies inhibitors over which he has less personal control – ie, availability of funds, quality of student help or institutional support – whereas women indicate as inhibitors situations and conditions where they might exercise some control – involvement in teaching, committee work and family tasks.

Facilitators and barriers: a focus on the social context of academe

In an attempt to explore these differences while controlling for the unequal distribution of men and women in academe (particularly with respect to the type or prestige of employing institution as well as the differential distributions of men and women across ranks, ages, field and institutional selectivity), we conducted a multiple regression analysis of women's publication rates on a series of social and demographic variables. This allowed us to probe more carefully the factors that inhibit or facilitate women's research productivity, thereby explaining why some women are more productive than others, particularly at certain stages of the career cycle. We found that the following factors were positively associated with women's research productivity:

Table 6.4 *Factors identified as inhibitors to research productivity among highly productive faculty, all fields. N = 299 (percentages)*

	Total	Men	Women
Resources (lack of)	13.4	11.2	16.4
Assistance (lack of)	6.5	6.7	6.0
Travel	1.4	1.7	0.9
No time (in general)	36.3	39.1	31.9
No time (family)	6.8	3.4	12.1**
No time (teaching)	26.7	22.3	33.6*
No time (administration)	30.8	25.7	37.9**
Limitations in skills	14.4	14.0	14.7
Colleagues (competition; lack of support)	13.4	11.2	164
Lack of student assistance	13.4	15.1	10.3
Lack of funds	33.2	36.3	28.4
No institutional support	8.9	10.1	6.9
Other	13.7	10.6	18.1

N = 176 males, 123 females.
* = significantly different to men (*p = .001) (**p = .08).
Source: Survey of Academic Personnel, Higher Education Research Institute, UCLA, 1980.

- expressing a strong need for advancement;
- spending more (than average) time on research and writing;
- higher rank (having been promoted to full professor;
- research funds;
- subscribing to more journals than the average academic;
- having opportunities for external consulting;
- being located at a selective university; and
- (young) age.

The following factors were negatively associated with women's research productivity: having come from student status directly to one's present position; and being single.

From these findings several important conclusions can be drawn.

1. Obtaining research funds provides one with resources such as a secretary, a research assistant and travel opportunities which can facilitate the research and writing process.
2. Spending less time advising students and serving on committees allows one to spend more time on research and writing.
3. Consulting and being in a selective or prestigious university brings greater visibility, more resources, and contacts with more eminent scholars – which often bring offers for publications.

4. Being driven – that is, wanting to advance rapidly or having strong status or achievement needs – can motivate one to become more productive.
5. Having reached a higher rank (ie full professor) also allows one to be more productive, mainly because the privilege of rank can exclude academics from unwanted departmental responsibilities, and because professors of higher rank generally teach less and choose to teach seminars with graduate students rather than large undergraduate introductory courses. These conditions free senior academics from the more time-consuming activities, and thus allow more time for writing and publishing.
6. At the same time, higher rank does not necessarily mean older age influences productivity: younger female academics who now may face less sex discrimination (and who also may be more driven precisely because opportunities are now opening in academia) also tend to be highly productive.

But why does being single constitute a 'barrier' to women's productivity? We found that married women have a tendency to produce more articles than single women, perhaps because they lack some of the advantages to which married women have access. Women without a male partner may be more likely to be excluded from the 'boys'' network, important connections and critical information. Academic women who are married have fewer obstacles to the social networking and collegiality that plays such an important role in facilitating productivity in academe.

Further, academic women are more likely to be married to other academics, which may enhance their access to networks. Their marital status makes them able to participate in important departmental socializing and networking without being socially threatening. Academic women whose husbands have the time flexibility granted by academe may also be more able to share or more easily distribute family responsibilities, thus reducing many of the obstacles to productivity other researchers have associated with marriage. Moreover, as academic women generally have highly educated spouses, even if their spouses are not academics, they may provide intellectual stimulation and support for intellectual activities as well as sufficient income to relieve them of 'normal' household and family responsibilities.

Subtle discrimination operates against single women, as they are seen as different from the modal academic who is a married man. Singlehood, particularly for women, is sometimes feared and misinterpreted, and it further isolates and keeps many women out of the 'charmed' circle of men. Its greatest disadvantage may be that singlehood prevents women from joining the networks that facilitate achievement and advancement.

The fact that networking plays such an important role in facilitating academic success is seen clearly in several of the facilitators and barriers mentioned earlier. Research funds provide academics with resources and opportunities to network with their departmental and national colleagues. Consulting opportunities broaden one's network of contacts, as does being located at a selective university. Access to such networks may be restricted among those whose first professional job followed directly from student status. Academics who have not had the opportunity to make new or additional contacts before coming to their posts clearly are disadvantaged vis-a-vis those who have taken other positions and thus expanded their networks even before coming to their permanent jobs.

This may be particularly the case for women, since the paternalistic relationships often forged between academic mentors and female graduate students can deprive women of the practical experience and confidence associated with being treated as scholars of true and equal merit. If this means women new to academia have less confidence and fewer skills for establishing relationships of respect and collegiality with their associates, it may be a critical obstacle to developing future networks of academic colleagues. Moreover, to the extent that single female graduate students are even more disadvantaged than male graduate students in developing mentoring and collegial relationships – since male professors (who still predominate) are generally wary of developing close mentoring and collegial relationships with single women – we can also understand the patterned differences between single and married women in academia.

Clearly, then, if access to social networks, free time and financial resources are critical facilitators to productivity in academe, singlehood and coming to one's present position directly from student status are so-called barriers precisely because they prevent women from developing or accessing social networks. Given our concerns about differences in productivity for women at different stages of the life and career cycles, what is particularly significant about these barriers is that they are more likely to affect women at early stages of their careers, while the facilitators tend to come at later stages. Indeed, by definition, coming directly from student status obviously is a problem only for new academics; and newer academic women are also more likely to be single (at least at the present time period when women often delay marriage until after embarking upon careers).

Beyond structural barriers: the role of perception in achievement strategies

Our research findings also suggest that the inability of certain women to utilize resources and establish networks may be due to more than so-called structural factors, ie their lack of access to these resources and networks at early stages of their career. Women may have very different perceptions of the academic world and what it takes to become successful, perceptions that can lead them to make very different (and often detrimental) choices at critical stages of their careers than to those that men take. Women may therefore be prevented from identifying and utilizing critical facilitators – or at least from understanding the most expedient strategies to increased research productivity and enhanced reputational standing.

Patterned differences in productivity further suggest that different perceptions of academe influence women's decisions and actions only at certain stages in their career and life cycles – particularly the early stages. Single women have the lowest mean rates of article publication of any group, independent of rank. However, they also have the highest mean rates of published books over their whole career. This finding is important because it suggests that single women publish at high rates, but that the types of research or scholarly publication they undertake are fundamentally different from those of married women and men.

There appear to be several reasons for this, each of which highlights the ways that the perceptions and structural circumstances of single women push them to achieve success in academia. Single women, who generally do not have family obligations and may therefore perceive themselves as having more time, choose to devote their energies to large-scale efforts such as writing books. The fact that married men are also more likely than married women to publish books supports this notion, since having a spouse who takes care of household responsibilities frees men to devote larger amounts of time and energy to book writing.

Still, time alone does not fully explain the difference in book-publication rates between single women and married men. It could be argued that having less access to funding sources, as single women do, forces them to write books rather than shorter research reports.

However, a more likely explanation is the tendency for single women to drive themselves early on to make large-scale and visible contributions. Because single women may be somewhat more isolated from networks and resources, they may feel that the best way to secure an unchallenged place for themselves in a male-dominated, predominantly marriage-oriented academic world is to make large and highly visible academic contributions. Consistent with the 'superstar' interpretation, at the assistant-professor level a greater proportion of single women receive funds as principal investigators than either married men or women. On the other hand, a much larger proportion of married men and married women have access to funds without being principal investigators than single women do.

Further evidence of the 'superstar' syndrome is also seen in the daily academic activities of single women. At the assistant-professor level, single women are much more likely than married men or women to be involved with research and teaching at specialized, extra-departmental research and studies centres, like Women's Studies centres. Of course, we expect the rates for women's involvement in such centres to be higher than men's. Yet in the first and critical stage of the professional career, single women are twice as likely as married women to undertake such responsibilities. (Married women do become involved in these activities, but they do so later in their careers.) Moreover, single women at the assistant-professor stage have a greater tendency to spend large amounts of time in teaching preparation and committee work than do both married men and women.

All these factors indicate that single women feel compelled, or are free to become 'superstars': to be highly committed to teaching, to research, to creating immediate and national-level visibility, and to undertake the administrative responsibilities that often accompany such teaching and research work. Ironically, it is their single status that actually affords them the time to do so. Yet by spreading themselves thinly across all these areas, single women may actually be reducing their opportunities to reach parity with married women and men in visibility, reputational standing, or even overall publication rates. As noted earlier, academic reputations are more often made through article and chapter publication than through books. Moreover, the time commitments associated with running research centres and becoming exceptional teachers can cut into research productivity.

This suggests that single women's perceptions about how best to build reputational standing translate into highly individualistic strategies of status attainment in academe. Unfortunately, such strategies, centred around the achievement of 'superstardom', do not necessarily prove to be the most effective way of enhancing a career in the highly social, closely networked world of academia (see Hood 1985). Married women may have learned this because they have had no choice but to maximize their limited time and rely on social networks for advancement.

Gender differences in status attainment: some concluding remarks

Does all this mean we should hold single women responsible for their own disadvantaged position in academia? Certainly not. Gender stratification in academe is a larger and more complex problem than lack of information or misguided perceptions, as such. The academic environment is dominated by males. Women are a minority – and an isolated one at that – and thus they must depend on their own efforts to advance rather than on the existent organization and social structure of academia. It is frequently suggested that in a male-dominated academic world, women have to do 'better' than men just to prove their equal worth, a consideration that may help explain the 'superstar' syndrome.

The concern with proving oneself may be greater for single women, whose choice (at least temporarily) of career over family often brings tremendous pressures for advancement and success. It follows that use of individualistic and high-powered strategies for success may be perceived as both logical and necessary for women, considering that they lack equal access to the organizational structure of academia, to insider's knowledge about it, to its institutional resources.

But what does it all mean, theoretically, for our understanding of how and why certain women, in particular single women at early stages in their career, do not achieve the same status as men? Most clearly, it indicates that such women are negatively affected by a unique combination of factors. They are excluded from networks even more so than married women. This directly influences both the realities and perceptions of the opportunities open to them. Limited access to networks compels single women to rely on alternative, individualistic strategies more than married women.

It is the fact that such strategies are neither the most appropriate nor the most expedient ones for advancement in the academic world that brings negative results for these single women. Responsibility lies with neither the individuals nor the social context, alone, but the ways that social context produces and interacts with the achievement strategies of particular women – and in the process, impedes overall success.

Such a disjunction between strategy and context is not a problem for men, since their strategies of advancement have both emerged from and produced the organizational and social context of academia over the last several decades. Neither is it such a large problem for married women, at least to the same extent, mainly because the advancement strategies they employ are more similar to men's, and thus more appropriate for the existent context.

While these conclusions may appear rather disheartening, particularly for single women, if understood in a historical context they need not be considered inevitable or immutable. The fact that women in general and single women in particular have employed different strategies of advancement is explained by the social structure of the academic world. American academe has neither accumulated the collective experience nor developed the informal social mechanisms to cope with the rather recent phenomenon of large numbers of women. As time passes things will undoubtedly change. With expanding ranks of highly educated women, and with more women substituting careers for marriage (or even just delaying the latter), the number of single women entering academia is bound to increase. As single women become more common in academic departments, men and women should be able (if not compelled) to interact with each other in a non-threatening, collegial manner. This should reduce the exclusion of single women from male-dominated networks and information, encouraging them to employ parallel strategies to those of men and married women.

Moreover, as time passes we can expect more women in academia as a whole, which will give women a basis for establishing their own networks, even if male networks remain unavailable to them. Such possibilities for expanding networks and for giving women experience and skills for employing more expedient strategies of advancement have already been enhanced by another recent trend; the rise of the 'new' scholarship on women. The attractiveness of this new area, the recent establishment of a number of scholarly journals devoted to women's issues, support (albeit declining) from funding agencies, and expanded interest on the part of publishers all offer new opportunities for women to establish networks, get practice in terms of editing as well as soliciting articles, and increase writing output. These, in turn, are important experiences that provide women with skills and insiders' knowledge, previously controlled and monitored by men, that help them sharpen their expertise and ability as scholars. Indeed, in our recent work we found that these historically specific changes help explain why women in recent years have been able to attain levels of reputational standing similar to men's, unlike the situation at earlier time periods (Davis and Astin 1987).

In the upcoming years we might expect to see academic women of the future pursuing strategies that would enable them to participate in the production and social organization of the academic world more fully. On the other hand, we also might see the social organization of the academic world change in such a way that new and expedient strategies for advancement might differ for both men and women, reflecting a more egalitarian and accessible academic world that is bound to emerge with the rise of women in academia. The latter possibility suggests, in fact, that what at first may have appeared in this discussion to be a problem for women in certain stages of their life and career cycles may more accurately be seen as a problem associated with stages of 'societal development', so to speak. Accordingly, as women increasingly enter academia and other occupational sectors in society heretofore dominated by men, and as women become more common in the workplace, we might expect barriers to their advancement in domains like academia to be reduced.

The real question, however, is whether women will be able to enter such occupations in proportions that reflect their qualifications and merit. If large-scale absorption of women into previously male-dominated worlds is recognized as the first step towards erasing gender stratification within occupations, it is not altogether impossible that initial barriers to occupational entry might be fortified by those who seek to protect their privileged domain. If so, we may see a return in research to questions of gender stratification across occupations. At least for now, we need to explore patterns and reasons for gender stratification *within* occupations. Such research should assist us in establishing policies and practices to eliminate the internal obstacles to achievement and advancement and thus enable women to make the contributions they are capable of making.

Notes

1. Different levels and stages of advancement in academia, like salary, rank, and promotion (including tenure), as well as number and type of publication, are clearly identifiable and often standardized in the academic world. Moreover, the level of training required for entry into academe, as well as the accomplishments necessary for advancement, like publishing, are generally more standardized and quantifiable in academe than in many other professions.

2. This project is coordinated by Helen S Astin, Professor of Higher Education at the University of California at Los Angeles (UCLA) under the auspices of the Higher Education Research Institute. Significant portions of the research were funded by the Ford Foundation and the Exxon Educational Foundation.

3. Our findings about no gender differences are significant because this was the group (ie, highly productive, or most esteemed) that Cole suggested exemplified gender differences in reputational standing most clearly.

4. In making this argument, we used a multiple repression analysis to test seven different indicators of reputational standing, and found that gender (female) did not significantly influence any of the measures of reputational standing (See Davis and Astin 1987).

5. Single women are defined as never married women. Divorced, separated, or widowed women are not included in this category.

6. We do not include figures for single males because they constitute such a small proportion of all academic males.

7. The academic system in the United States works on the tenure system. New professors are generally hired on contracts ranging anywhere from five to seven years, and during that preliminary stage they are ranked as assistant professors. Upon demonstration of sufficient research and intellectual competence (generally, publications are assessed for quantity and 'quality'), a professor is granted tenure, and moves to the rank of associate professor. Thus, a tenured professor is an associate professor or full professor.

8. With respect to parental education an interesting and recurring finding is the lower maternal education of the productive group. Prior research (Astin 1969), has documented and explained this finding as reflecting greater upward-mobility needs among the more productive scholars.

9. In our 1980 survey we asked respondents to identify in their own words what has made it possible for them to be productive or what has impeded their productivity. The open-ended responses were grouped into 16 categories reflecting facilitators and 12 categories of inhibitors – obstacles to productivity.

References

Astin, Helen S (1969), *The Woman Doctorate in America*, New York: Russell Sage Foundation.

Astin, Helen S and Bayer, Alan E (1979), Pervasive sex differences in the academic reward system: scholarship, marriage, and what else?, in *Academic Rewards*, Darrell R Lewis and William E Becker, Jr (eds), Cambridge, Mass.: Ballinger Publishing Company.

Astin, Helen S and Davis, Diane E (1985), Research productivity across the life and career cycles: facilitators and barriers for women, in *Scholarly Writing and Publishing: Issues, Problems, and Solutions*, Mary Frank Fox (ed), Boulder and London: Westview Press.

Astin, Helen S. and Snyder, Mary Beth (1982), Affirmative action 1972–1982: a decade of response, *Change*, July/August, pp 26–59.

Cole, Jonathon R (1979), *Fair Science: Women in the Scientific Community*, New York: Free Press.

Cole, Jonathon R and Cole, Stephen (1973), *Social Stratification in Science*, Chicago: University of Chicago Press.

Converse, Philip E and Converse, Jean M (1971), The status of women as students and professionals in political science, *Political Science* 4 pp 328–348.

Davis, Diane E and Astin, Helen S (1987), Reputational standing in academe, *The Journal of Higher Education* 58, May/June, pp 261–275.

Fox, Mary Frank (1985), Men, women, and publication productivity: patterns among social work academics, *The Sociological Quarterly* 26, pp 537–549.

Fox, Mary Frank (1985), Publication, performance, and reward in science and scholarship, in *Higher Education: Handbook of Theory and Research*, J. Smart (ed), New York: Agathon Press.

Hood, Jane C (1985), The lone scholar myth, in *Scholarly Writing and Publishing: Issues, Problems, and Solutions*, Mary Frank Fox (ed), Boulder and London: Westview Press.

Jacobi, Maryann and Astin, Helen S (1985), Career patterns of academics: differences in age, gender, and social cohort, unpublished manuscript, Higher Education Research Institute, UCLA.

Long, J Scott (1978), Productivity and academic position in the scientific career, *American Sociological Review* 43 pp 889–908.

Reskin, Barbara (1977), Scientific productivity and the reward structure of science, *American Sociological Review* 47 pp 491–504.

Robinson, Lora H (1973), Institutional variation in the status of academic women, in *Academic Women on the Move*, Alice Rossi and Alice Calderwood (eds).

Chapter 7

The Juggling Act:
Work and Family in Norway[1]

Suzanne Stiver Lie

In many Western countries, married women with children are now the rule rather than the exception among women scholars. The focus of this paper is on career and family role compatibility of Norwegian academics. Special emphasis is given to how the organizational structure of both the university and the society affect women's academic productivity. The extent to which the productivity patterns of women are affected by their family obligations is examined along with the effects of marital status and childrearing responsiblilities.

Traditionally, it was thought that the costs of combining familial and scholarly pursuits were so high that there was actually a prohibition against marriage for men, among whom scholarship has long been a prerogative (See Chapter 11). In Europe, scholarship had its first origins in the monastic life of the church. The scholar was cloistered away from the mundane world in order to dedicate himself to learning. In such pre-stigious centres of learning as Oxford and Cambridge, celibacy was actually required for the dons until late in the 1800s, some 300 years after clergymen in the Anglican church were allowed to marry.

By the late 1800s the cloistered scholar had been replaced by the impoverished, hard-working academic (male) (see Ardener 1984 and Sciama 1984) and 'professionalism took over where monasticism had left off as a force antithetical to marriage' (Sciama 1984, p 84). Conveniently, wives serviced these new academics' everyday needs to give them time and mental space. Concurrent with the growing demands of scientific professionalism, pressures from women and a few 'men of conscience' begrudgingly resulted in the opening of the university system to women (see Chapter 1). However, it was commonly held that professionalism and wifehood were incompatible. Women scholars were seen as fundamentally different women – plain and undesirable. This view was prominent well into the 1960s. Today, that image has changed. Career women, married or not, are seen as glamorous and enviable. But the belief persists that for academic women, marriage and career do not mix. Family is seen as the major impediment to women's full participation in academia. Supporting this perception is the frequently documented finding that women are less productive than men.

The productivity puzzle

Academicians are evaluated primarily in terms of their productivity and reputation (see Chapter 6). Numerous studies have found women to be less productive than men (Cole 1979; Cole and Zuckerman 1987; and Franklin 1988). The results of several studies show that married women and women with children publish as much or more on average as women who are single and childless, (Cole 1979; Cole and Zuckerman 1987 and Luukkonen-Gronow 1987) leading Cole to conclude that lower productivity is not due to marriage and family responsiblities, at least not directly. In the preface of the second edition of *Fair Science* (1987) he describes the productivity differences between men and women as a puzzle because he finds no objective evidence that academic women are discriminated against either.

The purpose of this chapter is to explore sex differences in productivity among Norwegian academics with an eye toward solving the productivity puzzle posed by Cole (1987). Consistent with recent arguments advanced by Davis and Astin (Chapter 6) and Long (1987), data from two samples of Norwegian academics suggest it is not gender per se, but variables associated with the life course such as age, marital status and children's age, as well as organizational climate factors which contribute to productivity differences.[2]

Data and method

The current study of Norwegian academic women is based on an analysis of two investigations: a national survey conducted in 1982 of academics' participation in university life (Kyvik 1988; 1990)[3] and an investigation of career and family role compatibility of university women graduates with advanced degrees (Rørslett and Lie 1984).[4] The Kyvik study focused on the research training, resources, productivity, administrative and teaching responsiblities and organizational situations of 1569 tenured faculty (199 women and 1370 men).[5] The role-compatibility study explored structural factors *outside* the academic organization affecting work. Of the 2000 university women graduates in that study, 90 were employed by the universities in tenured positions.[6] These 90 women, together with the male and female faculty in the Kyvik study, provide the basis of this analysis.

Women and men's cultural mandates

In academe the male is used as the standard of comparison for the evaluation of women. This standard is a difficult one for women to achieve, and they are frequently disadvantaged by it because their performance is constrained by obligations outside the academic community. Women who choose to function in the public sphere are still expected to perform the roles dictated by their place in the home. Therefore, it is not possible to understand the academic woman within the context of the university alone.

In understanding the strategies which women academics utilize in combining career and family, the concepts of 'rationality of care' and 'means–end rationality' are useful (Ve, in preparation). These constructs highlight the difference in female and male thought and action patterns. They spring from a patriarchal society where men are responsible for production, women for reproduction. Men are socialized according to a means–ends rationality, where efficiency is the basic aim or value. By contrast, women are the typical bearers of rationality of care (care for and with human beings – children, the sick, the disabled, the elderly). The concept of rationality takes on a different meaning when women's reality is considered.

The Scandinavian welfare state

The welfare state provides the context in which the lives of Norwegian academic women are played out. Its underlying ideology is based upon the ideals of neutrality and equality. It guarantees that benefits are equitably distributed among individuals (work for all, secure working conditions, medical care and universal retirement provisions). In reality, however, things work differently for women. The welfare state presupposes a genderized society where men are responsible for production, women for reproduction (Skrede 1988). Gender is used as a distributional key. The model of the welfare state is premised on the full-time employed *male* provider. This model does not take into account that half of the population has a very different reality and life cycle. As a result, it is difficult for women to participate in the labour market given the lack of nursery schools and poor pension rights accorded to part-time employees, etc.

Policies of equality

The policies of equality in the welfare state have similar political origins and have been inspired by the same visions and ideals (Skrede 1988).

Welfare-state policies and policies of equality were, however, not co-ordinated. Different ideologies of equality led to different types of policy with divergent goals and content – *formal* equality, *conditional* equality, and *full* equality (Ellingsæter and Iversen 1984).

Formal equality means that the same rules and laws apply for women and for men (eg access to education and paid employment). This established the legal basis for the two other policies. Conditional equality is premised on the notion that men and women have different responsibilities toward the family, as well as separate occupational responsibilities: women may work, but family comes first. Full equality means that women and men have equal rights and duties to participate in the labour market, are equal and active members of society as a whole, and share family responsibilities. Over time the concept of welfare has modified these policies of equality to take into consideration women's special situation. State feminism is the most recent expression of the policy of full equality. The political apparatus incorporated some feminist ideas such as paternity leave and made them policy (Hernes 1987).

While these policies of equality have influenced the development of the welfare state, their influence on the underlying patriarchal structure of the model has been slow to be realized. The oldest group of women in this study were socialized according to the principle of formal equality; conditional equality influenced the socialization of the other two groups. Today, ideologies of full equality influence all age groups, to varying degrees.

The productivity gap

In Norway, as in the United States, academic men are more productive than women. Using a publication index which measures productivity adjusted for type of publication and multiple authorship over a three-year period (1978–81), Kyvik finds that men publish an average of 5.0 article-equivalents compared to 3.5 for women. Thus, women publish 30 per cent less than men. This differential, however, is affected by faculty status, rank and age.

The picture is modified considerably when academic discipline and rank are taken into account. Consistent with Toren's findings in Chapter 5, the difference in Norwegian male and female publication rates is smallest in the natural sciences (20 per cent). Women in other areas publish 30 to 35 per cent less than their male colleagues. However, women associate professors are just as productive as men in that rank. In the social sciences women are actually more productive than men.

Furthermore, there is a clear connection between rank and productivity. Full professors are more productive than associate professors who in turn publish more than assistant professors. This pattern applies to women and men alike.

The connection between academic rank and productivity is not simple. As Kyvik points out, people reach a high academic position as a result of high productivity. The fact that fewer women are full professors is a result of their lower rate of publications. However, a high academic rank is in itself conducive to high productivity. The theory of 'cumulative advantage' (Cole 1979) then applies. That is, scientists seek recognition by publishing. Professional recognition leads to greater access to economic resources, assistants and network connections, which again has consequences for productivity. The processes of cumulative advantage and disadvantage are essential in understanding differences in productivity.

Age plays an important role in productivity. Men reach their peak in productivity between 45 and 49, while women follow some five years later, 50 to 54 years. For women, childcare delays productivity.[7]

Promotion is closely related to productivity. Comparison of the piecharts in Figure 7.1, resulting from the author's secondary analysis of Kyvik's data, reveals striking sex differences. The promotion pattern of men aged 45 to 49 is very different to that of women in the same age group, but closely resembles that of women aged 60 and older. Not until age 60 do women reach the same rank achieved by men in their mid to late 40s. The lag in promotion is apparent by age 35 and the gap increases rapidly until women are trailing 10 years or more behind men in the promotion stakes. Only 4 per cent of full professors were women in 1982.

The usual explanations for promotion delays focus on lack of formal qualifications, lower research productivity and the limited pool of women applicants. As Kyvik shows, this lag is also apparent in women's productivity pattern. It may be that these two trends, delayed productivity and delayed promotion, are related to the course of women's lives which differ dramatically from men's.

Kyvik explores several factors that might account for sex differences in productivity including intellectual capacity as measured by grades at university entry, integration into the academic community, degree of international contact, funding, availability of research assistance, time for research and childcare.

In his view, differences in productivity cannot be explained by differences in intellectual capacity. The women in his study had better grades at university entrance than their male colleagues. Male academics, on the other hand, had better examination results at higher degree level than female academics, but these differences were small. Kyvik speculates that the difference may be explained by the fact that for women, higher degree studies often coincide with marriage and

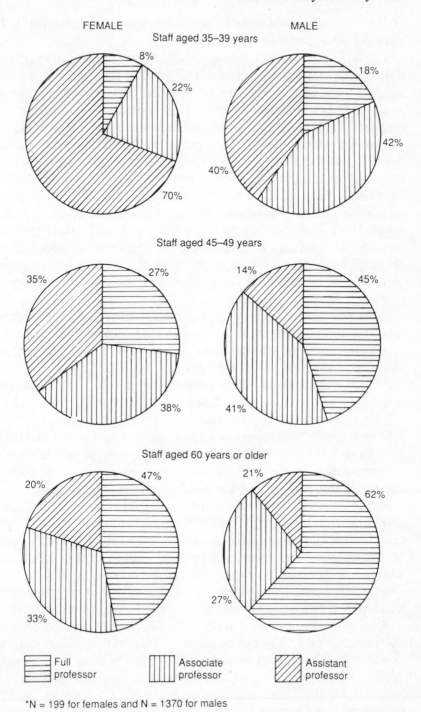

Figure 7.1 *Academic tenured staff in Norway according to gender and selected age groups in 1982*.*

*N = 199 for females and N = 1370 for males.

childbirth. An analysis of the 90 academics in the Rørslett and Lie (1984) data indeed show this to be the case.

Womens' integration into the academic community may be poorer than that of their male counterparts. They may miss out on the collegial support conducive to publication. In the Kyvik investigation fewer women (63 per cent) than men (75 per cent) had regular contact with colleagues at their institution regarding their own research work. Lie (in preparation) found that 47 per cent of the 90 academic women in the Rørslett and Lie (1984) study maintained that they had experienced sceptical or negative attitudes from colleagues because they were women. Perhaps in order to compensate for this lack of acceptance, they seek contact elsewhere. Although more women than men had regular contacts with colleagues at other research establishments in Norway, women had a level of contact similar to men's with colleagues internationally. Of course, these contacts may not have been sufficiently 'mainstream' to be credibile because they were probably with other women.

Economic resources and the availability of research assistants are other factors that might explain productivity differences between men and women. Kyvik's study shows that more men (81 per cent) than women (70 per cent) received funding from outside their universities. Research assistants and PhD students constitute another important 'resource' in the universities. They make valuable contributions to their teachers' research projects, particularly within medicine and the natural sciences. Men advise more graduate students than women and they are also more likely to regard mentoring as an integral part of their own research function. Interestingly, those who receive the most assistance from their students are also the most productive researchers.

University staff divide their time between research, teaching and administration. Contrary to other findings (Davis and Astin, Chapter 6; Cole 1979), Norwegian men and women spend about the same number of hours per week on teaching and administration, but female academics spend an average of two hours less per week on research. This is equivalent to the difference in the greater average number of hours per week that men work (49.5) compared to women (47.0).

Academic men are more likely to be married than academic women (87 per cent and 68 per cent respectively) and they also have more children. Yet, compared to academic women in other countries, there appear to be fewer single, never-married women in Norway. For instance, in the Davis and Astin sample of US women academics (Chapter 6), one-third were never married compared to only 16 per cent of Norwegian women.

Male academics are also more likely than academic women to have children (89 per cent and 79 per cent respectively), and to have larger families. Kyvik found that both men and women with young children under the age of ten reported problems with family responsibilities, 43 per cent and 56 per cent respectively. Family responsiblities for those with children over ten seemed to be less problematic, but still caused more difficulties for women. Long (1989) in his study of graduate students shows that the presence of young children has an adverse, indirect effect on the productivity of female, but not male scientists during graduate study.

Based on multivariate analyses, Kyvik concludes that childcare responsibility is the factor that best explains the difference in productivity between men and women. Overall, women with children are more productive than women with no children. It may be the age of the child (or children) that makes the difference.

Most of the international studies referred to earlier did not take children's age into account. One exception to this is Fox and Faver (1985) who studied American social-work faculty members and controlled for children's age. They found that having children at younger ages is positively related to women's productivity. In his analyses, Kyvik distinguishes academics with children under ten years from those with children ten years or older. Women with at least one child under ten produced 47 per cent fewer article-equivalents than their male colleagues in the same situation. This difference is reduced to 14 per cent among men and women who have children aged ten or older. When the analyses take academic rank into account, sex differences disappear. Women with older children are as productive as men in the same category.

Interestingly, women with no children are less productive than those who do have children, and married women are more productive than single women. Though most studies have shown that single women publish less than women with children, Davis and Astin (Chapter 6) find that, when controlling for type of publication, single women in the social sciences had the highest rates of published books over their entire career than either men or women with children. This is not the case in Norway. Women with children publish more books than single women.

Kyvik's findings suggest that it is critically important to differentiate between children's age to understand the impact of motherhood on women's productivity.

Although it appears that childcare is the most important factor affecting married women's productivity, the academic organizational setting is not as advantageous for women as men. Women are less integrated in their institutions, receive fewer resources and spend less time on research than men. Although the differences are small, it appears that women are subject to the processes of *cumulative disadvantage* to a greater degree than men. As Long (1989, p 20) points out,

'Small sex differences . . . consistently work against the achievement of females and for the achievement of males.'

Job versus home across the life course

Crucial phases of academic women's lives were analysed separately in the Kyvik study. This gives only fragmented information. A life-course perspective provides a unified approach. Important events, such as education, employment, domestic work, marriage and childbirth, are recorded, allowing us to chart the obstacles between career and family over time.

The 90 women in the current study were asked to record their work history and major life events. From this information typical time-lines were constructed (Figure 7.2).[8] Based on an analysis of these work histories, three categories are identified:

1. continuous academic career;
2. non-tenured employment combined with academic career; and
3. discontinuous career.[9]

Women's life histories indicate that the majority have careers characterized by *discontinuity*. The life histories and time-lines depicted in Figure 7.2 stand in sharp contrast to the male academic's uninterrupted career. The life course of women with children is intimately tied to the important processes of birth, nurturing and care. Even single and married women without children most often have discontinuous careers.

In all, 64 per cent of the women have careers characterized by discontinuity. Most came late to academe. The reasons vary – childcare breaks during and/or after studies, part-time studies and part-time employment combined with childcare and job experiences outside academe prior to entering the academy. Once in academe their careers were also frequently interrupted by childcare demands. Often, it is a *combination* of these events which distinguishes women's lives from the more orderly progression of men.

The married women in this sample live in family/partnership situations characterized by 'two careers on one pillow'. Ninety-six per cent of their spouses are university educated and 88 per cent hold leading positions in the public sector, in the professions, in business, etc.

Not suprisingly, these women cope with the multiple demands made upon them using the strategies characteristic of their generation. Different age groups have different life experiences: they belong to different generations which are affected by a different set of conditions and ideological influences. Through the lives of three generations of women academics – an older group (50 and over), an in-between generation (in their 40s), and a younger group (in their 30s) – we see how developments of the Norwegian welfare state and ideologies of equality set parameters for their ability to combine family and career. Eighty-two per cent of the older generation, 62 per cent of the in-between generation and only 48 per cent of the younger generation have had interrupted careers.

The older generation (50+): 'in–out' strategy

The oldest group of women academics differ from their same-age peers in that they attained a high level of education and employment at a time when societal expectations dictated that family and employment were incompatible. These women, born in 1932 or earlier, grew up in a period when the family was the total responsibility of women. They adapted their interests and needs to the demands of their husbands' careers. If they entered the paid labour force they paid other women to do 'their work' at home. The arrival of children often forced their temporary withdrawal from work. As nursery schools were uncommon, there were long interruptions in their careers. Rationality of care formed the core of their 'in–out' strategies to meet the conflicting demands of career and family.

The 28 women in the older generation were spread across all academic ranks. The majority (68 per cent) had children. Most took eight or more years to complete their higher university degrees (the range was five to 24 years). Disruption of studies was common due to war, financial constraints, and, less frequently, childcare. Marriage occurred towards the end of their studies. Children (generally two or three) followed shortly after, and precipitated withdrawal from paid employment. Childcare leaves lasted from three to 18 years, and many of the women worked in other fields prior to entering the academy. Thus, they arrived late.

Of the seven full professors over 50, all had disrupted careers. They began their academic careers in their 30s and were tenured in their late 30s. All obtained doctorates[10] in their late 40s following anywhere from seven to 16 years' work beyond the Master's degree.[11] Most were in their 50s by the time they were promoted to full professor. Still, compared to women of the same age, but lower rank, their careers progressed rapidly. The life line of the typical female full professor of the older generation is presented in Figure 7.2.

Only two of the ten older-generation women associate professors have doctorates. All have three or more children. The largest group of

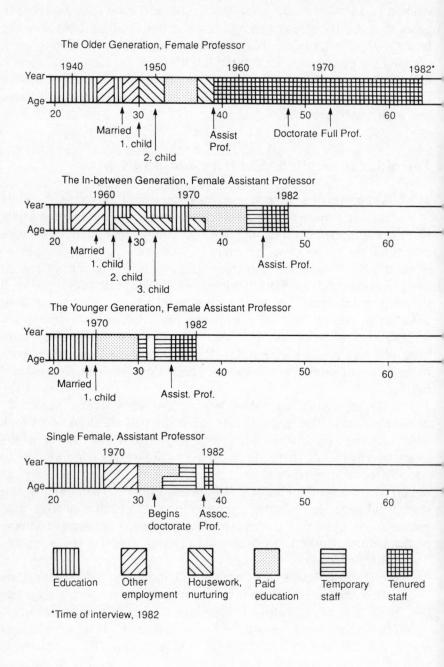

Figure 7.2 *A comparison of typical life lines of women academics by generation.*

older women (11) are assistant professors. Of these, eight entered academe after age 40. Most did not become assistant professors until their late 40s or early 50s, following completion of their stipend periods. Their childcare breaks were extensive (as many as 18 years) and these breaks were often combined with long periods of working in other occupations.

The in-between generation (40+): 'part-time' strategy

The in-between generation grew up during a time when the old gender pattern was still in force, although it began to erode as they reached maturity. The explosive development of the welfare state began in the 1950s and 1960s with the introduction of retirement and vacation rights, legal protection against dismissal and socialized medicine. All this was accompanied by broad educational reforms. Women were encouraged to get an education and welcomed into the labour market, where due to post-war expansion they were sorely needed, particularly in the public sector.

A new proletariat of women was created by the disappearance of servants from middle-class homes. Women with families and careers found themselves over-burdened, and there were few nursery schools or childcare centres to help. They reacted by having fewer children and working part time. This 'part-time' ideology resulted in stronger ties to the labour market and a different formulation of the rationality of care dictum.

Women of the in-between generation constitute the largest group of women academics, 37 in all. Seventy-eight per cent have children; 62 per cent have had a disrupted career. Most have used a part-time strategy to deal with the conflict between work and family. Many married and had children as undergraduates. Their studies were prolonged (seven to 12 years), and often interrupted because of husbands' studies abroad. Like the older generation, many had other occupational experiences before beginning an academic career.

In their early 30s when they entered academe, most obtained tenure in their late 30s. Only three have earned doctorates. Their life line is depicted in Figure 7.2. Several (seven) of the women of the in-between generation at the assistant-professor level had academic careers from the start. The life-course lines of these women are similar to those of their younger colleagues decribed below.

The younger generation (30+): the price of career commitment

The women in their 30s grew up at a time when the old ideal for women was passé but before a new one replaced it. They were a product of the educational explosion and were exposed to the women's movement's demands for liberation and full equality. As a result, most of these women maintained fairly continuous links with the labour market. By the time they had established their careers benefits for women with young families had increased substantially, especially in the public sector. Welfare programmes were expanded to include *both* maternity and paternity leave and time off was granted for parents of such children, although the dearth of nursery schools continue to pose a problem.

The 25 women in the generation of younger academics are committed to self-realization and careers. Although most (73 per cent) have children, over half (52 per cent) have worked consistently within academe since graduation from university. All but five are assistant professors. Many had to accept non-tenured positions at the outset of their careers due to the 'academic freeze' occasioned by declining enrolments. Because so many of them are in the humanities and social sciences, where the competition for tenure and promotion are greatest, they may be particularly disadvantaged compared to their male peers (Figure 7.2).

Ten of the younger women have had discontinuous careers, although their career breaks were of short (one or two years) duration. The price associated with career commitment is stress arising from dual demands. As one assistant professor with two youngsters observed: 'Time is something I just don't have enough of. My life is stressful and nervewracking.'

Of the five young women who are associate professors, all but one has her doctorate. The fact they obtained their doctorates early is, no doubt, the reason for their rank.

Single academics

Contrary to what might be expected, single women's careers do not parallel the unencumbered ones of most men. Of the 16 single women in the sample, only two had continuous careers. Four spent a period of non-tenured employment within academe, but the majority (ten) had discontinuous careers. Theirs is also a pattern of interrupted studies (six to 15 years) and many years of work in other professions (four to 16 years). Although the reasons differ, they too came late to academe.

Eleven of the 16 started their academic careers in their middle 30s. Most were tenured as assistant professors after the age of 35. Three-fourths are found in the older and middle-aged groups and over 60 per cent are at the lowest rung of the academic ladder. The time-line for a typical single academic is found in Figure 7.2.

The case of single women deserves further mention. Their problems are often overlooked. According to one:

You take for granted that women with children have more difficulties. . . . From my own and the experience of my single women colleagues, I know that the situation for unmarried women without children is very difficult. We have no one to support us, so we have to take outside jobs in order to finance our education because the scholarships available are not sufficient. We are not the centre of anyone's attention, are discriminated against socially and cannot choose between home and or occupation.

Several explanations have been suggested for why single women publish less than women with children: married women receive practical and moral support from their spouses, married women have a more stable social life, family life increases self-respect, married women are less of a threat to their male collegues because of their marital status, and lastly, 'selectivity' factors may be at work such that academic women who have children may have better health, more energy and stamina than women without children (Luukhonen-Gronow 1987).

This analysis of the life course of three generations of women substantiates Kyvik's finding that it is difficult for academic women with young children trying to combine career and family. Women's careers are delayed due to family responsiblities and consequently they fall somewhat behind men. Let us examine in more detail the solutions academic women use to cope with the conflict between family and career.

Coping strategies

Sharing at the ground level

The division of labour within the family partially determines how much difficulty women have juggling career and family. Not surprisingly, the work was generally divided along traditional lines. Women had responsiblity for running the home and caring for the children. They did most of the cleaning (46 per cent), daily shopping (69 per cent), food preparation (70 per cent), washing (68 per cent) and planning/administration of the household (90 per cent). Their husbands/partners do help: they pay the bills (42 per cent), assume responsibility for household repairs (67 per cent), and car repairs (74 per cent).

When it comes to childcare, the partners of women academics make their greatest contribution. They share equally at bedtime and in play activities. Younger men, in particular, share more in childcare activities. Men do the fun jobs with children, but when it comes to transporting children to school, women are more likely than men to interrupt their work schedules. The woman academic who is a single parent bears the burden alone.

Childcare

The fact that academic women's productivity is low when they have small children is not surprising when one considers the problems they face arranging childcare. The older generation either left children in the care of housekeepers or, more often, stayed home themselves until their children were self-sufficient. The in-between generation did not have access to household help and frequently reacted by having fewer children and by working part time in various phases of their career.

Childcare has been a particular problem for younger women, who are the most likely to have been continuously employed. Though benefits which support two-career families have increased substantially, Norway has yet to give priority to solving the *major* problem facing working parents – adequate public childcare. Norway has facilities for only 25 per cent of those who need it. This is the lowest rate in Western Europe, with the exception of Portugal. Their neighbour, Sweden, has a 75 per cent coverage (Kaul and Brandth 1988). So, the majority of the younger generation have had to rely on private childcare arrangements (64 per cent), such as childminders, au pairs, neighbours and relatives.

Most women utilize a combination of childcare arrangements to fulfil their complex needs. As one woman noted:

We have had childcare minders, short-term nursery/childcare minders, short-term nursery/grandma, that is, several solutions because of the lack of all-day nursery schools. And these arrangements have been of varying quality.

Because academic women earn a relatively high wage and often have access to two incomes, they do not qualify for public nursery schools. As a result, trying to arrange and maintain adequate care for their children looms as the largest and most frustrating problem for these women. They describe the problem as exhausting, problematic, traumatic, stressful and a struggle.

One assistant professor with two small children who is presently working on her doctorate sums up the problem this way:

The difficulties and uncertainty tied to the lack of nursery schools is what I regard as the most stressful and depressing about occupational life. . . . I am willing to work hard to qualify myself for a top position in society, but when my children suffer because of poor childcare, I become paralysed. If we are ever to experience equality in this country, it is imperative that there are enough nursery schools.

Conditions are no easier when children start school. Short days and irregular time schedules mean that children come and go at different hours. They do not have a full school day until they are ten. Lack of nursery-school facilities and short and irregular school days are examples of structural conditions which make the situtation of working mothers difficult.

When children are ill, mother is the most likely one to stay home (32 per cent), although housekeepers/day help (22 per cent), au pairs (15 per cent), relatives, particularly grandmothers (11 percent) and babysitters (12 per cent) are also used. Fathers (3 per cent) are rarely part of the solution. Although there has been an increased reliance on fathers (36 per cent) to care occasionally for sick children among academic women of the younger generation it is still not 50/50.[12]

In reality women's nurturing role never ends. Over 70 per cent of the older generation and over 30 per cent of the in-between generation have some responsibility for the elderly and sick relatives.

One disillusioned female associate professor lamented:

I was looking forward to the day when my children were older, then surely I would have more time for other things than work and family. But no such luck, now it is my elderly parents I have to look after. This entails time visiting them, doing their weekly shopping, paying bills, providing transportation, etc. And they are still able to take care of themselves to a great degree.

The younger generation are most likely to be free from responsibilities, but even some of them (15 per cent) care simultaneously for children and parents. And single women do not escape nurturing tasks – 75 per cent of older single-women academics in our sample care for aging relatives. Whether single or married, academic women have caring functions that persist throughout their adult lives.

Conclusion

Generally, academic women are less productive than men. However, the results of a number of studies examining sex differences in research productivity have indicated that unmarried and childless women are less productive than married women and women with children. This finding challenges the assumption that women's differential scholarly productivity is a direct result of familial distractions.

While sex differences in scholarly productivity may not be due to family responsibilities alone, Kyvik's data clearly suggest that they are important inhibitory factors during critical stages of women's life courses. This finding calls into question Cole's (1979) assertion that family responsiblities are not a factor in explaining women's (lower) research productivity compared to men's.

The celibate don in his monastic cell was free to pursue his scholarly work unfettered by the demands of home and family. This facilitated his productivity no doubt, but today few women (or men) enjoy the luxury of such a singularly focused existence. In spite (or perhaps because) of the frustration attendant to 'making it' in a male-dominated system, women's scholarship and women scholars are shifting the paradigm throughout the academy. As a result the future of the academic endeavour is encouraging, although at the level of individual women progress is painfully slow.

A life-course analysis highlights how the complicated daily life of academic women dictates their participation in academe. An analysis of three generations of women academics lends support to Kyvik's findings. Women's reproductive and nurturing tasks do affect all phases and choice situations during the life course, resulting in a cumulative deficit across their careers. Although strategies differed as the welfare state and ideologies of equality changed character, all three generations of these women were bound by their rationality of care.

But change is occurring. The younger generation starts an academic career at an earlier phase of their lives and their careers are more continuous. When they take childcare breaks, they are of a shorter duration than those of earlier generations. We see glimpses of a more equitable division of labour within young academic families. Yet women continue to have the major responsibility for the time-structured work in the home. These women may be more liberated than earlier generations but they pay a price in the form of stress. Thus, gender, per se, may not affect productivity uniformly but only at critical junctures in the life course.

From a life-course perspective, women are at a *cumulative disadvantage* in academe. For most, a late start, long periods of employment outside academe, childcare breaks, and caring and administrative responsibilities in the home make it more difficult for them to establish their careers than men. This in turn results in less time for research, fewer contacts, fewer resources in the form of assistants and funding. A complex web of institutional, cultural and personal forces create barriers for women's advancement in academic careers. These barriers need to be understood and challenged if 'equal opportunity' within academe is to be realized.

Notes

1. The author would like to thank Karen Nossum Bie, Svein Kyvik, Fride Eeg-Henriksen, Elisabeth Fürst, and Tone Skau Wetlesen for their useful comments on an earlier draft of this paper.

2. Alternatively, it has been suggested that unlike men, women are simply not willing to devote themselves exclusively to work, regardless of their familial obligations. This explanation is based on the premise that women's values dictate how they choose to spend their time (O'Leary and Primack, in preparation). Thagaard (1987), however, points out that it is often difficult to differentiate between choice and felt obligations.

3. The data set from the Kyvik investigation was made available to me by The Institute for Studies in Research and Higher Education, The Norwegian Research Council for Science and the Humanities.

4. Analyses of the present study were supported by the Norwegian Research Council for Science and the Humanities.

5. Norwegian academics receive tenure from the assistant-professor level.

6. A stratified random sample of Norwegian women graduates was drawn by the Norwegian Central Bureau of Statistics.

7. American investigations have shown the productivity gap between men and women tends to increase with age (Cole 1979; Cole and Zuckerman 1987). However, these studies have only examined the first 12 years of men's and women's careers, exactly the years when nurturing responsiblities are the most time-consuming. As shall be shown later an increased productivity gap does not seem to be the pattern for Norwegian academics.

8. The time lines are composites of several individual cases. This was done to highlight typical features and to prevent the possibility of person identification.

9. Category 1: A continuous academic career includes the stipend period which has varied over the years from ten to five years after the completion of a higher university degree (more or less equivalent to a Master's degree) and subsequent tenured academic positions; category 2 includes non-tenured positions within academe as either part-time instructor, researcher or substitute associate professor in addition to the conditions described in category 1; category 3, discontinuous career, includes those who have one or a combination of the following: interrupted studies of more than a year, experience in other occupations before or after beginning an academic

career, and career breaks exceeding the legal maternity leave. (A year or less of study interruptions is not regarded as abnormal and is therefore not recorded as a break (regardless of reason).

10. The doctorate is not as common in Norway as in the USA. In 1985 only 40 per cent of tenured males had doctorates and 14 percent of the tenured women. Once taken in 'splendid isolation', parallel with or in addition to one's work, the new doctoral study, resembles the American and British PhD programmes with a structured study programme (Olsen 1988).

11. A higher degree (equivalent to MA) in the natural sciences takes about five-and-a-half years; six to seven years for the social sciences and humanities.

12. This increase may have connection with the 1977 Norwegian Act of the Working Environment (arbeidsmiljøloven) which regulates the care of sick children. Under the law each parent can take free up to ten days of the calendar year to care for sick children under the age of ten (for single parents, 20 days). Parents have to divide this time equally.

References

Ardener, S (1984), Incorporation and exclusion: Oxford academics' wives, in H Callan and S Ardener (eds), *The Incorporated Wife*, London: Croom Helm.

Cole, J R (1979 and 1987), *Fair Science: Women in the Scientific Community*, New York: Columbia University Press.

Cole, J R and Zuckerman, H (1987), Marriage, motherhood and research performance in science, *Scientific American*, vol 255, no 2.

Ellingsæter, Anne Lise and Iversen, Gunnvor (1984), Endringer i kvinners arbeidsmarkedstilpasning, *Samfunnsøkonomiske studier*.

Fox, Mary Frank and Faver, Catherine A (1985), Men, women, and publication productivity: patterns among social work academics, *The Sociological Quarterly*, vol 26, no 4, pp 537–49.

Franklin, M N (1988), *The Community of Science in Europe: Preconditions for Research Effectiveness in European Community Countries*, Aldershot, Hants: Gower.

Hernes, Helga (1987), *Welfare State and Woman Power: Essays in State Feminism*, Oslo: Norwegian University Press.

Kaul, Hjørdis and Brandth, Berit (1988), Lov og Liv: Ensammenlikning av omsorgspermisjoner i Norden, IFIM SINTEF – Gruppen, Nord, p 9.

Kyvik, Svein (1986), Postgraduate education in Norway, *European Journal of Education*, vol 21, no 3.

Kyvik, Svein (1988), Vitenskapelig publisering blant kvinnelige og mannlige universitetsforskere, NAVF, Melding, p 2.

Kyvik, Svein (1990), Motherhood and scientific productivity, *Social Studies of Science*, vol 20, no 1, pp 149–60.

Lie, S and Rørslett, M B (1987), Women graduates: elite or second rate? (the case of Norway), in *Nordisk Pedagogik*, no 1, pp 27–36.

Lie, S (in preparation), Perceived discrimination in academe: Norwegian women academics.

Long, J S (1987), Problems and prospects for research on sex differences in the scientific career, in S Dix (ed), *Women: Their Underrepresentation and Career Differentials in Science and Engineering, Proceedings of a Workshop*, Washington DC: National Academy Press.

Long, J S (1989), The origins of sex differences in science, paper presented as GTE Lecture at the Dep of Science and Technology Studies at Rennselaer Polytechnic Institute, Troy, NY.

Luukkonen-Gronow, T (1987), University career opportunities for women in Finland in the 1980s, *Acta Sociologica*, 30, pp 193–206.

Olsen, Terje Bruen (1988), *Doktorgrader i Norge: En kvantitativ oversikt*, NAVF Notat 9/88.

O'Leary, V E and Primack, R B (in preparation), Sex differences in scientific productivity: values make the difference.

Rørslett, M B og S Lie (1984), *På solsiden: Kvinners kamp for kunnskap, hvor førte den?* Oslo: Cammermeyer forlag.

Sciama, L (1984), Ambivalence and dedication: academic wives in Cambridge University, 1870–1970, in H Callan and S Ardener (eds), *The Incorporated Wife*, London: Croom Helm.

Skrede, Kari (1988), Likestillingsforskning i velferdsstats perspektiv – innfallsvinkler og forskningsoppgaver, Seminar om likestilling og kvinneforskning i et velferdsstatsperspektiv, Sondvolden 13–15, april 1988. Arrangør: Norges råd for anvendt samfunnsforskning.

Thagaard, Tove (1987), Kvinner i forskningen: Om kjønnsforskjeller i publiseringsaktivitet, *Tidsskrift for sam funnsforskning*, vol 28, pp 72–86.

Ve, Hildur (in preparation), Gender differences in rationality on the difference between technical limited – and responsible rationality.

Zuckerman, (1987), Persistence and change in the careers of men and women scientists and engineers: a review of current research, in S Dix (ed), *Women: Their Underrepresentation and Career Differentials in Science and Engineering, Proceedings of a Workshop*, Washington DC: National Academy Press.

Chapter 8

Role Priorities and Career Patterns: A Cross-Cultural Study of Turkish and Jordanian University Teachers

Feride Acar

This article provides a comparative study of the career aspirations, role perceptions, role-conflict experiences and coping behaviours of two samples of academic women in Turkey and Jordan. The article is organized in four parts. In the first part, some background conditions specific to Jordan and Turkey are described. In the second part, the characteristics of the samples are detailed and the general methodology is explained. In the third, the results of the study are presented. In the conclusion, the implications of the results for academic women are discussed.

The topic of women academics in developing countries has not attracted much attention as a subject of scholarly inquiry. This lack of interest is owed partly to the fact that the academic women in many of the societies are typically too rare to provide a programmatic research agenda or arouse an individual researcher's curiosity.

Turkey

Even in Turkey where 32 per cent of all academic personnel in the universities are women (Acar 1989), studies focusing on Turkish academic women are uncommon (Acar 1983; Köker 1988). Turkish professional women, who comprise an elite sector of urban working women, have received somewhat more attention (Öncü 1981; Kandiyoti 1982; Kıray and Abadan-Unat 1985; Kağıtçıbaşı and Kansu 1976–77; Kuyaş 1982; Erkut 1982; and Çitçi 1981). While the presence of large numbers of professional women is not a uniquely Turkish phenomenon, many analysts have drawn attention to the 'anomaly' of finding impressive proportions of women attorneys (20 per cent) and doctors (30 per cent) (Kağıtçıbaşı 1989; Kandiyoti 1982; Öncü 1981) in a Middle Eastern society with a patriarchal Islamic cultural heritage and conspicuously high differences in literacy rates between men and women.[1]

Various political, economic and social factors have been suggested as causes of this rather unusual professional employment pattern of Turkish women.

The conventional interpretation of the rise in women's education and professionalization in Turkey often attributes it to the secular ideology and Westernizing reforms of Kemal Atatürk.[2] A series of reforms enacted by the state of the Turkish Republic following its founding by Atatürk in 1923 were aimed at giving women equal status with men. Having replaced the Islamic religious code (Shari'a) with a secular civil code, republican reforms aimed to improve the social and political conditions of women in Turkish society by outlawing polygamy, establishing universal suffrage and guaranteeing equality of the sexes before the law. As a consequence of this policy the state ideology and the elite subculture it defined strongly encouraged women's higher education and career-orientedness as part of their modernization mission. It is also claimed that the result of this sudden and unrestricted push to recruit women into the professions prevented the sex-typing of occupations in Turkish society (Kağıtçıbaşı 1989).

A structural explanation for this phenomenon also points to the interest of male-dominated political authorities in recruiting and training higher-class women rather than lower-class men (Öncü 1981). Certainly the pragmatic need for qualified personnel could have been influenced by the class bias of political authorities. Indeed, as late as the 1980s evidence indicates that professional women in government service continued to be drawn primarily from elite middle- or upper-class backgrounds (Çitçi 1981).

In addition, the ready availability of cheap household help from women of lower socioeconomic backgrounds coupled with that of female relatives in extended Turkish families facilitated elite women's participation in the labour force. It is argued that through these support mechanisms women were able to get into demanding career tracks without posing a serious threat to the traditional relations between sexes in the family and society (Erkut 1982; Kandiyoti 1982; Öncü 1981).

Jordan

As a traditional society with a predominantly Muslim Arab heritage, Jordan propagates an official ideology of modernization with emphasis on education and, recently, political equality of women. Jordan is one of the few Arab countries in which individual women have been encouraged to attain high-status professional careers in the public and private sectors. However, educated and working women in this society are still very new phenomena; cultural values pertaining to women's work outside the home continue to be quite restrictive in all social categories.

There are only a limited number of studies available exploring issues pertinent to urban working women – and none on academic women – in Jordan. In the existing studies the methodology is usually quantitative, and the emphasis is on the sectorial distribution of women's employment. The results of these studies show a continuous increase in the number of working women, and a clear shift from agricultural and manufacturing to service-sector jobs such as secretarial and clerical positions during the past two decades (Nasir 1968; Said 1984; Zaghal 1984).

The entry of women into these fields is also a result, in part, of the outflow of Jordanian males to other Arab countries as migrant white-collar workers (Zaghal 1984). Despite the growth of urban jobs open to women, their labour-force participation remains low in Jordan. Working women are found primarily in the traditional sex-typed fields and middle-level occupations of primary and secondary school teaching, nursing, and needlework. This is consistent with the prevailing cultural norms that define women's place as 'in the home' and the dictates of the Islamic law of sex segregation (Haj-Ismail 1987; Nasir 1968).

Method and samples

This chapter brings together two case studies conducted on Turkish and Jordanian academic women in the period from December 1983 to December 1985. Data employed in these studies were generated through in-depth interviews with 'convenience samples' of academic women in these countries. Since the technique of in-depth interviewing depends heavily on accessibility of and personal rapport with the interviewees, these considerations determined the selection of the samples and the number of respondents is limited. In the Turkish case the subjects were 15 full-time faculty members at the Middle East Technical University and Ankara University (Acar 1983), selected with regard to age, field of specialization, academic rank and marital status. The Jordanian sample, on the other hand, comprised 16 of the 20 Jordanian women faculty members at Yarmouk University (Acar 1986).[3]

The interview schedule was identical for all subjects. The interviews lasted from one to three-and-a-half hours. Although the sampling plan did not allow for representativeness and generalizability of the results to academic women in either society, the interviews provided a basis on which to compare the characteristics and experiences of Jordanian and Turkish academic women that is rich in content and may be used to supplement what is known about these groups from a more 'objective', quantitative perspective.

The Turkish respondents were between the ages of 35 and 45. They might best be described as professionally mature and successful, as 12 had been employed in academic positions for more than seven years and ten had achieved the rank of associate or full professor. The 16 women in the Jordanian group were professionally and chronologically younger than those from Turkey. Their ages ranged from 27 to 40 and they had only been employed in academe for an average of four years. Most were assistant professors and instructors. There was no Jordanian woman full professor at Yarmouk University at the time of the study.

All of the women in both samples had at least one graduate degree and over half had a PhD. Most of these degrees had been earned at Western universities. As a result, most of the women academics had been exposed to Western values and attitudes toward women's family and career roles. Women in both samples were daughters of middle- and upper-middle-class urban families. Their parents were educated and relatively enlightened and identified with the reformist and modernizing trends in Jordan and Turkey. Most of the fathers of the Turkish women were university educated. The Turkish mothers were high school or university educated women who belonged to the first generation of 'emancipated' republican women in Turkey. The parents of the Jordanian women were comparatively less well educated and more heterogeneous in background than the Turks.

Of the 12 Turkish and eight Jordanian women who were married, almost all had husbands who were highly trained professionals, often also faculty members. Eight of the Turkish and four of the Jordanian women were married to fellow academics. While most (ten in the Turkish sample and seven in the Jordanian) of the married women in the samples had children, the maximum number of children per woman in the Turkish sample was two. One Jordanian woman had five children.

The comparative study

Although on the surface it may appear that there are more similarities than differences between the women in the Turkish and Jordanian samples, on closer inspection many of these similarities prove to be illusory.

Career Motivation

All the women in the Turkish sample indicated that they had never doubted they would have careers. They said that they had never thought of 'not working' or becoming a 'housewife' (Acar 1983). In fact, the majority said they had defined their career goals as university teaching at quite an early age. The observation of a 67-year-old woman professor,

'I've wanted to be a professor since I was a child' is shared by many Turkish respondents. These women were clear in attributing their motivation to the impact of educated, 'open-minded' parents, particularly fathers, who had guided them. 'My career choice was not even a conscious one. I grew up with the decision,' said one associate professor whose father was also a university professor. Details of the personal life histories of these women elaborated elsewhere (Acar 1983) attest to their high motivation and strong career orientations.

In contrast, the academic women in the Jordanian sample indicated that they had very little initial interest in an academic career. Instead they attributed their career decisions to a series of external influences (Acar 1986). Among such influences, Jordanian women mentioned such things as the opportunity to go abroad; a chance to live in a campus town because of a husband's education; or a need to continue with their education because this was the only way their parents would consent to an independent lifestyle or travel. For instance, one unmarried Jordanian lecturer who had returned home after getting her Master's degree in the US said,

I am now planning to go abroad to get my PhD, but I am waiting for a family decision. A while ago, I got a contract for a job [in another Arab country] but my family said 'no way'. It actually offered very good money and I would have liked to try it. But I could not. You see, it is OK to go abroad to study but not to work.

Most of the women in the Jordanian sample openly admitted that they would rather have done something other than teach. They would have preferred employment in industry or the more applied professions.

The origin of these differences in orientation lies in the social-structural and cultural differences between the two societies. Modern Turkey has officially espoused the liberal values of the West and encouraged women's emancipation through legal and political action throughout most of this century. Regardless of what social, economic and political causes laid the grounds for its establishment, this ideology of emancipation provides the backdrop for the self-definitions of several generations of educated, urban middle-class women in Turkey. As products of this elite subculture the women in the Turkish sample reported themselves to be highly career motivated and ambitious from the beginning of their career lives. They saw the pursuit of a career as their primary goal, and received support for their ambitions from significant others, who expressed pride in their accomplishments. Their marriage and family decisions were consistent with the primacy of their career goals even though most had not refrained from marriage. One instructor stated: 'My decision to marry [my husband] was influenced by my career decision. I thought to marry someone who would not obstruct my career.' Another professor said she had planned and given birth to both her children during summer breaks and added,

I sent my first-born infant home to be taken care of by my parents for a year so that I could continue with my PhD work in the US. It was terrible, but I had to do it. What else could I do ? I could not interrupt my work.

These Turkish women viewed research, teaching and administration as equally important aspects of their academic careers, and set high standards for their own performance (Acar 1986). In contrast, the Jordanian women academics indicated that, for them, the traditional wife/mother role took precedence over career. Consistent with these values, they had or expected to have more children than their Turkish counterparts, and reported setting lower standards for their own career performance. Although they expressed interest in their careers, they saw that role as secondary to their family obligations. In the words of a 34-year-old Jordanian assistant professor with four children:

It is better to have your family happy than to have people say "she is a good scientist". Family is always more important than career for a woman.

Jordanian women did not assign first priority to their career roles, even in the initial stages of their careers. Most Jordanian academics reported support from family members in their academic pursuits but more often than not the support was for the woman's advanced education rather than her career. This is in keeping with other research findings indicating that women's work outside the home is still considered less important than home responsibilities by most and accepted only in some contexts – elementary and secondary school teaching and government posts – in Jordan (Barhoum 1983).

Thus, the career motivations and life choices of the Jordanian women were shaped by the demands of their traditionally defined gender roles. In contrast, the early career motivations of the less traditional Turkish sample were relatively independent of their familial roles. The role concepts and priorities of each group were shaped and supported by the dominant values in their respective social, political and intellectual milieus, resulting in different patterns of career development among women from the two societies.

Role conflict

As the role priorities of the Jordanian women were clearly defined, they experienced little career/family role conflict. Family took precedence. In contrast, Turkish women reported experiencing severe role conflict as the demands of both their careers and families escalated. Most of the married women reported a change in their role expectations and behaviours as their wife and mother roles evolved. Life became 'different' from what they had expected or what they thought it was 'in the beginning.' This gradual change spelled a redefinition of expectations and behaviour whereby the career role was no longer incontestably primary. Although the women in the Turkish sample strongly denied that they relegated career to a secondary status in their lives, they did display an increase in the extent to which they attributed equal importance to their family concerns. Consistent with this shift in career priority they perceived that their women colleagues appeared to pay less attention to their careers than did their male colleagues, although they denied this was true of themselves.

According to a 33-year-old married associate professor in the Middle East Technical University,

I don't think men and women faculty members I know have different perceptions of their career roles. At least here everyone I know would want to give priority to research but married women have more role conflict. Being married or single makes a lot of difference for women. For myself, I think, career and family are equally important roles, but many women behave differently in actuality.

One plausible explanation for this change in role-related pressure among more mature Turkish academic women may again be found in the culture. The Turkish women were raised in a subculture that encouraged and supported both their education and their career involvement as politically and socially significant (Tekeli 1981; Tekeli 1986). The economic status of urban elite families made it possible for them to adopt this liberated ideology without much disruption in the social order to which they were accustomed (Erkut 1982; Kandiyoti 1982; Öncü 1981). Raising and having a daughter or marrying a woman with a professional career was a valuable asset in the subculture (Erkut 1982; Kıray 1982). However, once the demands of the professional career became disruptive, many of these professional women found their families' support eroding.

A Turkish respondent raised with such supportive familial attitudes voices the experience of many when she said:

I had no problems with my parents at the beginning. They were proud of what I was doing, they supported me in every way they could. However, things changed somewhat after I had children and they grew up a little. My parents thought the children were being neglected. They even offered to pay me whatever it was I was earning at the university if I would quit my job. But I never thought of quitting or interrupting my career.

The Turkish academic women reported that this erosion was particularly evident as their husband's career demands increased and their children's demands became more complex with age. These events often coincided with the period during which their own career demands were escalating, following receipt of their advanced degrees. It was a time during which women reported increased homemaking responsibilities and increased demands to provide support to their spouses. Many of the Turkish women were not prepared to deal with the increase in role conflict occasioned by these shifts in their role demands as they matured.

Strategies for coping with role conflict

The two most prevalent methods of coping with role conflict among the Turkish academics were compartmentalization and integration (Acar 1983). Women who compartmentalized literally separated their lives into two spheres and developed a separate identity for each. Women labelled as integrators tried to cope with role conflict by developing consistent behaviour patterns that cut across both roles.

Among the Turkish academic women, the compartmentalizers were at least as insistent that their roles receive equal priority as were the integrators. When role conflict occurred they tried to resolve it by redefining their roles. Such redefinition involved a reduction in perceived role demands and a lowering of personal standards for performance in both career and family roles. In the career-role context, often such accommodations involved the neglect of research and administrative priorities in favour of teaching. In the wife/mother role, accomodation meant the neglect of some housework and home entertaining as well as a redefinition of mothering.

The response from a compartmentalizing Turkish associate professor illustrates this attitude:

My career revolves around mostly teaching and some research. Both of these are important for me. For me, academic administration is not. It would upset my schedule, create a lot of problems. This would disturb me. I am under enough stress trying to balance teaching and research. Often I can't even give enough time to research. Who needs to be an administrator?

Another woman, a full professor said:

When my children were younger they resented my schedule. I still feel terribly guilty when I remember the sight of twenty little fingers sticking from underneath the door of my study while I locked myself in to work in the evenings and my children wanted to be with me. But I was there when they were sick, I rushed to their emergencies, I just did not have as much play time with them as other mothers.

While these women redefined their roles, their standards for role performance remained quite high; compartmentalizing academic women of the Turkish sample invariably displayed competitive attitudes with regard to male colleagues. Separating their lives into compartments appeared to enable some to adopt more traditional wife–mother roles at home but in no instance did these women show tolerance for secondary status in the career context.

Integrators also redefined their roles, but not as rigidly. In the process of this redefinition integrators tried to develop a more consistent lifestyle, based on their refusal to adopt two separate identities. The integrators tended to be younger than compartmentalizers, more likely to be second-generation 'emancipated' women and more likely to have been exposed to feminist discourse.

One such respondent – a 30-year-old instructor – said:

Academe is not a profession, it is your life. Some women do not understand this. My intellectual and personal relationships coincide with one another. I do not separate them. For instance, I see some [academic] women fulfil the demands of the daughter-in-law role in rather traditional terms. They do not find it conflicting. I think it is conflictual to adulthood and I cannot separate my life like that.

These women also did not aim to appear 'desexed' in their career roles like the compartmentalizers often did. In the latter group, the following response characterized many women's perceptions of their career role identities: 'A professional woman should not attract attention with her dress, make-up or general femininity. People should not be aware of her womanhood at work.' By contrast, an integrator claimed:

Women have many advantages over men in this profession. They can attract more attention so often they communicate better; they don't mind changing their mind so they are more flexible and usually they are more easily accessible to people. If they use these 'feminine' characteristics they are better teachers and better administrators than men. I do not think there is anything wrong with using these assets.

Despite these differences in coping strategies both groups of Turkish women reported an acute awareness of their role conflicts. In effect, like other Turkish professional women, they mostly tried to cope with this conflict by 'shouldering an overload of responsibilities' (Erkut 1982).

The Jordanian women academics experienced little discontinuity in their role perceptions because they were not aware of competition between the demands of different roles and feelings of discomfort resulting from irreconcilable pressures, and therefore did not experience role conflict. Women in this basically patriarchal society were expected to assign higher priority to their stereotypically feminine role (Haj-Ismail 1987; Nasir 1968; Said 1984) and academic women were no exceptions, even though they were educated in the modern world and had high career status. Consequently, in a sociocultural environment that almost uniformly accepted the traditional gender-role definitions, these women did not need to integrate or even compartmentalize their different roles; they merely conformed to the dominant values. Because their career roles had been shaped around their family role demands, such conforming Jordanian academic women placed themselves outside the 'race' in their professional lives. As a result, their career performances were non-competitive.

Certainly, other factors such as the traditional structure of the academic establishment contributed to the Jordanian women's professional marginality. But the priority given to the traditional women's role by the women themselves also appeared to be a most influential factor here. Married Jordanian women did not experience role conflict because they did not perceive or experience their career roles to be in competition with their familial roles. They had been socialized to put the traditional female role first and they conformed to the traditional expectations their culture held for them.

However, the fact that eight of the 16 academic women in the Jordanian sample were not married is significant and suggests that they may have been avoiding the 'inevitable'. As one unmarried Jordanian woman – a 27-year-old assistant professor – put it: 'For me it [career] is first priority now. If I were to marry, I expect it would change. So I am delaying it. Another 30-year-old single assistant professor said:

For me, career comes first because I decided on a career before I married. . . . I have also decided that I do not want any children. I broke up an engagement for this reason. I did not get married mostly for career reasons. I believe I cannot manage both.

Not surprisingly, the career commitment of the Turkish women was much stronger than that of their Jordanian counterparts. After 43 years of service in the university one women professor said she was '. . . only retiring to be able to completely devote myself to academic interests; to work without interruption, to publish more.'

These Turkish women saw their careers as inextricably tied to their identities. For instance a 43-year-old associate professor who was the department chair during a period of rather violent student activity on campus and was once even a target of violence herself said 'Through all this I never thought of quitting the university. Where else would I go?'

The Turkish women viewed their educations as investments and thought they would feel guilty were they to waste those investments by withdrawing from the academic world, even to pursue an alternate career. So steadfast was their academic career commitment that one might question the extent to which it reflected liberation, as opposed to an alternate form of oppression: the kind of role oppression more characteristically associated with contemporary men who are slaves to the dictates of the male role.

Attitudes towards gender equality

All of the academic women interviewed, regardless of nationality, said that they believed in the fundamental principle of equality between the sexes. However, their definitions of equality differed.

Most Jordanian academic women and the compartmentalizers in the Turkish sample understood equality in terms of formal occupational criteria only. As the universities in Jordan and Turkey are public institutions, established and operated by the state, their formal rules and regulations do not permit overt discrimination based on sex. Thus, if one uses this criterion alone, gender equality appears to be a given as subtler indications of discrimination may not be acknowledged.

Interestingly, the Turkish compartmentalizers were different from their Jordanian counterparts in that they defined formal equality more stringently. For example, they were more likely to include the administrative dimension in their career role definitions and to insist on equality of opportunity in this respect too. In contrast, Jordanians viewed administrative positions as 'beyond their reach' or defined them as 'not fit for women'. As a result, these women were also less resentful of discrimination in administrative appointments than the Turkish academics.

On the other hand, only a few of the Jordanian respondents and half of the Turkish academic women, mostly those classified as integrators in the latter case, subscribed to a more abstract definition of equality at home or at work. Their criteria included the likelihood of a woman being taken seriously by male colleagues, gaining access to information concerning organizational matters, and wielding influence in decision-making and agenda-setting in the work place. These women identified many signs of discrimination against women in their organizations and were very critical of them.

Most Jordanian academic women and Turkish compartmentalizers were also likely to endorse traditional gender-role definitions and were less sensitive to demonstrations of inequality between spouses although they all said they had egalitarian marriages. Women in both these categories generally conceded to their spouses' authority and priorities at home. However, Jordanian women admitted and legitimized this situation more readily. According to a 29-year-old assistant professor:

My husband normally does not have the Middle Eastern attitude. Most of the time we are like roommates at home. We share most responsibilities but I serve him in front of people. We agreed on that, because people will say since I have a PhD and he does not, he is being put down. We both thought that it is better not to appear as a new social phenomenon.

By contrast, integrators in the Turkish sample who often had the least traditional marital roles and relations were sensitive to and unwilling to tolerate much subtler reflections of inequality. A married Turkish associate professor said:

I think inequality in a marital relationship like ours lies in who is more influential in setting the norms, and this depends on who can think of better things and impose them on the other, who has more self-confidence.

Conclusion

The role priorities and career patterns of Turkish and Jordanian women academics were compared in the study. Clear differences were observed, stemming in large measure from the dominant ideology governing women's roles in the two societies.

In Jordan the merits of education for girls were viewed in terms of their contribution to women's roles as mothers and homemakers. Jordanian women who had careers set their priorities in favour of their traditional gender roles. As a result, Jordanian academic women were not competitive with men, nor were they ambitious. Their performance of career roles was relatively passive and at the individual level, they were psychologically quite content.

Jordanian academic women in this study saw themselves as women first and foremost. Thus they tended to compare themselves with other women. Even when they admitted their career performance to be below their capacities, they were not disturbed and did not entertain guilt feelings.

Turkish academic women situated at the crossroads of traditional Islamic patriarchy and formal emancipatory discourse of Kemalism were the end-products of a unique social–historical experience. The effective challenge to the traditional values presented by the content and rhetoric of republican ideology made it possible for elite Turkish women to harbour distinctly non-traditional ambitions and role perceptions. However, since political and legal changes pertaining to women's lives in the public sphere were often unaccompanied by equally effective structural and normative changes in the private sphere, elite women in Turkey were not free from traditional female role obligations. Hence, experience and awareness of severe role conflict characterized all the married women in the Turkish study.

It has been observed in this case study that compartmentalizing and integrating Turkish academic women tended to exhibit different degrees of self-esteem. Compartmentalizing women generally expressed higher contentment than integrating women in terms of both career and gender roles. While they also tended to attribute their own success to their personal qualities and achievements, they believed qualified women had a fair chance in the system.

In contrast, integrators in the Turkish sample had the lowest self-esteem. Since they refused to reduce the demands of either role, family or career, but tried to achieve success according to universal standards in both, they were unsuccessful. However, these women did not see their achievements or failures as results of their individual traits, instead they were inclined to have a political – and feminist – awareness of their situation. Therefore, they were more actively change-oriented than their compartmentalizing sisters.

Notes

1. In Turkey, the literacy rate for women is 68 per cent as compared to 86 per cent for men according to the 1985 census. Although there has been a decrease in the difference between the literacy of men and women over the years (48 per cent and 75 per cent in 1975; 55 per cent and 80 per cent in 1980), the present difference is still among the highest in the world.

2. Some analysts also point to a continuity in the official ideology of Turkey dating back to the latter years of the Ottoman Empire (Kandiyoti 1988; Tekeli 1986).

3. Faculty member was defined as someone occupying the academic rank of instructor or above in both samples. In the Jordanian study two women were unavailable at the time (on leave, etc), one could not be reached, and one woman refused to be interviewed.

References

Acar, Feride (1983), Turkish women in academia: roles and careers, *METU Studies in Development*, Vol 10.

Acar, Feride (1986), Working women in a changing society: the case of Jordanian academics, *METU Studies in Development*, Vol 13.

Acar, Feride (1989), Women's participation in academic science careers: Turkey in 1989, paper presented at *Improving Employment Prospects for Women in a Changing Society: The Years Ahead*, an international conference organized jointly by the OECD and the Turkish Employment Organization, Istanbul, November 7–8.

Barhoum, Mohammad I (1983), Attitudes of university students toward women's work: the case of Jordan, *International Journal of Middle Eastern Studies*, Vol 15.

Çitçi, Oya (1981), Turkish female civil service employees, in N. Abadan-Unat (ed), *Women in Turkish Society*, Leiden: E J Brill.

Erkut, Sumru (1982), Dualism in values toward education of Turkish women, in Ç Kagıtçıbaşı (ed) *Sex Roles, Family and Community in Turkey*, Bloomington, Ind: Indiana University Turkish Studies, 121–32.

Haj-Ismail, Hanan A (1987), The participation of women in the government sector in Jordan, unpublished MS Thesis, Ankara: Department of Public Administration, Middle East Technical University.

Kağıtçıbaşı, Çiğdem and Aykut Kansu (1976–77), Cinsiyet Rollerinin Sosyalleş-mesi ve Aile Dinamiği: Kuşaklararası Bir Karşılaştırma, *Bogazici Universitesi Dergisi*, 4–5.

Kağıtçıbaşı, Çiğdem (1989), Women's intra-family status, education and employment in Turkey, paper presented at *Improving Employment Prospects for Women in a Changing Society: The Years Ahead*, an international conference organized jointly by the OECD and the Turkish Employment Organization, Istanbul, November 7–8.

Kandiyoti, Deniz (1982), Urban change and women's roles in Turkey: an overview and evaluation, in Ç Kağıtçıbaşı (ed), *Sex Roles, Family and Community in Turkey*, Bloomington, Ind: Indiana University Turkish Studies.

Kandiyoti, Deniz (1988) Women and the Turkish state: political actors or symbolic pawns?, in N Juval-Davis and A Athias (eds), *Women–Nation–State*, London: Macmillan.

Kıray, Mübeccel (1982), Changing patterns of patronage, in Ç. Kagıtçıbaşı (ed), *Sex Roles, Family and Community in Turkey*, Bloomington, Ind: Indiana University Turkish Studies.

Kıray, Mübeccel and Nermin Abadan-Unat (1985), Social structure, in Klaus-Detler Grothusen (ed), *Südosteuropa Handbuch – Türkei*, Göthingen, Vandenhoeck and Ruprecht.

Köker, Eser D (1988), Türkiye'de kadın, eğitim ve siyaset: yüksuk öğrenim kurumlarında kadının durumu üzerine bir inceleme, unpublished PhD dissertation, Ankara: Ankara University, Institute of Social Sciences.

Kuyaş, Nilüfer (1982), The effects of female labor on power relations in the urban Turkish family, in Ç Kağıtçıbaşı (ed), *Sex Roles, Family and Community in Turkey*, Bloomington, Ind: Indiana University Turkish Studies.

Nasir, Sari (1968), Social survey of the working women in Jordan, *Jordan University Faculty of Arts Journal*, vol 2.

Öncü, Ayşe (1981), Turkish women in the professions: why so many?, in N Abadan-Unat (ed), *Women in Turkish Society*, Leiden: R J Brill.

Said, Nimra T (1974), The changing role of women in Jordan, paper presented to the *VIII World Congress of Sociology*, Toronto, August.

Tekeli, Şirin (1981), Women in Turkish politics, in N Abadan-Unat (ed), *Women in Turkish Society*, Leiden: E J Brill.

Tekeli, Şirin (1986), Emergence of the feminist movement in Turkey, in Drude Dahlerup (ed), *The New Women's Movement*, London: Sage Publications.

Zaghal, Ali S (1984), Social change in Jordan, *Middle Eastern Studies* 20, 4, 53–75.

Part IV
A Closer Look

Chapter 9
African-American Women in Academia: Paradoxes and Barriers*

Pamela Trotman Reid

There is an impending crisis in higher education. As one researcher recently noted, 'In an increasingly Black and Hispanic America, the academy remains a near-lily-white institution' (Hirschorn 1988). In fact, throughout the world, attempts to change the domination of university faculty by white men have been resisted. In the United States, for example, fewer than 4 per cent of professors are of African descent in a national population in which African Americans constitute about 12 per cent. (Only 2 per cent of full-time professors with PhDs are Black). Within various disciplines the numbers of Black professors are so low that reports of gender are not typically provided.

There are multiple reasons to promote an increase in the numbers of Black faculty. Among those are predictions from demographic studies which strongly indicate that White women and ethnic minorities must fill the gap left by declining numbers of White men. The growing 'brain drain' of the academy, ie, students of talent going to business and other avenues of employment, is most severe for Blacks, particularly Black men who may be viewed as abandoning the educational field to women. Hirschorn asserts that there is little hope that enough Black PhDs will be produced in the near future to fill the need for minority faculty for the 3,300 colleges and universities in the USA. Sheila Widnall (1988) concurs in his assessment of the academic situation. Both recognize that the difficulty cannot be corrected quickly. In fact, they agree that a solution must begin with the recognition of need to move more minority students through the academic pipeline. While the impending shortage has been discussed widely in the United States, international attention may be necessary when considering an educational agenda for Black people around the world.

*I wish to acknowledge the assistance and feedback of Dr W LaVome Robinson on earlier versions of this chapter.

The numbers game: demographic information

African-American women participate in academia at every level. They may be found as administrators, as professors and as students. However, the overall rates of participation, which increased during the 1960s and 1970s have remained fairly constant in the 1980s and are predicted to decline relative to other groups into the 1990s. The US Department of Labour (1988) reports that Black women who teach at the college and university level have increased by only 20 per cent from 1980 to 1986 (10,000 to 12,000). Statistical data for administrators are not so clearly differentiated. Overall, in education and related fields Black female administrators have increased from 17,000 to 25,000 (US Department of Labor 1988). As students, Black women earned 5.7 per cent (n = 442) of all doctorates in 1975–1976. In 1985–86 they earned 5.4 per cent (N = 593) – this was virtually no change (American Council on Education 1987). Data from the National Science Foundation (1988) indicate that the number of Blacks earning doctorates has declined since 1978. Although Black men account for most of the decline, the number of Black women earning doctorates has also dropped over the past five years.

Black women throughout the USA earned fewer advanced degrees each year after 1984, particularly in science and related fields. For example, African-American women earned only 499 doctorates in science and engineering in 1986, compared to 564 in 1982 (National Research Council 1988). At every level, the educational attainment of African American women and men has consistently trailed behind both White men and White women. Although Black women appear to surpass Black men in several areas these differences are relatively inconsequential when the total picture of African-American achievement is considered. For example, of all doctorates earned in 1984, 1.9 per cent (14,000) were earned by Black men and 2.3 per cent (18,000 by Black women.

The future does not promise much improvement for Black women's educational attainment levels. The total enrolment of African-American women in institutions of higher education has increased less than 1 per cent in the years from 1976 to 1986. During that same period White women have increased by 3 per cent, Hispanic women by 18 per cent, Asian women by 16 per cent and Native-American women by almost 11 per cent (US Department of Education 1988). Among 18–24-year-old high-school graduates, the number of Black women enrolled in college (which includes junior college students) barely increased from 331,000 in 1982 to 340,000 in 1986. With few Black women in the pipeline, there are few opportunities for new faculty in the coming years. At the present time Black females constitute only 5 per cent of the total student enrolment in American colleges and universities. Many of them have little expectation of obtaining advanced or professional degrees (Guy-Sheftall and Bell-Scott 1989). Given the necessity for most Black women throughout the world to attend predominantly White institutions if they have academic aspirations, it is clear that they are unlikely to encounter Black role models or to have opportunities to examine their own experience as African-American women.

Systemic barriers to academic success

The barriers to achievement for women of African descent include systemic problems stemming from family expectations and community demands. It would be useful if these barriers could be grouped neatly according to source; however, the overlapping and complex nature of each prevents such simplistic categorization.

Graduate student and faculty perspectives

It has been documented that poor academic preparation limits entry into academia, but at the graduate and faculty levels poor preparation may take forms different from those affecting undergraduate students. Students accepted into graduate programmes must often struggle to receive the same attention as their White peers. The scarcity of Black faculty has been blamed, in part, for some of the difficulties which many Black graduate students experience in finding a faculty mentor or sponsor. White professors often assume that they cannot guide Black students in their research work, especially if the student indicates any interest in examining African-American issues. This issue may be compounded by parallel concerns of male faculty directing research on women. Some White faculty may have abdicated their responsibility for teaching Black students research and practice skills. Because these students wish to reflect the Black experience in their studies, White faculty uninformed about the African-American community may excuse themselves from dealing with these areas and these students. This abdication is itself a subtle form of discrimination.

The special demands on Black professors and administrators represent another form of insufficient preparation. Often, young Black professors are not ready for the demands which will be made upon them: demands from Black students who are searching for a role model and mentors of their own; from White students who may be suspicious and challenging of the authority of a Black professor; from faculty colleagues who demand proof that their new colleague is worthy of their respect, some of them certain that she/he never can be; from university administrators seeking to validate their actions by including minority faculty on every possible committee; and, finally, from the African-American community requesting support and seeking professional guidance. As in graduate school, this lack of preparation comes from a lack of mentoring and, further possibly the lack of a professional network to serve as a source for comparison and consultation. It also stems from a lack of preparation for the task of ordering priorities and dealing with conflicting demands. While a number of African-American women and men have earned advanced rank and tenure at prestigious American universities, some potentially outstanding Black faculty women and men have been defeated by the academic system.

Inadequate resources

In part the financial strains on African-American students come from the lack of support given them by their academic institution. Even the generous offers of some universities are insufficient to cover all student needs. For Black women with responsibilities to provide a return to their family for earlier investments, the cost of devoting additional years to study may be prohibitive. This impact must be all the greater for Black women from countries with fewer resources devoted to their education. For example, in South Africa where the per capita income of full Africans is only 10 per cent of that of Western Europeans (Simpson and Yinger 1985), the chances of a Black woman becoming a university professor are minuscule.

Brazziel and Brazziel (1987) note that Black American students are more likely to study far from home. This is also true for students of African descent around the world given the typical location of universities in European communities. Leaving family and friends is often more stressful for women who have been socialized to remain close to home and hearth.

The combination of poor financial support plus the distance from familiar surroundings is undoubtedly important in Black students taking longer to complete a graduate degree. For example, the average African-American student takes two years longer than the Anglo-American student to achieve the first university degree. Subsequent degrees, thus, must also be delayed. Consequently the Black candidate for university positions appears less capable and less attractive than their White counterparts who completed their education requirements in a more timely fashion.

Strategies for increasing faculty and graduate students

At the student level, colleges have experienced varying levels of success with programmes designed to recruit and retain ethnic-minority students. A few campuses have attempted to create a welcoming atmosphere for African-American students. Most have focused on providing a generous financial aid package. Although it is clear that an interest in increasing ethnic-minority involvement on campus exists on the part of many administrators, it is also obvious that some students and faculty do not concur with this commitment. Attention has been focused recently on protests and racist incidents initiated by White students against Black students and faculty. Denise K Magner (1989) reports that while the students who perpetrate these racist acts are actually a minority, the indifference of the majority appears to offer silent support to their actions. The task which remains to be accomplished by those who value diversity in higher education is to convince the majority of participants (students and faculty) that ethnic diversity enriches us all. This requires debunking the notion that administrators are 'doing a favour' for Blacks and other minorities by including them in the academic process.

For Black faculty women the efforts directed at their recruitment are typically more intensive than are plans to facilitate adjustment and retention. The isolation and insensitivity which may be faced by an African or an African American at a predominantly White campus is intensified by the greater position of visibility and responsibility. Adding further to the stress is the fact that Black women, like other women on campus, are seen as anomalies in the predominantly male environment. The role of double token (Black and female) is a difficult one. Yet, there are some actions which institutions could take to address this situation. Since the isolation as a double token is often most distressing, assistance in making 'connections' should be provided. Awarding assistance and support for networking activities, eg funds for attending professional conferences and meetings, would also be useful. Most importantly, however, building a local university network of ethnic minorities at various levels throughout the campus will help to establish a supportive environment for African-American professionals and students.

Racism and sexism: re-emerging and persistent traditions

During the 1960s and 1970s progress was made with respect to opening US colleges and universities to divergent groups (Huber 1983). The overt refusal to admit Black students and the covert quotas placed on the admission of White women were gradually modified and eliminated. However, recent years have evidenced a decline of tolerance and a resurgence of blatant racist and sexist behaviour (Damon 1989; Magner 1989).

Black women, unlike White women or Black men, are in the position of facing the deleterious impact of both racism and sexism. The prejudiced behaviour, attitudes and resulting effects must be handled by Black women in both the personal and professional spheres of their everyday lives in academia. In recent decades researchers have carefully documented the consequences of sexist behaviour; the impact of racism has also been noted. Few studies, however, have addressed the dual impact which may be far more devastating than the predicted combined effects. C H Smith (1982) suggests that this lack of data on professional Black women in higher education is symptomatic of their status. Even without any clear documentation of combined impact, the barriers of racism and sexism may be seen through behaviour on the campus and felt through the control of attitudes.

Both racism and sexism have functioned well for gatekeeping in the classroom. Under the guise of 'standards', ethnic minority women and men have been labelled or stigmatized as unfit for entry into higher education. Subtleties in racial discrimination may be even more damaging than blatant actions. Professors, who are too clever and sophisticated to use derogatory names for African Americans, may take every opportunity to point out real and imagined racial deficiencies to their classes. Or, they may direct racial comments and queries to the sole Black student in the class as though it were that student's responsibility to defend or to represent her/his entire ethnic community.

During recent years, according to the National Institute Against Prejudice and Violence, the incidents of campus racism in the US have reached the hundreds (Damon 1989). Media reports about ethnic violence towards university students in European countries have also surfaced. Simultaneously, accounts of violence towards White women have also increased. At the professional level, discrimination may take the form of disparagement or negation of the efforts of the Black faculty/ administrators, especially when they focus on ethnic issues. For black women all of the difficulties of racism must be combined with the real potential for sexism (including, but not limited to, sexual harassment) from both her White and Black male colleagues.

When faced with discrimination, Black women may find that there are not many ways to seek redress. There may not even be sympathetic listeners with whom they may share their experiences. Attempting to label a hostile act as either racist or sexist may indeed pose a true dilemma for there is no single term which conveys how these hostile and negative belief systems may interact and feed each other. If a Black woman claims racial discrimination, she may find that no other Black faculty has been employed in her academic unit. Thus, with no basis for establishing a pattern or case of discrimination, she may be viewed as paranoid. If she makes a claim for sex discrimination, she will need assurances that the White women in the academic unit will support this claim. A usual strategy for academic discrimination is the presentation of negative information to cast the individual as an isolated case of inferiority. With this technique the racist/sexist may excuse their individual acts of discrimination by claiming it is justified: 'We would be pleased to support a Black candidate/female candidate for this position, if only we could find a qualified one.' Taking one case at a time obscures the fact that no candidate/student ever meets the ideal unless that candidate is White and male.

The most blatant form of discrimination is direct exclusion. Denial of admission to programme at the student level, failure to offer employment and, for those few who have gained faculty rank, denial of promotion and tenure. In addition to blatant exclusion, other significant examples of discrimination may be found. Black women may find that as faculty they have few opportunities offered them as collaborators or participants in important projects. For example, supervisors, colleagues or department heads may hold the conscious or unconscious belief that a Black female can contribute only if the issue is one relevant to race. Graduate assistantships may be awarded to minority women only when special 'set aside' money is available. Whether blatant or subtle, however, the result is an atmosphere which fosters mistrust and separateness.

Personal barriers to academic success

Double jeopardy or double whammy*? Cynthia Epstein (1976) argued that Black women were ahead of White women because their double status (Black and female) worked in tandem to ward off sexism and racism. None of the data has supported this early claim. In fact, it may be that the contrary is more accurate (Reid 1984 and 1988). Dual allegiance as Blacks and as females has generally functioned to keep Black Women in the background of both the civil-rights and the women's movements. Similarly, in higher education, not only institutional but also personal barriers and conflicts have beset African-American women.

Problems of identity and self-concept

The need to establish an identity is important for Black women in today's society. The many pressures to meet the standards of attractiveness set by White women, to accept the levels of achievement permitted

---

*A US term denoting a belief that Black women are more effective or positively impactful due to their double-minority status.

by Black men, and to acquiesce to the demands for conformity to community standards, may leave little room for a Black woman to find herself. The questions about who she *should* become, who she *could* become, and who she *will* become are left to each woman. There are few models to assist her in determining how to balance the conflicting roles. A study by Reid and Robinson (1985) of Black professionals indicated that the successful African-American women demonstrated a much narrower range of life choices compared to African-American men. Black women who had received either a doctoral degree or a professional degree were more likely than men to have a middle-class family background. They were less likely to be married and to have children, although, if they married, their spouse also held a professional degree.

In setting one's own identity, then, the African-American woman must determine her goals and have the confidence to achieve them. Hafner (1989) found that in both 1971 and 1983 being Black predicted a higher level of aspiration for females, but not for males. One might expect that high aspirations would develop from a strong and positive sense of self. However, African-American women students from two-year colleges and Black colleges, were found to have lower-than-average self-concepts.

Fleming (1983) also found that Black women from Black colleges were low in sense of self. She found that African-American women in Black colleges actually experienced a significant loss in assertive abilities over time, while those who attended White colleges increased their assertiveness from their freshmen through to their senior year. Fleming suggests that for African-American women within the Black college environment there is a re-enactment of the dilemma which has so often faced White women. That is, the supportive environment for Black women at Black colleges encourages them to achieve without becoming too assertive. The resulting Black women tend to be passive and dependent rather than assertive and ambitious. Fleming finds it ironic that Black colleges, established to facilitate academic development, may actually undermine the Black woman's social development. In contrast, the adverse conditions of predominantly White colleges, while more likely to induce self-reliance and assertion in African-American women, produce simultaneously feelings of dissatisfaction and self-doubt. These findings suggest that much analysis and evaluation is necessary to determine which circumstances are best to facilitate academic and personal success for Black women.

Lack of social support networks

Allen and Britt's (1984) literature review on studies of Black women in academic settings indicated that the lack of support systems is especially problematic. Given the low number of African Americans in most institutions, it is not always possible to find another African-American woman with whom to associate when empathy or experience is needed. The scarcity might be expected to promote cooperation among Blacks and others who are considered outsiders, yet this does not always occur. In fact, the practice of pitting one group against the other for designated scholarships, faculty positions or other recognition has frequently evoked an adversarial relationship. This competitiveness may occur between Black and White women, and between Black women and Black men. For example, at one White institution several Black male faculty joined together to malign and denigrate the achievements of their Black female colleague (personal communication). Their actions contributed to the challenge of her right to tenure and to her low comfort level at that university.

Black women as deviants

Equally as devastating as blatant hostility to the confidence of a Black woman, are the covert types of discrimination. With disguised discrimination the underlying assumptions and attitudes cannot be addressed directly. Wilson (1975) asserted that subtleties in personal racism can be difficult, almost impossible to prove. Just as a professor may easily rationalize why a Black student receives a lower grade for essentially the same work as a White student, denial may also occur when a Black woman's performance disconfirms the negative expectancies and stereotypes. The credit for her accomplishments may be attributed to sources other than her ability.

One explanation of such distortion may be that achievement on the part of a Black woman leads to an attitude imbalance. According to Heider's (1958) balance theory, there is a strong inclination for people to maintain consistency, or balance, among the elements of their cognitive system. Therefore, when a Black woman demonstrates competence, achieves status or power, the conclusion drawn by those unaccepting of this display of ability is not that she is competent, powerful and hardworking; instead, it becomes necessary to restore balance by changing the attitude system. One possible change is to view this woman as the exception, not really like Black people or not really deserving. Either of these attitude alterations will restore cognitive balance and keep intact the stereotypical perspectives.

It is unfortunate, but sometimes true, that high-achieving Black women may cause a similar attitude imbalance among their same-race peers. Some African Americans have learned to construe high achievement or academic success as inappropriate, labelling it as characteristic of Whites (Gardner 1988). The successful cohort member, then, may have to choose to be successful or to 'be Black'. What often goes unrecognized is that the community members have unconsciously accepted the stereotype for themselves and their cohorts.

The scenarios of distortion and denial serve to underscore the role of African-American women as deviants in the academy. Laws (1975) described 'single deviant' women as those who constituted a minority in a working world dominated by men, and 'double deviants' as those women who worked in this world expecting to receive equitable rewards and recognition. Black women, then, must certainly be triple or quadruple deviants in an academic world dominated by men and by Whites. The deviant African-American woman who elects to pursue a career in academia must recognize that her existence may be viewed as criticism for those who take other career paths. Because they stand apart as different, Black women in academia may have difficulty establishing networks which will serve to their benefit and support.

Combating isolation through networks

When investigators interviewed Black female administrators (Mosley 1979), Black female professors (Alperson 1975) and Black female undergraduates on White campuses (Scott and Horn, cited in Smith 1982), they found that Black women typically feel isolated, stereotyped and unaccepted. Across the academic levels Black women perceived a lack of relevance or support from campus women's groups indicating that the women's movement was not believed to represent the interests of all women. Since women's groups have most often focused on White women's issues, the lack of participation by Black women can be readily explained. One survey (Mosley 1979), however, indicated that White women provided the most support to Black women, White men the least; Black men came somewhere in between. Mosley suggested that Black men were not always comfortable with female assertiveness and ambition. White men, on the other hand, experience discomfort with both Blacks and women.

While feelings of isolation have led some Black women to abandon an academic career, others have coped with the isolation by developing ties within their families and with the outside African-American community. For other African-American women in academia, adjustment is facilitated through long-distance social support networks. Such networks may serve to provide mentors, professional female colleagues and sympathetic listeners who may not be available at the local level. These Black women need to interact with other Black women who can understand the complexity of their position.

Diversity among Black women

It has been common in psychology and in education to find common pathways, to rely on generalizations and to break down entities into their common components. While this is a useful strategy for concepts and behaviour, with people, it does not always produce appropriate categories. For example, women of African descent are especially anxious to display their unique and distinctive characteristics, compared not only to other ethnic-race groups, but within their own groups. While many researchers and professors have treated Black women and men as though they represent some monolithic population, there is a slowly dawning recognition that diversity exists (Komarovsky 1985).

Black women may vary in many areas, particularly notable are differences in social class, religion and culture. Even among African-American women these varieties of experiences may lead to different attitudes, behaviours and values. If people ignore these differences, they may be lead to an assumption that shared 'Blackness' will result in automatic social or political connections. The results may be embarrassing, uncomfortable or disastrous, depending on the importance of the situation. For example, at one mid-western US university admissions officials made a serious error when they assigned two African-American women to be first-year room mates. They assumed that putting the young Black women together would assure companionship and camaraderie. However, one of the young Black women was a Catholic who enjoyed 'rock' music; the other was a member of a fundamental sect opposed to many forms of popular entertainment. Pairing these two on the basis of race alone resulted in an unpleasant first-year experience for each. Although there certainly are experiences which Black women from many cultures hold in common, particularly racism and sexism, these may not be a sufficient basis for establishing or maintaining meaningful relationships with one another.

Black women in academia: success against the odds?

African-American women in academia have made incredible accomplishments against institutionalized odds and have overcome numerous personal challenges. The barriers against which they have pushed, however, have been much the same for the past 50 years. As Beverly Guy-Sheftall and Patricia Bell-Scott observed (1989), even in the 1930s Black women were faced with multiple sources of difficulties. They quote Lucy Slowe, a Dean of Women at Howard University in the 1930s. Slowe asserted that 'Black women come to college with several problems: (a) inexperience in civic life affairs; (b) a conservative background which fosters traditional attitudes toward women; and (c) a debilitating psychological approach to life.' Current problems may not be framed in exactly those terms, yet institutional, family/community, and personal issues remain of paramount importance for Black women.

The women who have succeeded in the educational system have typically been older and unmarried. Furthermore, they may not hold aspirations as high as their male peers, nor are they likely to have mentors. Whether climbing the academic rungs to tenure and higher rank, or advancing in administrative positions, African-American women may expect to take longer than their White or Black male colleagues (Revere 1987; Williams, 1986). Nevertheless, Black women are slowly becoming a more visible and effective force in higher education. According to the American Council on Education (1987), there were 22 minority women presidents of post-secondary institutions in 1981. Ten of these were African Americans.

Summary of academic circumstances for African-American women

Decreasing numbers of African-American women have completed the doctorate each year since 1984. These declines are especially problematic in the face of more Black women graduating with undergraduate degrees. In addition to fewer Black women electing to pursue advanced degrees, the degrees earned are typically limited to traditional female-dominated areas like education, nursing and social sciences. The prediction for future academic life is that insufficient numbers of African Americans will earn doctorates to fill the needs of a population growing in ethnic diversity.

The difficulty in pursuing graduate degrees is compounded for Black women by the likelihood that they will be underprepared both academically and emotionally. Further, like many ethnic-minority men, they will have inadequate financial resources to sustain them through the long years of study to the doctorate. Added to the strain of low levels of social support, little guidance or encouragement from mentors, and the conflicting demands of family responsibility are the dual burdens of racism and sexism.

Personal pressures should not be minimized as we recount the difficulties of institutionalized bias. The distortion and denial used to attack non-traditional African-American women may be debilitating and brutal. Professional and personal networks, including White women and African-American men, may be supportive and helpful. Yet competition among these groups also exists and needs to be recognized. Most important, however, is the need to establish and assert the identity and individualism of each African-American woman.

The future for African-American women in academia

The prospects for the future of African-American women in the academy is fairly dim at the present time. Indeed, all women of African descent must face difficult and stressful challenges to achieve success in the academic world. In the USA, recent actions of the federal government have reduced the levels of financial support for higher education and at the same time lessened the commitment for ethnic diversity. In other countries, resources have not been committed to educating Black women. Another generation has grown up without recognizing that there are advantages to expanding opportunities for people who have different cultures, perspectives and backgrounds. Within the university itself, the energy remains directed towards recruitment at faculty levels, with insufficient attention toward training faculty or retaining them. This has resulted in a 'revolving door' for Blacks.

With respect to increasing the representation of Black women and men, many colleges appear satisfied with slow progress as long as they are not seen as falling behind the others. Yet, there are some germinal ideas and events which give us hope for a change in a positive direction. For example, the Institute of Higher Education Research and Services at the University of Alabama in the USA has developed a structured training programme in response to the underrepresentation of women and ethnic minorities in research and development. Their programme includes financial support, training opportunities, access to mentors, time for development of skills, absence of undue stress and the commitment of the personnel involved (Diener and Owens 1984). Other colleges and universities are also experimenting with programmes to enhance opportunities for Blacks on their campuses.

Recommendations for increasing numbers of African-American women

1. *Early identification programmes for all levels of recruitment combined with strategies for retention*
   Although universities and colleges typically have well-developed early-identification programme for high-school students, which include visits, summer programmes, and the like, there are few if any such programmes for graduate students and faculty.

2. *Positive and encouraging institutional atmosphere*
   It has been suggested that the single most important factor in retention of ethnic-minority-women and men is the institutional

atmosphere. Olson (1988) suggests that there is typically a need for a university-wide coordinated approach to understanding and appreciating diversity. Both faculty and students must recognize how they can contribute and gain from a community effort.

3. *Financial support packages*
   Retention strategies must include realistic consideration of the economic support necessary for keeping ethnic-minority women, who are likely to have family commitments, in school.

4. *Opportunities for networking*
   For students and faculty this means that a 'critical mass' of African-American women and men need to be recruited simultaneously. In addition, support for networking outside the university is also necessary.

5. *Open and frank discussions concerning racism and sexism*
   The university or college community must examine the practices in which it traditionally engages and assess the degree of stereotyping and misinformed assumptions which are being perpetrated.

6. *Concerted and systematic efforts to incorporate gender and race in the curriculum*
   Individual courses on gender and race may suffice as a temporary panacea for incipient racism and sexism. The long-range goal, however, must be to have the issues of race and gender included as part of every relevant class discussion.

References

Allen, L and Britt, D W (1984), Black women in American society: a resource development perspective, in A U Rickel, M Gerrard, I Iscoe (eds), *Social and Psychological Problems of Women: Prevention and Crisis Intervention*, Washington DC: Hemisphere, pp 61–84.

Alperson, E D (1975), The minority woman in academe, *Professional Psychology* 6, pp 232–56.

American Council on Education (1987), *Minorities in Higher Education. Sixth Annual Status Report*, Washington DC: Office of Minority Concerns.

Brazziel, M W and Brazziel, W F (1987), Impact of support for graduate study on program completion of Black doctorate recipients, *Journal of Negro Education* 56, pp 145–51.

Damon, W (1989), Learning how to deal with the new American dilemma: We must teach our students about morality and racism, *Chronicle of Higher Education XXXV* (May 3), p B 1–3.

Diener, T and Owens, O H (1984), Preparing women and minorities for educational research and leadership: a case study, *Journal of Negro Education* 53, pp 491–8.

Epstein, C F (1976), Positive effects of the multiple negative: explaining the success of black professional women, in F L Denmark (ed), *Women-volume I: A PDI Research Reference Work*, New York: Psychological Dimensions.

Fleming, J (1983), Black women in Black and white college environments: the making of a matriarch, *Journal of Social Issues* 39, pp 41–54.

Gardner, M (1988), Technology and the at-risk student, *Electronic Learning* 8 (3), November/December, pp 27–30.

Guy-Sheftall, B and Bell-Scott, P (1989), Finding a way: Black women students and the academy, in C S Pearson, D L Shavlik and J G Touchton (eds), *Educating the Majority*, New York: American Council on Education/ Macmillan, pp 47–56.

Hafner, A L (1989), The 'traditional' undergraduate woman in the mid-1980s: a changing profile, in C S Pearson, D L Shavlik and J G Touchton (eds), *Educating the Majority*, New York: American Council on Education/ Macmillan, pp 32–46.

Heider, F (1958), *The Psychology of Interpersonal Relationships*, New York: Wiley.

Hirschorn, M (1988), The doctorate dilemma: why there aren't enough black professors, *The New Republic*, June, pp 24–27.

Huber, J (1983), Ambiguities in identity transformation: from sugar and spice to professor, in L Richardson and V Taylor (eds), *Feminist Frontiers: Rethinking Sex, Gender, and Society*, Reading, MA: Addison-Wesley, p 330–36.

Komarovsky, M (1985), *Women in College: Shaping New Feminine Identities*, New York: Basic Books.

Laws, J L (1975), The psychology of tokenism: an analysis, *Sex Roles*, pp 51–67.

Magner, D K (1989). Blacks and Whites on the campuses: behind ugly racist incidents, student isolation and insensitivity, *Chronicle for Higher Education XXXV* 33, pp 1, 28.

Mosley, M H (1979), Black women administrators in higher education: an endangered species, in W D Smith, K H Burlew, M H Mosley and W M Whitney (eds), *Reflections on Black psychology*, Washington DC: University Press of America.

National Research Council (1988), Summary report 1986: doctorate recipients from US universities, *Black Issues in Higher Education* 6 (2), p 20.

National Science Foundation (1988), Profiles – psychology: human resources and funding, *Surveys of Science Resources Series. Special Report*, Washington DC; US Government Printing Office (NSF 88–325).

Olson, C (1988), Recruiting and retaining minority graduate students: a systems perspective, *Journal of Negro Education* 57, pp 31–42.

Reid, P T (1984), Feminism vs minority group identity: not for black women only, *Sex Roles* 10, pp 247–255.

Reid, P T (1988), Racism and sexism: comparisons and conflicts, in P A Katz and E A Taylor (eds), *Eliminating Racism: Comparisons and Conflicts*, New York: Plenum Publishing, pp 203–21.

Reid, P T and Robinson, W L (1985), Professional black men and women: attainment of terminal academic degrees, *Psychological Reports* 56, pp 547–55.

Revere, A B (1987), Black women superintendents in the United States: 1984–85. *Journal of Negro Education* 56, pp 510–20.

Simpson, G E and Yinger, J M (1985), *Racial and Cultural Minorities: An Analysis of Prejudice*, fifth edn, New York: Plenum Press.

Smith, C H (1982), Black female achievers in academe, *Journal of Negro Education* 51, pp 318–57.

US Department of Education, Center for Education Statistics (1988), *Trends in Minority Enrollment in Higher Education, Fall 1976–1986*, Washington DC: Office of Educational Research and Improvement, April.

US Department of Labor Bureau of Labor Statistics (1988), *Current Population Survey*, March.

Widnall, S E (1988), AAAS presidential lecture: voices from the pipeline, *Science* 241 (September), pp 1740–45.

Williams, L E (1986), Chief academic officers at Black colleges and universities: a comparison by gender, *Journal of Negro Education* 55, pp 443–52.

Wilson, C E (1975), Racism in education, in B N Schwartz and R Disch (eds), *White Racism: Its History, Pathology and Practice*, pp 302–14.

Chapter 10
Beyond the Boundaries: Lesbians in Academe

*Celia Kitzinger**

Listening to lesbians talk about their academic jobs, reading their work, and thinking about my own experience as a lesbian academic, two themes become evident: we speak of academia both as a source of our oppression and also, paradoxically, as providing opportunities for our liberation. On the one hand we document the systematic exclusion of lesbians from higher education and our oppression within it, while, on the other, we celebrate our own survival and achievements within the academy. While we analyse the ways in which academic theory has been used to sustain heterosexist and patriarchal ideologies, we also attempt, as lesbian academics, to devise theories which derive from and explain our lesbian experience. This chapter explores the perils and promise of academia for lesbians. What does it mean for us as lesbians to align ourselves with 'the processions of the sons of educated men' (Woolf 1938)? How does academia exclude and oppress us, and how can we fight back? What is the price of survival as lesbians in academe? What is involved in coming out as a lesbian academic? And with what authority do we speak as lesbian academics – to whom, and *for* whom?

First, it is important to acknowledge that lesbians in academia are systematically oppressed, and also to relate this to the oppression suffered by lesbians outside academia. Lesbian academics' guilty sense of our own privilege as academics seems sometimes to lead to a heavy emphasis on our own oppression, and a concomitant refusal to examine our privileges. My own experience is that academia is one of the easiest jobs in which to exist as an out lesbian – offering, as it does, a liberal tolerance of my 'lifestyle' and acceptance of my right to 'academic freedom', which makes my overt lesbianism relatively painless.

*I would like to thank Harriette Marshall, Kate Gleeson, Jenny Kitzinger and Sheila Kitzinger for their comments on an earlier draft of this paper. Full responsibility for its contents and for the opinions expressed is mine alone.

Throughout my academic career I have encountered little more than trivialization, ridicule and minor forms of sexual harassment – plus the suspicion that because my work is politically motivated, it is not proper 'science' (see Kitzinger, 1989). While the latter has certainly impeded my career, and resulted in periods of unemployment, I have never been beaten up, or sacked from work because of it. I have never suffered the extreme hostility, verbal abuse or physical attack endured in the workplace by some of my non-academic lesbian friends (Kitzinger 1990).

Oppressed as a lesbian among academics, I am privileged as an academic amongst lesbians. There is, of course, a sense in which those few of us who are 'allowed' into academia gain entry as tokens, while the systematic exclusion of other lesbians (especially Black and working-class lesbians) is built into the system. Our experience of oppression as academic lesbians has to be interpreted and understood, then, against the backdrop of our privilege.

The oppression of lesbians in academia is, nonetheless, both real and sometimes severe. Its clearest manifestation is our invisibility: knowing too well the consequences attached to openness, and fearful of the repercussions, most lesbian academics are silent about their sexuality. Most do not discuss their lesbianism with colleagues, and certainly not with students; most do not introduce lesbian issues into teaching, or allow it to feature in research or publications. By contrast, heterosexuality in academia (as elsewhere: Hearn and Parkin 1987; Kitzinger 1990) is overtly displayed and taken for granted as the natural and normal way to be. It manifests itself in engagement and wedding rings, photographs of spouses and children on the desk, casual conversation about weekend activities and gossip about new boyfriends or girlfriends, impending weddings, and flirtations between colleagues. Heterosexual relationships are reinforced, too, when colleagues enquire after husbands or wives, or support each other through difficult experiences – a birth or death in the family, a divorce or remarriage. Rarely are gay or lesbian relationships given a similarly high public profile. In teaching, assumptions are made about students' heterosexuality, and students can pass through their entire degree course without ever hearing even a mention of lesbianism (Clarke 1989; Hickok 1982; Faderman 1982). Even in women's studies courses, where one might hope for greater awareness, academics demonstrate a 'mostly uncritical and apparently unalterable ... commitment to heterosexuality' (Frye 1982). In research and publications, dedications to 'my wife without whom ...', or blatant sexism and heterosexism in the text, or simply the incorporation into theoretical positions of unconscious heterosexist biases – all serve to flaunt heterosexuality.

In the face of this pervasive heterosexual consensus, most lesbian academics are silent. As Adrienne Rich (1980, p 8) has pointed out, whether you are black, or disabled, or lesbian, when someone 'describes the world and you are not in it there is a moment of psychic disequilibrium, as if you looked into a mirror and saw nothing.' In remaining silent, we collaborate with this, implicitly agreeing that there is no one in the mirror – that we do not exist.

Becoming an academic means being willing to jump through the hoops of a higher-education system set up so as to systematically exclude those who refuse to accept and perpetuate status-quo ideologies. Lesbian activists have described how academia

brooks only token deviance from its norms, just enough to demonstrate its democratic principles or its "innovative" atmosphere. It offers survival and acceptance (graduation, a job, prestige) to those who will quietly take their place on the assembly line or who are themselves willing to be mutilated into professionals (Gearhart, 1983, p 4).

Many lesbians are excluded from academia because of the operation of these 'institutional filters': they drop out, or are thrown out, of secondary school; they abandon, or never enter, higher education; they are denied entry or expelled from doctoral programmes and academic teaching posts. The filtering process is well under way by the time a young woman reaches adolescence: some (myself included) are expelled from secondary schools because of our relationships with women and our refusal of heteroreality; others simply find the oppressive assumptions (rooted in values that are middle-class, white, and male as well as heterosexual) too alien and alienating, and drop out. Young women can go through school without ever hearing a positive word about lesbianism and, in the UK, the passing of Section 28 of the Local Government Act, which bans the 'promotion' of lesbian or gay-male sexuality in schools, makes it difficult for teachers to challenge heterosexism, even if they wanted to (Kitzinger 1987a). Most, of course, are happy to promote *hetero*sexuality and to pathologize lesbianism: the general secretary of one of the leading British teachers' trades union (the Professional Association of Teachers) announced recently that:

If there is any active homosexual who thinks that his or her behaviour is normal, the sooner that idea is knocked on the head the better. . . . Active homosexual behaviour is deviant. Anyone who teaches young people otherwise is an evil influence in the nation (Dawson 1989, p 24).

Lesbians who survive schooling, make it to college, and then come (or are forced) out of the closet, may find that they have 'seriously impaired their standing in their respective academic departments as well as threatened further job placements' (Nuehring et al 1975, p 64). One lesbian, now a university English professor, describes how, as a student, she was 'kicked out of TWO universities *because I was a Lesbian* and denied entrance to two others, *because I was a Lesbian* and that fact was on my transcripts. Finally, I lied to get into City College in New York City' (Penelope 1986, p 60).

Students who are not thrown out often become increasingly alienated and angry at the anti-lesbianism they encounter. One recent survey of 125 lesbians and gay men in a university community found that three-quarters reported experiencing verbal abuse because of their homo-sexuality, 26 per cent were threatened with violence and 17 per cent had personal property damaged – this in spite of the fact that the vast majority reported hiding their gay/lesbian status from other under-graduates and faculty. (Very few [6 per cent] of those who had been victimized reported the incident to appropriate university officials; most feared further harassment if they did so). Nearly half of the respon-dents in this study said they had made specific life changes to avoid dis-crimination of harassment including avoidance of locations in which lesbians or gay men meet, presenting themselves as heterosexual, and refraining from associating with known lesbians or gay men (D'Augelli 1989). Under conditions like these, students feel little incentive to carry on in academic life. Even where lesbians are not explicitly harassed, ignoring lesbian experience and assuming students' heterosexuality also serve to alienate and disturb lesbian students. The sense of being an 'outsider', an alien to the heterosexual assumptions of academe, makes the choice of a professional career seem unrealistic to many lesbians. Confronting not only their outlaw status as *lesbians*, but also their alien position as *women* (and possibly also as Black or working-class), many lesbians never consider professional academic careers as a realistic option.

Those who do finally make it through the system to hold academic posts (or who come to think of themselves as lesbians only after acquiring such jobs) may then discover that simply being known to be lesbian is sufficient to seriously damage their careers. Many lesbians are fired, not rehired and denied tenure because of their lesbianism (McDaniel 1982). As a result, some lesbians resort to deception: 'some of us,' says Margaret Cruikshank (1982b, p xvi), 'keep two résumés, one "straight" and one including all lesbian and gay publications. Others change titles so that the word "lesbian" is replaced by "woman".'

The decision to keep one's lesbianism secret is the majority choice in academe. Avoiding the sometimes severe penalties of openness, these lesbians incur instead the different and more insidious costs of secrecy:

Caught between silence on one side and fear on the other, the typical closeted gay academic spends his or her professional life in a state of constant duplicity, internally and externally divided by a lie that is not spoken, by an act of deception that is never acted out. . . . Talks about nights out, living arrangements, lovers, divorces is carefully censored to control how much real information is given out. (Bennett 1982, p 5).

In choosing not to come out as lesbian to one's students, this duplicity, and the personal cost of silence, are often painful. One English lecturer describes an occasion when a student, referring to a poem which used the word 'pansy', said in class: 'isn't it awful to name faggots and queers after such a sweet flower.'

I went numb. I stared at her, momentarily unable to speak. My impulse was to scream, to let her know that I took this affront personally. . . . I was personally assaulted, and whatever I did to correct her, I was still left shaken and raw. 'I will not allow those attitudes or that language to be expressed in this classroom', I told her. But I did not say, 'I am one'. (McDaniel 1981, p 197).

'Coming out' in academia has different meanings for different lesbians. From some, it means simply allowing others to know about their lesbianism – saying 'I am one'. Coming out in this sense is rarely a one-off event: there are always new colleagues and new students. We are forced to make daily decisions about whether or not to say, whether or not to interrupt the assumptions being made about our presumed heterosexuality, weighing up the risks and possible repercussions of each and every situation. Because coming out has to be continually redone, many lesbians are neither 'in' nor 'out', but in some inter-mediate situation: some people (often colleagues) know or suspect they are lesbian, others (usually students, and senior academics with the power to influence career prospects) do not. Many academics never actually say that they are lesbian, but simply allow it to be assumed: 'everybody knows that Sarah is who I live with, so I suppose they've put two and two together'; 'people must know I'm a lesbian – I've never said so, but I've never hidden it either.' However, 'to share the knowledge of one's homosexuality with non-gay people, but never to speak of it, is to tacitly agree that, like bad breath, homosexuality is something embar-rassing, best left unmentioned' (Hodges and Hutter 1977). By contrast, one young university research assistant told me: 'it is much easier to go up to people and say, "hello, I'm Rachel and I'm a lesbian", instead of waiting for the so-called "right time", because there never *is* a "right time".'

Many lesbians have written of explosions of violence against us, or occasional extremities of hostility in (and beyond) academia. By com-parison, the day-to-day realities of being an 'out' lesbian in academia, the continual and corrosive 'minor' heterosexism – what some call 'dripping-tap anti-lesbianism' – is rarely discussed. We tend to feel that unless our male students beat us up in the carpark after an evening class, or unless the vice chancellor of the university bans our courses, we are not 'really' oppressed, compared with what happens to other lesbians. My own experience, after more than 15 years of uncompromisingly 'out' lesbianism, is less dramatic, but is also part of the everyday oppression of lesbians in academia. At work I endure, with grim resignation, the same limited set or reactions from both staff and students; the men who see me as a challenge ('all you need is the right man'), or as the embodiment of their sordid pornographic fantasies ('I've always wanted to go to bed with a lesbian'); the married women with small children who fall desperately in love with the mirage of freedom they imagine me to represent; the heterosexual women who are wary, cautious and distant as though lesbianism might be infectious, and the 'liberated' ones who are ostentatiously friendly to prove they know it isn't. Most common of all, the anxious embarrassment of tolerant and well-meaning liberals, who insist that my sexuality is private – 'what you do in bed is your own business' – and can't see why I keep dragging it into the conversation. My predominant reactions, now, are of frustration and boredom.

When I was in my early twenties, I found a certain thrill, a frisson of excitement, in openly asserting 'the love that dare not speak its name'. Being out as lesbian functioned as an affirmation of my right to exist at a time when I personally lacked much confidence in that right – at times, it even felt exotically daring. All that has long gone. As I deliberately, dutifully, put myself in the firing line and rehearse with my students for the hundredth time the tedious arguments about genes and hormones, nature and nurture, I feel dragged down by the slowness of social change, and the steady erosion of even those small gains we thought we had won. The stale stereotypes and predictable platitudes seem never to change over the years – the same words, the same tones, only the faces are different. I continue to come out at work partly because it seems that I no longer have a choice (my reputation precedes me), and partly because it seems desperately important for lesbian students to see someone in authority, with a respectable job, who is open about her lesbianism and survives. Most importantly, I persist in openly affirming my lesbianism because I believe that those of us who have the privilege of an academic job have a moral responsibility to speak the truth about our lesbianism. An academic environment is one of the easier places in which to be out: unlike secondary-school teaching, no law (yet) prevents me from expressing strong pro-lesbian values in the classroom. I continue to come out at work because I still have the freedom to do so – and because freedoms must be exercised if they are to be preserved.

The fact that I (and others) can speak as academic lesbians is sometimes used to discredit what we say about our oppression ('what are you complaining about – we *let you* join our club?'). The fact that we can speak from the position we do is used to invalidate what we say. What is ignored in so doing is the silence of the vast majority of our lesbian colleagues. Fear keeps most lesbians silent and invisible: fears fed by the casual everyday heterosexism of academia, both individual (eg colleagues and students who make anti-lesbian comments) and institutional (such as superannuation schemes which pay no benefits to a lesbian partner, or relocation and scholarship schemes which pay expenses for employee and legally defined 'spouse' only. Few academic institutions have written policies about combating heterosexism; in the absence of any such explicit statements the onus for discovering whether one will be accepted or not lies with the individual lesbian.

Against the backdrop of pervasive anti-lesbianism in academia, most lesbians are unwilling to run the risk of finding out what the response might be. Heterosexuals who believe that their institutions are 'safe' places for lesbians (citing the existence of a few open lesbians like myself as evidence) sometimes tell other lesbians that their fears are unfounded, their apprehensions unjustified: they are 'paranoid' or 'scaremongering' when they talk about anti-lesbianism, 'cowardly' or 'defeatist' when they decline to make their lesbianism obvious to their hierarchical superiors. As long as there are no institutional policies protecting us (and plenty of anti-lesbian ones that discriminate against us), few lesbians will be pre- pared to find out whether their fears are unfounded or not. The appro- priate target for criticism is not individual lesbians who fear for their careers, but institutional policies that create and perpetuate those fears. Instead of berating lesbians for failing to come out, 'sympathetic' heterosexuals would do well to work for institutional changes.

I know only too well why other lesbians choose invisibility. At the same time, I acknowledge my disappointment and sense of betrayal when women in my own department confide in me about their les- bianism, but demand total secrecy, when they criticize me for bringing lesbianism into the public arena, so casting suspicion on them, or when closeted lesbians avoid me for fear of being 'tarred with the same brush'. Feeling hurt and angry by the rejection of our lesbian colleagues is far more painful than the insults we endure from men. I am disturbed, too, when other lesbians, denying themselves the opportunity to explore what their lesbianism might mean to their academic research, insist a priori that their lesbianism is 'not relevant', that it 'makes no difference'. I am distressed that many feminist academics, whose work is well respected, are also lesbian but never say so in print – their work often informed by a lesbian consciousness which they refuse to make explicit. The word 'woman' (or sometimes 'single woman') functions as a code- word for 'lesbian' in much closeted lesbian scholarship. I know why lesbians are silent or speak only in code: I know too that their choices make it harder for those of us who do speak out.

'Coming out' as a lesbian academic can, as above, be taken simply as referring to a woman's willingness to allow those with whom she works to know of her lesbianism. But there is another, broader sense in which an academic lesbian can 'come out': she can come out not just in her role as university employee, but also as teacher and researcher – that is, she can teach and write *as a lesbian*. Very few make this choice. For most the discourse of 'objectivity' offers a convenient cover: 'what I do in bed is irrelevant to how I teach evolutionary theory'.

However, much feminist scholarship (along with postmodernist movements across the academic disciplines) challenges this whole discourse of objectivity, pointing out the ways in which theories are not reflections or maps of the world, but rather artefacts of communal interchange which reflect the social, historical, cultural and political features of their originators (Bleier, 1989; Harding 1987): the apparent objectivity of the academic text is created through a series of rhetorical devices Kitzinger 1987b; chapter 1). Feminists have analysed the ways in which the academic disciplines are permeated with male assumptions and patriarchal worldviews – the so-called 'hard sciences' no less than the 'soft sciences' and humanities (Wallsgrove 1980): 'science it would seem is not sexless; she is a man, a father and infected too' (Woolf 1938). Many feminists 'come out' *as women* in academia: that is, they think, teach and write from a position in which being a woman is assumed to matter, and to make a difference.

To think like a woman in a man's world means thinking critically, refusing to accept the givens, making connections between facts and ideas which men have left unconnected. It means remembering that every mind resides in a body; remaining accountable to the female bodies in which we live; constantly retesting given hypotheses against lived experience. . . . And it means that most difficult thing of all; listening and watching in art and literature, in the social sciences, in all the descriptions we are given of the world, for the silences, the absences, the nameless, the unspoken, the encoded – for there we will find the true knowledge of women. (Rich 1978, p 245).

There is a flowering of feminist theory in academia, but one of the silences, the absences, in this as much as in patriarchal theory, is a silence about lesbianism. While feminist theory may validate our experience *as women*, many of us still feel excluded and ignored as lesbians. Lesbian experience is rarely made the central – the focal – point of feminist theory. At best, lesbians merit an occasional reference, a token gesture. Ironically, even when it is lesbians who have produced feminist theory (and it very often is) we have sometimes been so keen to include 'ordinary women' – to make what we say accessible and applicable beyond our own 'special case', not to alienate or antagonize heterosexual women – that we have ignored or discounted the specificities of our experience as lesbians. Often we do not even know what putting our lesbianism centre-stage might mean; many women find the idea of 'lesbian theory' unthinkable – just as feminist theory was unthinkable a few decades ago.

The lesbian academic who is willing to consider the possibility of constructing lesbian theory must face the challenge of identifying and rendering problematic not just the male but also the heterosexual assumptions that permeate her discipline, and must imagine how things could be otherwise if she were able to foreground her own lesbian reality. Just as feminist scholars find that 'adding women in' to patriarchal theory means rewriting the theory, so lesbians are finding that lesbian experience cannot simply be accommodated within the boundaries of heterofeminist theory – added on as an afterthought – but rather that taking lesbianism seriously necessitates an entire shift of focus, a rewriting of the theory. As Margaret Cruikshank (1981) has written: 'It may turn out that there is a distinctively *lesbian* view of science, art, literature, politics. What is clear already is that lesbian scholars are asking new questions.'

Although 'lesbian scholarship is now flourishing in almost all academic disciplines' (Freedman et al 1984), it is in the fields of history and, particularly, literary theory that it seems most highly developed. This may be accounted for by the fact that there are many more women (and therefore lesbian) academics in the humanities compared with the sciences, and consequently, just as courses on women writers were among the first in higher education to show a feminist perspective, so now they are the first to embrace the possibilities of lesbian theory. Early lesbian literary theory focused on the ways in which the oppression of lesbians has affected lesbian writing through what Willa Cather called 'the inexplicable presence of the thing not named' (quoted in O'Brien 1984): gender references are omitted (as in much of Amy Lowell's love poetry) or perfunctory gender changes introduced (as in Willa Cather's use of a male narrator in *My Antonia,* or Rosemary Manning's translation of a lesbian relationship into a heterosexual one in *Man on a Tower.* When we come out as lesbian academics, not just to the extent of allowing colleagues and/or students to know that we are lesbian, but also to incorporate our lesbianism into our teaching and research, we enter new linguistic territory and begin to speak on our own terms. As the lesbian poet and literary theorist Nicole Brossard has written, 'a lesbian who does not reinvent the word is a lesbian in the process of disappearing' (1988, p 122). Her own 'reinvention of the word' as a lesbian theorist means to write 'only under a woman's gaze, feverishly received. . . . If I desire a woman, if a woman desires me, then there is the beginning of writing' (1988, pp 42, 43).

But our problems in writing as lesbian theorists go beyond simply the

difficulty of exorcizing the heteropatriarchal worldview from our consciousness. One problem is that when we do so, when we produce
theory which starts from and continually refers to our experience as
women and as lesbians, we do not speak with authority, because to
speak with authority is to speak in a male voice – one that is authorized
by men. As academics we can speak with authority only by using the
language of patriarchy (white, middle-class, heterosexual and male),
referring diligently to male theorists, distorting lesbian realities to fit in
with those perspectives, and failing to acknowledge (sometimes even to
ourselves) our own difference.

One characteristic of male academic language is its obscurity: it is
often deliberately designed to be unintelligible to the majority of people.
As Linda Garber (1989) argues, 'we need to question the integrity of
subsuming our vital concerns to academic schools whose language is
inaccessible to our own communities.' Another characteristic of
academic language is its pervasive and largely unreflective incorporation of liberal ideology – a faith in 'objectivity', individualism, the distinction between the 'personal' and the political, and a belief in
progress. This means that while liberal lesbian-feminist perspectives
can (within limits) prosper in academia, radical-lesbian theory (eg
lesbian separatism) is far less readily tolerated (Kitzinger 1987b,
pp 191–8), and this 'fit' between higher education and liberal feminism
creates real constraints on what most radical lesbian feminist
academics can do within their workplace.

Political pressures, and the questioning of our 'authority' and 'objectivity' are also used to prevent us not just from developing and
publishing lesbian theory, but also from teaching it. As feminists have
recognized, teaching is always a political act:

Some person is choosing, for whatever reasons, to teach a set of values, ideas,
assumptions, and pieces of information, and in so doing, to omit other values,
ideas, assumptions, and pieces of information. If all those choices form a
pattern excluding half the human race, that is a political act one can hardly help
noticing. To omit women entirely makes one kind of political statement; to
include women as a target for humor makes another. To include women with
seriousness and vision and with some attention to the perspective of women as
a hitherto subordinate group is simply another kind of political act. (Howe
1983, p 110).

The decision of feminist academics teaching on women's studies
courses *not* to include lesbianism is also a political act. Women's
studies faculty often try hard to appease male heterosexist administrators all too ready to believe that 'women's studies is a lesbian plot',
and 'the threat of being labelled "lesbian" is used to keep women in line
and to keep those who are really lesbians from being visible (Beck 1989).

Feeling that their lesbianism will be used to discredit the already precarious position of women's studies in the university, lesbians may silence themselves, and as a result of lesbian exclusion women's studies 'actively and aggressively supports women in becoming and remaining heterosexual' (Frye 1982, pp 196).

In my experience with women's studies it seems common and characteristic for the women instructors to assume that widespread heterosexuality and the dominance of heterosexual conceptions have always been and will always be The Way It Is for humans on this planet, in particular for women on this planet. . . . It is also assumed that we should support (not just tolerate) speakers, films, workshops, classes, whole courses, which encourage women to prepare themselves to cope with life in the "dual career marriage", teach how to be married and a feminist. . . . Imagine a real reversal of the heterosexualist teaching our program provides. Imagine thirty faculty members at a large university engaged routinely and seriously in the vigorous and aggressive encouragement of women to be lesbians, helping them learn skills and ideas for living as lesbians, teaching the connections between lesbianism and feminism and between heterosexism and sexism. . . . Imagine us openly and actively advising women not to marry, not to fuck, not to become bonded with any man. (Frye 1982, pp 195–6).

Over the last decade, gay and lesbian studies courses have been developed in the US and, recently, North America's first Department of Gay and Lesbian Studies has been formed (*Lesbian and Gay Studies Newsletter* 16(2), 1). Some of these courses come close to Marilyn Frye's (1982, p 196) vision, in that they teach 'out of a politics determined by lesbian perception and sensibility'. However, 'like women's studies and ethnic studies, gay studies . . . weigh less heavily toward promotion and tenure, and they are taken less seriously by scholars-at-large' (Bennett 1982, p 6). In the UK (where tenure has already been abolished as part of the Tory attack on higher education), gay and lesbian studies are virtually inconceivable as practical realities.

It is hardly surprising that lesbian writers are generally very critical of academia. Many have written about the ways in which lesbians are systematically excluded, oppressed and vilified within higher education, and radical feminist and lesbian theory systematically obliterated. Mary Daly is one of the lesbian theorists most critical of academia. In her 'metadictionary' (a 'source book of New Words for Wise Women') she coins the word 'academentia' to describe 'the normal state of persons in academia, marked by varying and progressive degrees; irreversible deterioration of faculties of intellectuals' (Daly 1987, p 184). But many of those who write openly about their lesbian experience also hold academic jobs. The 'notes on contributors' at the back of general anthologies of lesbian writing typically reveal that somewhere between a fifth and a half of the contributors state that they have PhDs and/or academic jobs. By comparison, anthologies specifically about Black or working-class women's experience rarely include more than a tiny percentage of contributors with doctorates. A disproportionately large amount of lesbian theory is produced by privileged women, with access to time and facilities simply not available to the vast majority of lesbians.

The very lesbians who write most critically about the academy, who describe its betrayals and their own oppression within it, have nonetheless also to acknowledge the benefits it offers them, both personally and in terms of developing specifically lesbian and feminist theory. Mary Daly, described on the flier to her most recent book as a 'Fribourg-trained theologian . . . and academic scholar', acknowledges the receipt of a Rockefeller Foundation grant 'which not only enabled me to take an extensive leave of absence from teaching at Boston College but also to do the necessary travel for this project and to provide salaries for secretarial and research assistants' (Daly 1978, pp xvii–xviii). Acknowledgements like these bear witness to the extent to which an oppressive, hierarchical and heterosexist academic system can simultaneously offer space and facilities for lesbian writers to engage in explicitly lesbian projects, which become important texts within the radical-feminist and lesbian communities. Guilty, perhaps, at our own privilege, we have presented a one-sided picture of academic life, stressing our oppression as though it were a measure of our political purity: if they hate us, ban our courses and censor our writing, we must be doing something right. In portraying ourselves as victims, perhaps we hope to defuse the criticism of lesbians outside academia who challenge our 'academic' approach, require that we speak in a language which is accessible to them and demand that we be accountable to the lesbian and feminist movements which make our existence possible.

The problem, then, in theorizing about the relationship between lesbians and academia, is adequately to acknowledge both the considerable privileges (in terms of money, time, access and material assistance) accorded to lesbians *as academics*, and, at the same time, to acknowledge the penalties (in terms of discrimination, oppression, silencing and distortion) paid by academics *as lesbians*.

Lesbians are oppressed in academia because lesbians are oppressed in the world. At the same time, lesbians in academia have specific freedoms and opportunities denied to many. Virtually all employment under heteropatriarchy exacts a price from lesbians: in the way we must dress, the attitudes we must express, the system we uphold through the work that we do. All of us juggle our politics and our jobs in different ways, making various compromises and refusing others, insisting on certain values, allowing others to slide. Academia is neither uniquely corrupt, nor uniquely liberating: it offers a set of possibilities. As academic lesbians we must acknowledge the resources at our disposal, consider both their limitations and their political implications and, recognizing our relative privileges, use them to tell the truths about our lesbianism.

References

Beck, Evelyn Torton (1989), Asking for the future, *Women's Review of Books* VI (5), February, pp 21–22.

Bennett, Paula (1982), Dyke in Academe (II), in Margaret Cruikshank (ed), *Lesbian Studies: Present and Future*, New York: The Feminist Press.

Bleier, Ruth (ed) (1989), *Feminist Approaches to Science*, Oxford: Pergamon Press.

Brossard, Nicole (1988), *The Aerial Letter* (Trans Marlene Wildeman), Ontario: The Women's Press.

Clarke, Louise (1989) Academic Aliens, *British Psychological Society Psychology of Women Section Newsletter*, 4, pp 3–8.

Cruikshank, Margaret (1981), Lesbian studies: some preliminary notes, *Radical Teacher* 17, pp 18–19.

Cruikshank, Margaret (1982), Introduction, in Margaret Cruikshank (ed), *Lesbian Studies: Present and Future*, New York: The Feminist Press.

Daly, Mary (1978), *Gyn/Ecology: The Metaethics of Radical Feminism*, London: The Women's Press.

Daly, Mary, in cahoots with Jane Caputi (1987), *Websters' First New Intergalactic Wickedary of the English Language*, London: The Women's Press.

D'Augelli, Anthony R (1989), Lesbians' and gay men's experiences of discrimination and harassment in a university community, *American Journal of Community Psychology* 17, pp 317–21.

Dawson, Peter (1989), Standing by speech on soap 'Evil', Letter in the *Guardian*, 10 August 1989.

Faderman, Lillian (1982), Who Hid Lesbian History?, in Margaret Cruikshank (ed), *Lesbian Studies: Present and Future*, New York: The Feminist Press.

Freedman, Estelle B, Charlesworth Gelpi, Barbara, Johnson, Susan L and Weston Kathleen M (1984), Editorial, *Signs: Journal of Women in Culture and Society – the Lesbian Issue*, 9(4), pp 553–6.

Frye, Marilyn (1982), A lesbian perspective on women's studies, in Margaret Cruikshank (ed), *Lesbian Studies: Present and Future*, New York: The Feminist Press.

Garber, Linda (1989), Still coming out, *Women's Review of Books* VI(5), pp 17.

Gearhart, Sally Miller (1983), If the mortarboard fits . . . radical feminism in academia, in Charlotte Bunch and Sandra Pollack (eds), *Learning Our Way*, New York: The Crossing Press.

Harding, S (ed) (1987), *Feminism and Methodology*, Bloomington, Indiana: Indiana University Press.

Hearn, Jeff and Parkin, Wendy (1987), *'Sex' at 'Work': The Power and Paradox of Organisation Sexuality*, Brighton: Wheatsheaf.

Hickok, Kathy (1982), Lesbian images in women's literature anthologies, in Margaret Cruikshank (ed), *Lesbian Studies: Present and Future*, New York: The Feminist Press.

Hodges, A and Hutter, D (1977), *With Downcast Gays: Aspects of Homosexual Self-Oppression*, Toronto: Pink Triangle Press.

Howe, Florence (1983), Feminist scholarship; the extent of the revolution, in Charlotte Bunch and Sandra Pollack (eds) *Learning Our Way*, New York: The Crossing Press.

Kitzinger, Celia (1987a), Heterosexism in Schools, *Values* 2(1), pp 40–41.

Kitzinger, Celia (1987b), *The Social Construction of Lesbianism*, London: Sage.

Kitzinger, Celia (1989) Resisting the discipline, in Erica Burman (ed) *Feminists and Psychological Practice*, London: Sage.

Kitzinger, Celia (1990) Lesbians and Gay Men in the Workplace: Psychosocial Issues, in Marilyn J Davidson and Jill Earnshaw (eds), *Vulnerable Workers: Psychosocial and Legal Issues*, London: Wiley.

McDaniel, Judith (1981), Is there room for me in the closet? Or, my life as the only lesbian professor, in Cruikshank, M (ed), *The Lesbian Path*, San Francisco: Double Axe Books.

McDaniel Judith (1982), We were fired: lesbian experiences in academe, *Sinister Wisdom* 20, pp 30–43.

Nuehring, B M, Fein S B and Tyler, M (1975), The gay college student: perspectives for mental health professionals, *Counselling Psychologist* 4, pp 64–72.

O'Brien, Sharon (1984), 'The Thing Not Named': Willa Cather as a Lesbian Writer, *Signs: Journal of Women in Culture and Society – the Lesbian Issue*, 9(4), pp 576–99.

Penelope, Julia (1986), The mystery of lesbians II, *Gossip: A Journal of Lesbian Feminist Ethics* 2, pp 16–68.

Rich, Adrienne (1978), Taking women students seriously, in Adrienne Rich (1980), *On Lies, Secrets, and Silence: Selected Prose 1966–1978*, London: Virago.

Rich, Adrienne (1980), Foreword: on history, illiteracy, passivity, violence and women's culture, in Adrienne Rich (1980), *On Lies, Secrets, and Silence: Selected Prose 1966– 1978*, London: Virago.

Wallsgrove, Ruth (1980) The masculine face of science, in the Brighton Women and Science Group (eds), *Alice Through the Microscope: The Power of Science over Women's Lives*, London: Virago.

Woolf, Virginia (1938), *Three Guineas*, New York: Harcourt Brace Jovanovich.

Chapter 11

In Two Worlds:
Women Academics in India

Veena Gill

The teacher (acharya) is ten times more venerable than a subteacher (up-acharya), the father a hundred times more than a teacher, and the mother a thousand times more than a father.

Vasistha, an ancient Indian law giver

Since ancient history Indian society has accorded a teacher a position of social eminence second only to parents. The academic profession is among the most venerated and respectable in India. Women in this profession enjoy the position of a privileged elite. Their growing entry into the citadels of knowledge, both as students and teachers, is a consequence of changing social attitudes, economic resources and better educational opportunities due to conscious public policy and pressures by organized women's interest groups. Yet, within the gender hierarchy of academe, women academics emerge as a clearly disadvantaged group.

This chapter explores the position of women academics in India. In the first section, the history of the status and education of Indian women in ancient, medieval and modern periods is briefly traced, to set the context for understanding their situation. The second section presents an analysis of the patterns of recruitment, motivation and work experience of present-day women academics, as well as the role conflicts between career and family which confront them.

Data

This study is based upon individual unstructured in-depth interviews conducted in English and/or Hindi in January and February 1989 with 40 women academics from Delhi University. A few group interviews were also conducted. Questions were asked regarding attitudes towards their careers, family role conflict and professionalization.[1] In addition secondary sources were utilized.

From equals to outcasts: education and women's status in ancient and medieval India

Societal attitudes towards the academic profession as a 'respectable' occupation for women are related to the time-honoured traditions of respect and veneration that have been accorded to a 'guru' or learned one in Indian society. Historical research and records reveal an early and unparalleled tradition of learning to which women in ancient India had access (Altekar 1962).

Few in the West are aware that the history of women's education in India goes as far back as the Vedic period of 1500 to 600 BC. In Vedic society sons and daughters had equal opportunity for education. It was not unusual to find women teachers, philosophers and poets (Altekar 1962). Vedic women who received education could choose to be students for life, devoted to study and meditation: Brahmvadinis. Those women who received education until they were married were called Sadyovadhus. Early marriage was unknown. During the later Vedic period of 1000 to 600 BC (the age of Brahmans and Upanishads), the tradition of the early Vedic period continued. Men and women were admitted to philosophical discourse. Gargi and Maitreyi were two famous women philosophers of this period (Sharma 1981).

The post-Vedic period from about 500 BC to 500 AD, when the caste system became firmly established, marked the deterioration in the status of women. The *Manusmriti*, or the code of Manu, stipulates the rights and obligations of men and women. It is clear from this source that women were relegated a subordinate status compared to men. A girl was deprived of her right to an education. She was also denied the right to study scriptures and to remain unmarried. According to the code of Manu, her father had authority over her in childhood, her husband in youth, and her son in old age (Manusmriti IX, 3 quoted in Liddle and Joshi 1986). The exclusiveness of education in this period is evident from its restriction to Brahmins. This period marked not only the practice of gender inequality, where women had less human worth than men, but also the practice of rigid male social inequality, where the value of men was inversely related to their position in the caste hierarchy (Thapar 1966).

The rise of Buddhism in India had an important though limited impact upon the education and status of women. The Buddhist order assigned an honoured place to women in society. As the Bhikshuni-Sangh, or the order of the nuns or Upasikas (lay female devotees), women received access to opportunities for education, culture and social service. Some of the nuns achieved great distinction as scholars, poets, thinkers and writers. Equality of women was, however, only relative (Kuppuswamy 1986).

The decline of Buddhism and the advent of Muslim rule in India, in the eleventh and twelfth centuries, had disastrous consequences for women. Hindu social order and principles of ascribed caste status and gender inequality became even more rigid. The successive wave of Muslim invasions which culminated in the establishment of the Mughal Empire in 1526 probably made the Hindu society even more conscious of the need to preserve their own distinct customs, traditions and cultures. Early marriage, the dowry system, sati, purdah and kulinism were the major social evils prevalent among high-caste Hindus and upper-class Muslims (Sharma 1981).[2] These rigid norms did not apply to lower-caste rural women who, although uneducated, had the freedom to divorce and remarry (Kuppuswamy 1986). Low caste rural women participated in agricultural work together with their men. They had the freedom to travel and sell their agricultural produce in the neighbouring towns.

Similarly, women of the nobility had greater social freedom from conservative cultural traditions and regulations of their conduct. There are several examples of eminent women scholars, administrators and rulers from this period (Sharma 1981).

However, despite occasional references to educated and talented women, ordinary women suffered a deterioration in their status for at least 2000 years from 200 BC to about 1800 AD (Altekar 1962). Thus, this period reveals a complete reversal in the status of women from equals to outcasts by the turn of the eighteenth century.

Colonial rule: advancement of women's rights

The advent of colonial rule did bring about some changes in the status of women but progress was both erratic and slow. In the first century of British rule, from 1757 to 1857, Indian women were clearly unequal and subordinate to men. British policies toward women's rights and education were initiated very cautiously out of respect for social and religious norms.

In many provinces, because of the institution of purdah, the education of girls was expensive. Separate educational institutions for boys and girls were costly. High compound walls had to be erected to protect the girls from the view of outsiders. Transport had to be provided to and from school. Education was not within the reach of the ordinary working family. The tradition of early marriage among Hindus and Muslims was also an obstacle to the education of girls who were withdrawn from school at young age, not yet fully literate.[3] As a result, there were few women teachers.

At the same time, British rule brought with it liberal ideas and culture. Liberalization in attitudes toward women in the nineteenth century was due to the acceptance of the tenets of liberal Western philosophy by enlightened Indians, study of the old Indian texts by reformers, and study of the ancient Vedic society by revivalists.

Liberal-minded Indians initiated a social-reform movement with emphasis on social attitudes and customs towards women. The nineteenth century saw social legislation enacted that abolished some of the more abominable social customs for the first time in India. For instance, sati and marriages of minors under the age of 12 was made illegal.

Progress regarding women's education was slow. While the Charter Act of 1813 had entrusted the East India Company with the responsibility for educating Indian people, access to education was limited to men with the objective of providing English-speaking clerks and petty officials (Brown 1985).

Given the widespread prevalence of purdah, the first formal efforts to educate girls were in segregated schools. There were also several co-educational schools in this period. However, they were not endorsed by well-to-do Indians. Co-education was (and still is) a subject of great controversy.

An active policy of education for girls mentioned in the Education Dispatch of 1854[4] was not actually initiated until 1870. In that year, training colleges for women were established and women had access to training for employment as teachers in girls' schools. These policies were given a boost by the recommendations of the Education Commission of 1882.

Women admitted to higher education

Contrary to the Western experience, Indian women were admitted with little opposition to the university as early as 1877. Calcutta University permitted women candidates to sit for the entrance and BA examinations in 1877 and 1878, respectively. Bombay University followed in 1883. The first two women graduates of Calcutta received their degrees in 1883. Although London University admitted women in 1878, Oxford and Cambridge did not admit them for degrees until after the First World War (Government of India 1975).

Only a few thousand girls, mostly from urban upper- and middle-class families, entered the formal system of education between 1850 and 1870.

The situation in 1946 and 1947 in this context was no different. Educated women of this period were mostly Christian, Anglo-Indian, Parsi and upper-caste Hindu. These women had received an education in the face of opposition by conservative social groups. The main purpose for educating women was to make them more capable of fulfilling their traditional roles. Actual social or economic involvement was not expected of them. This attitude was also shared by the middle classes of that time elsewhere in Europe and America. Changing social attitudes towards women's education were also a consequence of the demand for educated wives by men employed in the colonial administration, who sought to enhance their social status. The ambivalence between traditional and modern views continues to plague present social attitudes regarding women's education, its social use and women's roles in society (Government of India 1949).

The national movement and women's rights (1917–47)

During the course of the national movement for independence from colonial rule, social and religious reform that had been initiated earlier was given new impetus. The Indian political leadership which was interested in the general social and economic reform of society was convinced that without extending the principle of equality to women, they would not be able to secure their political objectives of Swaraj (independence).

Although women's emancipation was a desired end in itself, it was also a political necessity. Only a minority of elite upper-class women leaders became members of the central government or parliament in independent India. For most other women it was back to domestic chores. The absence of an active women's movement and the failure of political organizations to recruit and mobilize them, prevented the majority of women from meaningfully exercising their political rights and participating in decision-making bodies.

Nevertheless, the recognition of women's political equality in the Indian constitution was a radical departure – from traditional norms of Indian society as well as the political norms of most advanced countries at that time. With the exception of socialist countries, no other state in the world had accepted women's equality without a fight (Government of India 1975).

The improvement of the status of women in India was the result of a culmination of efforts, which include the social and religious reform movements of the eighteenth and nineteenth centuries, official British policy and social legislation, and the political mobilization of women in the course of the national movement. The progress of women's education showed a significant improvement in the last quarter of the nineteenth century and first half of the twentieth century, from a 0.2 per cent literacy for women in 1882 to 6 per cent in 1947.

Women and education in modern India

The Constitution of the Republic of India, adopted in 1950, guarantees equality of opportunity to all citizens irrespective of race, sex, caste and religion. It further directs the state to endeavour to provide free and compulsory education within a period of ten years of the commencement of the constitution for all children up to 14 years of age. In 1959 the National Committee on Women's Education (Government of India 1959) reported with disappointment that there were only 36 girls educated for every 100 boys.

In view of the norm of seclusion of women, the National Committee recommended the provision of separate institutions for girls to help to break down parental prejudice against their education in co-educational institutions. This was seen as a way to provide occupational roles for educated women as these segregated institutions would employ only women. It worked. In 1948, women's educational institutions constituted only 10.3 per cent of the total; by 1968 they were up to 29 per cent.

The last two decades have witnessed a remarkable growth in the expansion of women's education, although sharp inequalities persist in the ratio of men to women, urban to rural, class to caste and across regions. Female literacy has grown from 7.8 per cent in 1951 to 24.9 per cent in 1981. Yet three-quarters of all Indian women and half of men are illiterate today.

Indian women in higher education

In the field of higher education progress in terms of women's enrolments has been impressive. A college- or university-level education in India is still, however, confined to a small minority of the population. Women graduates are mostly from urban upper- and middle-class backgrounds. Women graduates were a mere 0.3 per cent of the total female population in 1971 (Government of India 1975). Women's enrolment as a percentage of total enrolment has increased progressively from 23 per cent in 1974 to 29 per cent in 1985.

The number of women's colleges increased from 506 in 1975 to 696 in 1985, leading to a corresponding increase in the recruitment of women in the teaching faculties of these institutions (University Grants

Commission 1985). Enrolment of women at the university has been consistent from 1971 to 1984. Since 1985 the University Grants Commission has relaxed the maximum age limit for women by ten years for candidates for research fellowships and stipulated that at least 30 per cent of research fellowships are to be awarded to women candidates (University Grants Commission 1985).

These changes are the result of pressure by women activists in the university-teachers' representative bodies as well as recommendations from special committees of the University Grants Commission on problems relating to improving research qualifications of university academics.

The distribution of women's enrolment in 1985 was: arts 39 per cent, science 29 per cent, commerce 18 per cent, education 48 per cent, engineering and technology 5 per cent, medicine 27 per cent, agriculture 4 per cent, veterinary science 5 per cent and law 7 per cent (University Grants Commission 1985). This subject concentration is similar to Western countries.

Given the low level of female literacy as well as the rural–urban differences in India, women in higher education are a privileged elite. These women become an even more exclusive group when professionally employed. In 1970, women constituted only 17 per cent of professional and technical workers. The largest concentration of women workers is found within the teaching, medical and health fields as well as in clerical and telecommunication jobs. They are highly represented in medicine and teaching, 21 per cent (1977) and 18 per cent (1973–74, higher education) respectively. However, they comprise only 9 per cent of the civil service (1977, Indian administrative service) and only 2 per cent of management and executive jobs (1970–71) (Government of India 1975; Liddle and Joshi 1986).

As an occupational group women academics in 1980 were only 10 per cent of the total staff in Indian universities and 10 per cent in research institutes. Their position was relatively better in colleges of general and professional education where for the same year they represented 22 per cent and 14 per cent of their total staffs respectively (Association of Indian Universities 1987).

In 1951 women's enrolment for university education was at 11 per cent the total (Government of India 1975). Women as a percentage of university academic staff were 3 per cent in 1951. Figures for the same year for women lecturers in colleges of general education are 10 per cent and in colleges of professional education 7 per cent (Table 11.1).

Table 11.1 *Percentage of academic women employed in institutions of higher learning and research*

Year	Universities	Research Institutes	Gen. Edu. Colleges	Prof. Edu. Colleges
1950–51	3	*	10	7
1960–61	5	4	15	10
1970–71	8	5	20	12
1979–80	10	10	22	14

*Only one woman was employed.
Source: Association of Indian Universities 1987.

Recruitment and motivation of women in academe

This section presents the results of my study based upon a non-structured interview in English and/or Hindi of 40 academic women from Delhi University in January and February 1989, along with general developments regarding recruitment to higher education.

The academic profession is documented as the first modern occupation recruiting a high percentage of educated upper- and middle-class women (Government of India 1975; Kuppuswamy 1986). Two inter-related factors appear to have made this possible. First, an active state policy that defined expansion of educational opportunities for women as a prerequisite for social change and development. Second, the implementation of the policy to establish special educational institutions for girls and women.

In recent years the increasing entrance of urban educated women into paid employment reflects the change in social values as well as the growing economic pressures on urban middle-class families. Not all reasons for supporting womens' quest for higher education are however, altruistic. An important reason for urban middle-class parents to encourage and financially support their daughter's professional education, is to increase her marriage potential or economic independence (Dhingra 1972). The teaching profession, in particular, is a preferred occupational choice for women because Indian society deems it respectable. Another reason for this preference is that it allows women comparatively more time to satisfy their familial roles given the short work days and vacations. The social acceptability of women in the academic profession is further enhanced by sex segregation and minimal contact with men. In the University of Delhi there are 18 women's colleges who employ only women lecturers and readers (Bali 1986). Both these features of the profession conform to the cultural ideology of 'segregation' and 'domestication' of women advocated by the upper castes.

In the present study, 75 per cent of the married women academics interviewed were supporting a member or members of their own or their husbands' family, suggesting a strong economic motivation for their work involvement. A few decades ago, middle-class families considered economic support from single or married daughters taboo. Apart from the economic incentives, other motivational factors for gainful employment were evident from interviews with women academics. Some reasons were altruistic – such as using their educational knowledge for a social purpose – and others practical – such as the expected increase in autonomy in their lives and higher social status. For most Indian women the choice of an educational and professional career implies explicit financial support from their families. Higher education is expensive and in fields such as engineering and medicine can be a great financial burden for the parents.

Not all parents recognize an equal obligation to educate a daughter as they would a son. For instance, of the 40 academic women interviewed, 5 per cent met with family opposition. In 55 per cent of the cases there was a liberal attitude, 30 per cent divided, and in 10 per cent there was active parental support to daughters' education. The additional expenditure of educating girls as well as arranging their marriages and dowries is seen as a deterrent to enrolling them in expensive, long-term professional educations. While social attitudes are changing, Indian parents normally tend to emphasize occupational goals for their sons and non-occupational goals for their daughters. This conforms to the traditional role expectations of males as breadwinners and women as housewives by the middle and upper classes in India. It also conforms to their normative expectations that their sons will support them in their old age, while daughters are expected to live in the husband's household and serve the parents-in-law.

In the four decades since independence, gradual change has occurred in social attitudes and values towards education of women and their employment. Most of the women academics interviewed are first-generation urban and middle-class women in employment. While the educational background of their fathers ranges between high school and university, only two of the mothers had graduate and professional qualifications. The fathers are primarily employed as middle- and senior-level government professionals, technical workers and businessmen, most of their mothers are housewives. If attitudinal change is a function of one's education and occupational level then there is hope for the future.

Work experiences of women academics

In order to understand Indian women academics' attitudes towards work it is useful to examine the professional context in which they operate.

University academics in India are employed either by universities in their departments or in their constituent and affiliated colleges. At the top of the academic hierarchy is the professor, next in rank is the associate professor, reader or senior lecturer. At the bottom of the hierarchy are the ranks of assistant professors and lecturers. Promotion to senior posts is generally made through selection procedures on the basis of merit. Political and gender discrimination, while difficult to document, cannot be ruled out. College lecturers working in the under-graduate institutions constitute around 80 per cent of the academic community in India and the great majority of women academics are represented in this category (University Grants Commission 1985). They are thus responsible for doing the back-breaking introductory courses at the undergraduate level while at the senior levels their colleagues, mostly men, engage in the more creative research-oriented activities, postgraduate teaching and supervision of doctoral candidates. Both sex- and professional-status discrimination is evident. There are few women in the category of professor and reader. Analysis of the interview data suggests that college lecturers are also seen as less research-oriented and productive by their 'elite' colleagues working at the university departments.

Seventy-five per cent of the women lecturers in the sample complained that they are more constrained in their professional activities by the regulations governing their academic work compared to their senior colleagues. They feel they have little autonomy and control over their conditions of work. The division of higher education into undergraduate and postgraduate sections in Indian universities with responsibility for the former in colleges and that for the latter in university departments and institutes partially explains the lower status of college teachers as compared to academics in the university.

Upward mobility in the profession is uncommon. With few promotional opportunities, most college lecturers retire at the same professional status as they began their careers. This has not only encouraged qualified intelligent young persons into other more professionally and materially rewarding occupations but also resulted in apathy and low professional self-esteem among lecturers (Bali 1986; Nayar 1988). The university stipulation that a lecturer who does not qualify for a PhD or MPhil within eight years of appointment in that post will not be entitled to future salary increments has increased enrolments in doctoral programmes. An analysis of the interview data suggests that the motivation seems to be more pecuniary than professional, as few lecturers are engaged in post-doctoral research. An ironic fact that emerged in the interviews conducted with women lecturers was that importance of a research degree was limited to selection for appointment. Thereafter universities and colleges showed little interest in the teachers' research profile. Many women (75 per cent of the respondents) expressed frustration with the difficulties they encountered in securing study and academic leave for research. Women professors and associate professors in the sample expressed less discontent on this subject.

Most of the academic women (90 per cent of the sample) interviewed expressed satisfaction with their occupational status. They are pleased to be respectably employed. They enjoy their work as well as the prestige it has given them. They are aware of their privileged position compared to other women as well as their favourable position in the social-class hierarchy. However, many are less confident than their male colleagues about their professional status and they exhibit low self-esteem (60 per cent). Some were proud of their accomplishments in qualifying for their PhDs in as short a time as three years (10 per cent). Others complained that given their workload of teaching, and their family responsibilities, research was becoming increasingly difficult (60 per cent). In this context there was also a difference in attitudes between the younger (under 35 years) and older (35 and over) women academics.

The younger lecturers seemed highly motivated academically but expressed the most dissatisfaction in achieving their primarily male expectations for the ideal academic. One explanation for this is the fact that some were recently married and others had been employed for less than five years. Both circumstances might explain their lower rates of productivity compared to men. Other Indian studies have obtained similar evidence for moderate career orientations and lower research productivity among academic women (Bali 1986; Nayar 1988).

Discrimination

There was a clear ambivalence in these women's attitudes towards professional sex discrimination. While some denied inequality outright (5 per cent), others claimed that women were themselves responsible for the discrimination they experienced (15 per cent). Over half believed that had there not been special higher-educational institutions for women, unemployment in their ranks would be higher than at present. Others felt that they became victims of sex discrimination only after they had been recruited (20 per cent). Examples of this included being given classes and courses to teach that their senior colleagues (male) did not want to do, being given excess workloads, or not being included in academic committees and structures of decision-making. A few women also complained of discrimination by senior colleagues of their own sex.

The majority of academic women interviewed denied wage discrimination (90 per cent). However, a few stated that given their high educational qualifications, they deserved a higher initial salary (10 per cent). The constitutional guarantee for equality of opportunity for employment did not hold true in several cases.[5] Most (75 per cent) were of the opinion that generally, women have to be much better qualified for the same position than their male colleagues. One professor interviewed said 'Even though I was considered very well qualified, by several selection committees for higher academic positions it took me a long time to get the readership and then the professorship.'

Most expressed doubts also about opportunities of re-entry into the profession (over 80 per cent). Higher educational institutions, they maintained, preferred to recruit fresh postgraduates generally from their local milieu. Many of the women interviewed were unaware of their formal and legal working rights and few sought to challenge the authorities to redress wrongs (60 per cent and 20 per cent respectively).

Despite experiencing some radical discrimination, identification with women's issues – including their own professional problems through organized and active participation in women's groups and activities – was the choice of only a few of the women (less than 20 per cent). When queried about the reasons, for lack of active participation in women's groups, answers varied:

I would like to but don't have the time from my work and family commitments. . . .

I don't think it's proper for us in our profession to behave like trade unionists. . . .

I agree with the demands in principle but not the means for implementing them. . . .

I can't morally participate in a strike action leading to the closure of the University . . . believing is doing.

A women's association meeting is not the only place for initiating a struggle. . . .

The general reluctance of academic women to participate in organized activist groups has been noted in studies of other Indian professional women (Nayar 1988; Liddle and Joshi 1986). Most of academic women's demands for reform and change are subsumed within broader movements spearheaded by their general university teachers' associations and other voluntary women's organizations.

Several women interviewed saw formal women's organizations as elitist social-class and power structures. Some believed that government-initiated efforts to improve gender equality were farcical and motivated by political considerations. Others were sceptical of institutional structures not organized at the grass-roots level. Most (over 80 per cent) of the women interviewed were of the opinion that meaningful change can only come about if women persistently challenge discriminatory attitudes in their everyday behaviour at home, at work, in their family and in society at large. Active public participation is important to show solidarity with women's issues but is meaningless if not practised in one's personal life. It was clear from the interview data that many academic women struggle individually against subordination in their family lives where it probably matters and hurts most.

A few of the women interviewed had responded by openly defying their cultural traditions, some had hesitantly resisted conformity while others had sacrificed their own career aspirations for their husbands or families. As we shall see, it is this dichotomy between professional and family life that many of the respondents in this study complained about. The question of dual standards of behaviour also touches upon the question of commitment to change. Many of the academic women tend to identify their interests with maintaining the status quo and their privileges within it. What would the stressed married Indian woman academic do without her menial domestic help? Highly educated women are not all equally aware of their unequal status nor are they all equally motivated for resisting gender subordination. Their solidarity with the less fortunate of their sex is also ambivalent.

In two worlds: role conflict among academic women

Traditional sex-role socialization suggests that men should work, build careers and provide economic support for the family while women should attend to housework and rearing of children. These norms appear to be gradually changing in urban, middle-class Indian families today as is evident from the growing entry of women into professional employment, particularly academics. Women are taking up the dual role of work and family in increasing numbers, often experiencing the stress of role conflict in the face of their additional responsibilities.

Adjustment to normative and cultural expectations of traditional and modern roles, mother/wife, work/career is seen as the principal problem of professionally employed women. A lot of women experience great difficulty in combining these roles, often compromising in the performance in either or both (see Chapters 7 and 8). How have Indian women academics responded to the pressure of work and family?

The majority of the academics in this study are married (80 per cent), to men of equal or better professional status. Relatively few are unmarried or choose to remain so (15 per cent); a minority are separated or divorced (5 per cent). As compared with other women who are not professionally employed, women academics tend to marry late: a fact not unrelated to their aspirations and the demands of higher-educational and research qualifications as criteria for employment. Parallel findings were obtained by Nayar (1988) and Trembour (1984).

Most of those interviewed maintained their own independent households but had one or more relatives or members of the family residing with them (generally from the husband's side). Few (15 per cent) of the women lived in joint or extended family households with their in-laws. The unmarried women resided with their parents. Nearly all (85 per cent) were postgraduates from the university where they are presently employed. This is significant as it suggests the level of academic inbreeding and pattern of local recruitment. In fact, women not domiciled in the same city are denied admission to undergraduate study in some colleges which do not have residence facilities for them.[6]

Almost all the women (90 per cent) agreed that relative to other professions such as medicine, the nature of their job allowed them more time for their familial roles. For lecturers generally, the prescribed workload in colleges is 15 hours per week, although this varies considerably for members of the academic staff. At any rate, academics work relatively shorter hours and fewer days each year than most full-time workers. An academic year is about 240 days. Much of the work, such as lecture preparation and evaluation of manuscripts, is done at home. The degree of respectability that this profession enjoys and its suitability for women is partially due to this fact.

Sexual equality in family life was evident from these women's responses that in most matters they made decisions jointly with their husbands. However, this was not so for most of the women in the context of housework. Women coped with the pressure of dual work by relying upon support from their extended family network or by hiring domestic help. In most cases women were satisfied with their present arrangements. Although it was expressed by several that given the rate of industrialization, and alternative opportunities for employment, loyal househelp would be difficult to find and expensive to afford in the not-too-distant future. The subject of rearing young children, while pursuing an active research career was seen as a problem for only a few women who could not rely upon househelp or family support (15 per cent). This was in marked contrast to problems faced by working mothers of young children in the West (see Chapter 7). In the absence of daycare centres for small children under three years, most Indian middle-class families with working women have to employ an ayah (maidservant) or naukar (manservant) or else rely upon family support: mothers-in-law, aunts, and so on, for this purpose. As one of the women interviewed remarked:

I have worked for nearly equal number of years in India and the USA. . . . I must admit that it was more difficult to manage academic work and the family abroad than it is here. Both my parents and in-laws are more than willing to help with the children if need be. I can afford to employ a part-time house-help. . . . My children take the school bus to and from school. . . .

The women interviewed have in many cases also adjusted to their situation by lowering their aspirations of measuring up to the image of the ideal academic or mother/wife stereotype. Few considered it necessary – and some inappropriate – for their husbands to share equally with the housework and childrearing. To quote a 41-year-old history lecturer:

We have a comfortable modern flat, equipped with necessary household appliances and we can afford a part-time househelp. . . . She washes the clothes, cleans the flat and helps prepare meals. I don't expect my husband to help me with these household chores. What will his family and colleagues say? . . . Anyway, I have managed so long to combine my work and family life quite well. Although often it has involved compromise at home or at work. . . . At present, apart from the time I use for preparing my lectures at night, I do not have the time for other research activities. While the children are still at school I have to sacrifice my research aspirations. . . . Presently, I am content with being a good teacher to my undergraduate students.

A minority expressed the view that their husbands were willing to accept household responsibilities when the occasion arose.

There is no doubt that educated Indian women have come a long way in their struggle for gender equality. But, as the present study suggests, this goal has been only partially achieved. Higher education has undeniably given women new options for organizing their lives. Professional employment has given them enhanced status and economic independence, but the equality they experience is relative and conditional. Women academics in India live in two worlds: the one in which they are a privileged social elite, the other where they are less equal.

Notes

1. The sample covered a group of women of diverse age, religion and social, family and professional status. Ages varied from 23 to 55; half were under 35. The majority were Hindus, and the rest were Sikhs, Muslims and Christians. Two-thirds of the women were married. All were from upper- and middle-class backgrounds. Three were professors, 12 were senior lecturers/readers/associate professors and 25 were lecturers.

2. Sati is immolation of the wife together with the dead husband on his funeral pyre. Purdah is the observance of segregation of women from males.

Kulinism was a practice under which a kulin Brahman could secure several wives as well as wealth on the basis of his kul (clan) and status.

3. This is still considered an important factor denying women the opportunity of education in rural areas of India.

4. This Dispatch is one of the most significant features in the history of Indian education, since it accepted the responsibility of the government to promote primary education in general and that of the girls in particular.

5. Equal Remuneration Act (ERA) No 25, 1976.

6. This policy concerning admission to study is practised in several colleges of Delhi University.

References

Altekar, A S (1962), *The Position of Indian Women in Hindu Civilization*, Motilal: Banarsidas.

Association of Indian Universities (1987), *Educational Statistics at a Glance*, New Delhi: AIU.

Bali, A B (1986), *College Teachers: Challenges and Responses*, New Delhi.

Brown, J M (1985), *The Origins of an Asian Democracy*, Oxford: Oxford University Press.

Dhingra, O P (1972), *The Career Woman and Her Problems*, New Delhi: Shri Ram Center for Industrial Relations and Human Resources.

Government of India, (1949), *Report of the University Education Commission.*

Government of India, (1959), *Report of the National Committee on Women's Education.*

Government of India (1975), *Towards Equality*, Report of the Committee on the Status of Women in India, New Delhi.

Government of India, (1985), *Women in India*, New Delhi: Ministry of Social and Women's Welfare.

Kuppuswamy, B (1986), *Social Change in India*, Delhi: Vikas.

Liddle, J and Joshi, R (1986), *Daughters of Independence*, London: Zed books.

Nayar, U (1988), *Women Teachers in South Asia*, Delhi: Chanakya.

Sharma, R K (1981), *Nationalism, Social reform and Indian Women*, New Delhi: Janaki Prakashan.

Thapar, R (1966), *A History of India*, Vol 1, Penguin.

Trembour, M (1984), Women in education, in J Lebra (ed), *India: Continuity and Change*, New Delhi: Promilla & Co.

University Grants Commission (1985), *Report for the Year 1984–85*, New Delhi.

Chapter 12

Women Professors in the USA: Where Are They?

Jennie Farley

Opportunities for American scholars of both sexes are often considered to be better than those of their counterparts in other countries. In the most hidebound of European universities , there used to be one – and only one – professor in each field, who controlled the destiny of all aspirants to upward mobility. American institutions, it is thought, are bigger, more numerous and more democratic; therefore, the argument goes, it must be easier to get to the top. But is it? And are women afforded the same opportunities as men?

Many of us believe that the university is the institution in any society with the highest potential for preserving, transmitting and enlarging on what is best in the culture. At the same time, we recognize full well that the US academy, like those elsewhere, is one of the most rigid and conversative institutions. We all believe in universities, traditional though they be; we also believe that women should have a full and fair share in shaping them. In this chapter, I shall describe the occupational structure in a typical US university and show where women stand in the pecking order. I shall conclude with a report on some of the reforms that we are trying to institute. In the process of trying to reshape the institu-ion, we have learned that there are as many steps and distinctions among university staff members as there are among members of the armed forces, the church and the government. To change it, we must first understand it.

The system

Universities in the United States have three purposes:

1. To transmit the culture: that is, to teach undergraduates and graduate students in residence at the institution.

2. To push back the frontiers of knowledge: that is, to do research and dis-
seminate the results in scholarly publications.
3. To serve the public.

These aims are weighted differently at different types of institutions.
Teaching undergraduates is the primary or only function of many
colleges, while at a research university scholarly investigation is a
major activity. At a state university, a major function is extension: that
is, the extending of what is taught and learned on-campus to adults off-
campus. These functions are reflected in the career ladders on which
the faculty members find themselves at a comprehensive institution, as
shown in Table 12.1. Those whose duties are in extension are on one
ladder; teachers are on another; researchers, another. Those faculty
members who have all three responsibilities are on the professorial
ladder.

Table 12.1 *Faculty career ladders at an American university*

Service ladder	Teaching ladder	Research ladder	Professorial ladder
Senior extension associate	Senior lecturer	Senior research associate	Professor
Extension associate	Lecturer	Research associate	Associate professor
			Assistant professor
			Instructor*

*A post usually held by a candidate for an assistant professorship who is in the process of
completing the PhD at another university. Upon completion of the degree, the instructor is
promoted to the post of assistant professor. Assistant professors are on trial for six years, at
which time they are either terminated or promoted to tenured associate professorships.

Of course, the ten job titles listed in Table 12.1 do not exhaust all the
possibilities. Each of them can be modified with adjectives such as
'courtesy', 'acting', 'adjunct', or 'visiting', all of which mean essentially
the same thing: that the title-holder is extended some but not all of the
privileges associated with his or her title. In addition, there are librarians, attorneys, administrators, counsellors, clerical staff, technicians
and custodial staff – about 6,300 of them at an institution with 18,600
students in residence and some 2,485 faculty. The persons holding the
job titles listed in Table 12.1 are often lumped together as 'the faculty'.
Some, however, are more faculty than others, as shall be seen.

Those on the service ladder develop, coordinate, and administer
extension programmes; those on the teaching ladder offer courses –
often introductory-level courses in the study of languages or in
'freshman composition' but sometimes in other fields as well; and those
on the research ladder do only research work, usually but not always in
the sciences. Those holding the titles of extension associate, lecturer, or

research associate are expected to have credentials and experience equivalent to those of assistant professors; those one step higher on each ladder are expected to be equivalent in education and experience to associate professors. Note that there is no equivalent of the full professor on the other ladders. University administrators speak of the possibility of 'lateralling' over from one ladder to another, specifically from one of the other three ladders to the professorial ladder; this seldom happens in practice. Regulations specifically prohibit moving from the professorial ladder to one of the others.

Three other factors differentiate the professorial-ladder posts from all the others. The first is that assistant, associate and full professors all have three duties: to teach, research and participate in service. Second, those on the professorial ladder are eligible for consideration for (or have been granted) *tenure*: permanent appointment. Assistant professors are on trial for, at most, six years. At that juncture, they are either promoted to tenured associate professorships or required to leave – 'up or out'. Associate professors and full professors have something which is unusual in any occupation in the United States: lifetime appointments. The third factor which differentiates professorial posts from all the others is that professors make the decisions about recruitment, hiring and promotion not only of one another but of all those on the service, teaching and research ladders as well. Researchers can be let go when a grant expires; lecturers, when the demand for their courses abates; extension associates, when state money is reallocated; and assistant professors when the quality of their work is deemed not to meet the standards defined by the associate professors and professors. It is tenured professors and only they who vote on tenure. Dean and directors do not have the power either to appoint or promote professorial faculty at most major universities. At smaller institutions, administrators tend to be more powerful. But, in general, the more prestigious the institution, the more these crucial tenure decisions rest with the tenured faculty. Only the tenured faculty in a department can propose a candidate for promotion to tenure. The dean of the college and the president of the university and even the members of the ultimate governing body, the board of trustees, cannot overrule tenured faculty in the all-important matter of granting tenure.

Women in the system

As an example, I shall cite the status of women at my institution, Cornell University. Cornell is located in upper New York State in the small city of Ithaca, where it is the largest employer. Founded in 1868, it is now composed of seven undergraduate schools and colleges and five graduate divisions. It is unusual in that eight of these units are private (endowed) and five are public (state colleges linked to the State University of New York). In 1989, there were 18,601 students on campus, of whom 42 per cent were women. Cornell is one of the best-known institutions in the United States and abroad, being a member of the 'Ivy League', a group of universities generally acknowledged to be the most competitive in terms of admission of students, the richest in terms of endowment funds, and the oldest in our young country. Women constituted 24 per cent of the persons holding full-time faculty posts at Cornell on the four career ladders as shown in Table 12.2.

Table 12.2 *Women's place on the career ladders at Cornell, 1989**

		Women	
Ladder	Total	Number	Per cent
Service	247	96	39
Teaching	333	189	57
Research	289	69	24
Professorial	1617	249	15
Total	2486	603	24

*Source: Report on the Status of Women and Minorities at Cornell University, Office of the Associate Vice President for Human Relations and the Office of Institutional Planning and Research, May 1989, pp 29, 35.

It can be seen that women are least well represented on the most prestigious of the ladders: the professoriate. Where do they stand on that ladder itself? Mostly on the bottom step, as shown in Table 12.3.

Table 12.3 *Women's place on the professorial ladder at Cornell, 1989**

		Women	
Title	Total	Number	Per cent
Professor	849	56	7
Associate professor	418	86	21
Assistant professor	350	107	31
Total	1617	249	15

*Source: As for Table 12.2, p 29.

Of the 249 women on the professorial ladder, 107 (43 per cent) were assistant professors on trial. It can be seen that, at Cornell at the end of the 1980s, *women were 15 per cent of the professorial faculty but only 7 per cent of the full professors*. Is Cornell unusual? Of the 2,546 institutions of higher education in the United States surveyed in 1988, women held 26 per cent of the professorial posts.[1] But a detailed analysis of the sex composition of the faculties in the best-known institutions in the same survey shows that Cornell is not unusual when compared to other institutions of its type. It and its sister institutions averaged together had women as 17 per cent of the total professorial faculty and 8 per cent of the full professors. Cornell is like its peers, as shown in Table 12.4.

Table 12.4 *Full-time faculty (excluding instructors) in Ivy League and 'Big Ten' institutions by sex and percentage of full professors who are women, 1988**

	Faculty		Full professors	
	Total	Per cent	Total	Per cent
Ivy League	number	women	number	women
Brown	475	18.7	275	7.6
Columbia	906	19.2	507	10.8
Cornell	1488	14.9	749	5.7
Dartmouth	339	23.3	174	6.8
Harvard	894	15.9	518	7.9
U. of Pennsylvania	1002	16.7	535	9.7
Princeton	597	13.4	362	6.9
Yale	737	20.6	391	6.6
Total	6438	17.2	3511	7.8
Big Ten				
U. of Illinois	2973	17.7	1319	8.8
Indiana U.	1191	20.9	605	10.9
U. of Iowa	987	20.4	473	8.7
U. of Michigan	1574	17.9	816	8.6
Michigan State	1869	20.4	973	10.2
U. of Minnesota	1511	21.3	747	10.9
Northwestern	871	15.8	439	7.5
Ohio State U.	1886	19.0	744	7.4
Purdue U.	1374	15.4	562	4.6
U. of Wisconsin	2183	20.2	1159	9.6
Total	16419	18.9	7837	8.9
Grand Total	22857	18.4	11348	8.6

*Source: Tabulated from individual entries in *Annual Report on the Economic Status of the Profession, 1988–89. Academe*, Bulletin of the American Association of University Professors, March–April 1989, Appendix 1, pp 22–65.

Summarizing the results of the survey of all types of institutions of higher education from which these data are drawn, economist Hirschel Kasper noted that Category I universities (as all those in Table 12.4 are classified) show not only the 'smallest proportion of women faculty members' but also the largest salary differentials between the sexes.[2] Table 12.4 shows that the state institutions have a higher proportion of women faculty and women full professors than do Ivy League universities. It can also be seen from Table 12.4 that Cornell has the next-to-lowest percentage of women faculty and the lowest percentage of women full professors in the Ivy League.

Feminists at Cornell find it galling that progress has come so slowly in light of the fact that the university has been a pioneer in the education of women. There have been women students at Cornell since 1870, a full century before the other Ivy institutions admitted women on an equal basis with men. (several had coordinate women's colleges; the University of Pennsylvania had a special curriculum for women students.) Cornell was also a leader in developing courses on women[3] and the first major university to found a women's studies programme.[4] Yet our faculty is still a little more male-dominated than the other Ivies.

At Cornell, as it has been shown, women tend to be in the less prestigious teaching, research and extension posts rather than on the professorial ladder. Indeed, the more prestigious the ladder the fewer the women on it here. So it is in the country as a whole: while women constitute 26 per cent of the faculty in all institutions, they hold only about 18 per cent of the professorial faculty posts in the best-known institutions. The more prestigious the institution, the fewer the women on the faculty.

Changing the system

Activist women all over the world are seeking change. In Norway, Berit Ås envisions a feminist university, different from any institution now in existence (see Chapter 14). In India, a high priority is placed on help from the government (see Chapter 11). In the United States, many of us focus on seemingly small reforms. Bernice Sandler, director of the Project on the Status and Education of Women of the Association of American Colleges in Washington DC, has noted that reformers often elicit this reaction: 'These women want to change the whole university!' And, Sandler goes on, 'Correct. We do'.[5] But she urges specificity. She observes that academic women in the USA have resources they can draw upon for help: outside organizations, both local and national; campus-wide women's organizations, and official university committees on women's issues. The first includes such organizations as the

National Organization for Women (NOW), the Women's Equity Action League (WEAL), and the American Assocation of University Women. These organizations are sometimes discounted as being either too radical on the one hand or too powerless on the other to have any effect on policies framed by academic men. The second resource is student groups, which are sometimes discounted by academics as too uninformed to be taken seriously. The third group, the official committee on campus, is sometimes considered to be too conservative, since its members are sometimes hand-picked by the administration, perhaps because they won't make trouble. But, as Sandler has pointed out, these three sets of resources can be drawn upon to bring about change. She is perhaps the best-known American expert on how women can work from without and within at the same time.

I shall focus here on the inside group at my university to show the kinds of issues it can raise. The Status of Women Committee came into being at the request of a concerned woman trustee. In the eighteen years since it was founded, the committee has dealt with virtually every aspect of university policy and practice: admissions requirements, the representation of minority women in the student body and on the staff; equity in the allocation of financial aid, including grants, loans and employment opportunities for students; provision of equal opportunity for women in fields where they are under-represented such as science and engineering; and equity in the provision of student services, including opportunities for participation in athletics. For the most part, however, the committee has focused on the university as an employer. Concerns have included the extent to which clerical staff (now called 'office professionals' here) have access to career ladders, opportunities for professional development and full benefits; the problems of blue-collar women seeking to move into job titles in the skilled trades traditionally dominated by men; and the extent to which librarians, editors, and other women professionals not on the faculty are rewarded for their important contribution to the university community.

Committee members concerned with faculty women studied the career ladders and the statistics showing women's place on them. The committee has raised a number of hard questions:

- If extension associates, lecturers, and research associates have the same level of qualifications as assistant professors and the senior extension associates, senior lecturers, and senior research associates, the same level of qualifications as associate professors, how is it that women are appointed to 41 per cent of the posts on the non-professorial ladders and to only 25 per cent of the posts on the professorial ladder?

- Of all the faculty men at Cornell, 73 per cent are on the professorial ladder. Of all the faculty women here, only 41 per cent are on that ladder. Is it possible that the men are so much more likely to be generalists and the women, specialists?

- How is it that some women hold appointments which are part time on one non-professorial ladder and part time on another? If a woman is a half-time research associate and a half-time lecturer, why isn't she a full-time assistant professor?

The committee has also scrutinized the position descriptions and pointed out that:

- Having a requirement that an assistant professor of art shall have exhibited in a major art gallery in New York City effectively screened women out of the competition since at the time this requirement was stated, virtually no women had had such exhibitions.

- Having a requirement that an assistant professor of law must have had Wall Street experience also excluded women from the competition, since the best-known law firms there were the slowest to open their doors to women.

The committee has also raised questions about the ladder-steps themselves, seemingly so rational and well considered, and the unwritten requirements for placement on them. By custom, graduate students cannot be considered as candidates for assistant professorships at the institutions where they study. Professors look to those nearing completion of the PhD at other institutions for candidates. This is based on the belief that institutions should not become too inbred by hiring their own graduates, at least not until those graduates have had experience elsewhere. In this regard, the committee has asked:

- Are women holding Cornell doctorates who are on the non-professorial ladders being passed over in favour of men from other universities who have not yet completed their PhDs?

- Has consideration been given to the fact that the 'no Cornell PhDs without experience elsewhere' rule effects women more drastically than men? Women are often older when they complete graduate work; sometimes their family ties hold them to Ithaca. Thus that group is excluded from consideration by a rule which, while neutral on the surface, affects women more than it does men.

- Has the faculty been fully informed about the change in the nepotism rules? Formerly, by custom, two professorial appointments could not be held by people married to each other. One partner had to be content with a non-professorial ladder post. This rule, until it was changed quietly in 1970, affected women more than men.

The group has pressed for reforms which would make it possible not only for more women to be appointed to the professorial ladder but for the posts on the other ladders to be more dignified and secure financially. The committee has asked:

- If associate professors and full professors have lifetime appointments, couldn't the institution appoint its lecturers for more than a year at a time? Shouldn't lecturers – allegedly equivalent in qualifications to assistant professors – be paid on a per-course basis as assistant professors for teaching exactly the same courses?

- If associate professors and full professors are entitled to paid sabbatic leaves every seven years, shouldn't senior extension associates, senior research associates, and senior lecturers be entitled to the same opportunities for study and renewal?

- If senior research associates are truly equivalent in qualifications to associate professors, shouldn't the former be eligible to apply for outside funding as senior investigators and project leaders, as those on the professorial ladder can?

And the committee has considered historical data, noting that in the academic year 1971–72, women held 33 per cent of the posts on the non-professorial ladders while in 1988–89, they held 41 per cent of such posts. The faculty as a whole increased in size from 1,796 persons in 1972 to 2,486 in 1989. Women's share of the professorial posts rose from 7 per cent to 15 per cent in that period while their share of the powerful tenured associate professorships and full professorships grew from 6 per cent in 1972[6] to 11 per cent in 1989. Women's advocates are counselled to be patient. But they find it disheartening that, at this rate of change, it will be the year 3000 before women are as well represented on the faculty as they currently are in the student body. In this regard, the committee has asked for promotion data:

- Are the women extension associates, lecturers, and research associates being promoted to the senior posts on their ladders at the same rate as the men in these positions? How about the crucial promotions from assistant professorships to tenured associate professorships? Since these decisions are made by tenured professors, a group which is, as has been shown, 89 per cent male, can there be bias against women in these life-changing decisions?

Another function the committee has served has been to put faculty women in touch with one another. An example is the scheduling of yearly meetings of senior professors with newly appointed assistant professors. The older women advise the younger ones, especially about how to prepare for the vital tenure review. Time was when the counsel was general and even bromidic ('Do your best', 'Be a lady', 'Don't be too aggressive', and the like). In recent years, the advice has been direct and specific, to wit:

- 'Concentrate on your research at all costs. You will be asked to teach extra courses and serve on extra committees. Don't. Scholarly publication and only that will get you promoted'.

- 'Get in touch with scholars in your discipline at other institutions. Your colleagues will expect you to have a national reputation when you are reviewed for tenure'.

- 'Don't bank your whole life on getting tenure here. Consider the odds: some assistant professors don't even make it past the first review after they've been here three years. Others are "counselled out" at the end of five years, before they even come up for tenure. And, of the men and women who actually are considered for tenure at Cornell, half are turned down. Half'.

- 'If you are turned down, the decision is almost irreversible. If the students raise an uproar on your behalf, that won't help. It'll solidify faculty resistance to your promotion'.

- 'Don't serve on any committee, even the Status of Women Committee, if you can possibly help it, until you get tenure. Then do your committee work, especially on the Status of Women committee. We need you tenured and on our side'.

There is solid evidence that women who try to reverse negative tenure decisions have had little success. Despite equal-opportunity legislation, women academics lose in court much more often than they win. Yet their suits do serve to bring about institutional change and to smooth the path for the junior women (and men) who come after them.[7] Social historian Dale Spender has noted that astronomer Maria Mitchell, one of the first women professors in the United States, found discrimination against women scholars in the 1860s. Spender writes that Mitchell lectured widely, reiterating over and over that:

- It was a fallacy for women to believe that things would gradually improve: because men's attitudes about women's 'inferiority' had *not* changed, there was always the danger that men would take back some of women's hard-won gains. And because men still possessed the power, women were not in a position to stop them.[8]

The 1980s saw a rising tide of conservatism in many countries, especially mine. There was less vigorous enforcement of anti-bias laws and diminished pressure for the full and fair recruitment and selection processes required by 'affirmative action', which was often mistakenly identified as discrimination against white men. Maria Mitchell was right: individual women cannot stem the tide of discrimination alone. But women as a group can guard their hard-won gains and continue to effect small but important changes.

At my university, as the 1990s begin, advertisements for openings for faculty members do not include requirements which screen women out of the competition. Women on the non-professorial ladders can compete for lateral transfers to professorial posts. Lecturers and research associates can be appointed for three- to five-year periods.

Senior extension associates are eligible for study leave; senior research associates can apply in their own names for research grants for work they will direct and conduct. There is a senior woman administrator who keeps careful track of promotion rates and the extent to which full and fair searches are undertaken for candidates and the numbers of women of all races and minority men who are considered. She reports annually to the Staus of Women Committee and to the university's board of trustees.

These reforms can be traced directly to the agitation for them on the part of the Status of Women Committee and to the campus climate, affected by a five-year-long law suit waged by a group known as the 'Cornell Eleven'. The suit was brought by women who had been turned down for tenure or reappointment as assistant professors. Although none of the named plaintiffs gained reinstatement, the university was forced to pay a quarter of a million dollars to settle with them and the 35 other women who joined in the complaint. The suit was supported throughout by the American Association of University Women and by a group of staff, faculty, alumnae and student women.

What are the prospects for the future? A 1986 article in *Working Woman* cited US Bureau of Labor Statistics projections to help readers make informed career decisions. At that time, it was predicted that two occupations would dwindle drastically in size. The first was postal clerk: there would be 18 per cent fewer openings for clerks in post offices in 1995 than in 1985, no doubt because more communication would take place by computer. A second occupation was cited: college professor. There would be 15 per cent fewer openings by 1995.[9] This was based on the fact that there will be fewer students in colleges by then because there are fewer boys and girls in that age group. Students who will enter colleges and universities in 1995 are already born: they are 12 years old now and there are fewer of them than the institutions of higher education are set up for. More recent projections underscore the problem for women. The *Occupational Outlook Handbook* for 1988–89 predicts that openings for college and university professors will decline through the mid-1990s and then increase somewhat. However, by the year 2000, the number of openings for professors will be below the 1986 level.[10] Of course, then, as now, demand will vary by discipline. Those trained in the fields traditionally dominated by men – for example, science and engineering – will be sought after on campus as they are within the university.

Given these gloomy prospects, why do we want to fight our way into academic life? Because the university is a vital institution which has changed our lives. Women before us fought for generations for our right to study in them; now we fight for our right to move out of the basement of the professoriate into full partnership in shaping them. Many of us have battled long and hard for women's rights at Cornell, both on the inside, on the Status of Women Committee, and outside, supporting the law suit.

A junior colleague once, asked me if it had been worth all the struggle. The answer is yes. I have been a lecturer and an extension associate and a research associate. The professors who appointed me to those positions told me I would love the work. They were correct. I did. They also told me that those 'less demanding' posts were perfect for women with family responsibilities. Once I was told that women have a 'special knack' for teaching; another time, that women were really best suited to research. The national statistics bear out the perception that women are really best suited to adult education or extension work. The American Association of University Professors survey found that women constitute 26.4 per cent of the faculty in four-year institutions but 37.7 per cent of the faculty in two-year institutions.[11] Researcher Emily Abel has demonstrated that women are a disproportionately large percentage of part-time and temporary faculty at American colleges.[12]

I studied and worked at a university for many years before I realized that the people with power, those running it, were not those teaching introductory courses or those staffing the research projects, or even those with impressive administrative titles. The tenured professors run the place. It is they who elect the deans, define the discipline, study what they choose to study, shape the courses they teach the way they want them to be, hire everybody else and decide who among them is worthy of promotion. Women are few and far between among the tenured professoriate.

American academic women do so much of the work on campus and have so little voice in policy. We women want to help decide what questions are studied, how the university resources are allocated, what is taught on-campus and how, and with what ingenuity and to whom that information is extended off-campus.

In my corner of the world, it was a woman trustee, Charlotte Williams Conable, who first wrote a history of the women at the institution. She found that, although women were admitted as students much sooner here than elsewhere in the United States, there had always been problems for women students and women faculty. Conable discovered that the number of women admitted to study here was restricted to the number of beds available for them in the dormitories (a restriction that did not apply to men) and that these admissions quotas kept the number of women down and number of men up. The first woman teacher elevated to the professorial ranks at Cornell was botanist Anna Botsford Comstock, a Cornell graduate. She was appointed to an assistant professorship in the summer session in 1898. The trustees decided, however, that this was not a suitable title for a woman and demoted her to lecturer in the autumn. She taught in that position for thirteen years before finally being reappointed assistant professor in 1911, associate professor in 1917 and, in 1920, just before she was to retire, to full professor at last.[13]

The question posed in the title of this chapter can now be answered. Where are the women professors in the United States? They tend to be in the least well known institutions, often as part-time appointees. When they have fought their way into the best-known universities, they often find themselves, like Anna Botsford Comstock, doing professorial work – but off the professorial ladder. The few women who have made it to the top of the university ladders at Cornell have used their power to help other women. Constance E Cook served on the board of trustees and later briefly as vice president of Cornell: she pressed hard for a trustee investigation of the status of women and the formation of a committee to monitor progress. It is a woman associate vice president, Jocelyn R Hart, who gathers and makes available the annual data on the progress of women and minorities at Cornell. And it was two tenured women professors, Alice H Cook of the School of Industrial and Labor Relations here and historian Mary Beth Norton, who chaired the group supporting the Cornell Eleven, the junior women who sued their employer.

As the 1990s unfold, the law may prove to provide better protections for women academics. On January 10 1990, the US Supreme Court ruled unanimously that colleges and universities accused of bias in tenure reviews cannot keep the tenure review materials secret. Justice Harry A. Blackmun wrote wisely, 'if there is a "smoking gun" to be found that demonstrates discrimination in tenure decisions, it is likely to be tucked away in peer review files.'[14]

Can universities keep plaintiffs from knowing why they were turned down for tenure? The highest court in the land says no:

The ruling was a decisive victory for the Equal Employment Opportunity Commission and for many civil rights groups that had filed briefs arguing that the secrecy of the tenure process is a shield for discrimination that has kept women and minorities out of the tenured ranks.[15]

It has been a long struggle and one that is not, by any means, over. In 1989, there were only 974 women as full professors in the 18 American universities known as the Ivy League and the Big Ten – 974 women and 10,374 men. What will we do when we are half of those in power? Preserve the best and change the rest.

Notes

1. Annual report on the economic status of the profession, 1988–1989, *Academe*, Bulletin of the American Association of University Professors, March–April 1989, Table 14, Footnote 1, p 19.

2. Hirschel Kasper, High education goals: low salary increases: the annual report on the economic status of the profession, 1988–1989, *Academe*, Bulletin of the American Association of University Professors, March–April 1989, pp 3–7.

3. Catherine East, *A Chronology of the Women's Movement in the US, 1961–1975*, US National Commission on the Observance of International Women's Year, Department of State, Washington DC, 1975, p 5.

4. Florence Howe, Women's studies in New York State, *PS: Post-Secondary Education in New York State*, September–October 1975, p 1.

5. Bernice R Sandler, Strategies for eliminating sex discrimination: times that try men's souls, in Jennie Farley (ed), *Sex Discrimination in Higher Education: Strategies for Equality*, Ithaca, New York: ILR Publications, 1981, p 73.

6. Jennie Farley, Men, women, and work satisfaction on campus, *Cornell Journal of Social Relations*, vol 9, no 1, Spring 1974, pp 17–33.

7. Jennie Farley, Women versus academe: who's winning?, *Journal of Social Issues*, vol 41, no 4, 1985, pp 111–120.

8. Dale Spender, *Women of Ideas and What Men Have Done to Them*, London: ARK, 1983, p 382.

9. Where the jobs will be, *Working Woman*, January 1986.

10. *Occupational Outlook Handbook 1988–1989*, US Department of Labor, Bureau of Labor Statistics, Bulletin 2300, p 115.

11. As for Footnote 1, p 19.

12. Emily K Abel, *Terminal Degrees: The Job Crisis in Higher Education*, New York: Praeger, 1984.

13. Charlotte Williams Conable, *Women at Cornell: The Myth of Equal Education*, Ithaca New York: Cornell University Press, 1977, p 127.

14. Excerpts from court decision requiring universities to yield tenure data, *The New York Times*, January 10 1990, p B6.

15. Linda Greenhouse, Universities lose shield of secrecy in tenure disputes, *The New York Times*, January 10 1990, p 1.

Part V
Finding Solutions and Creating Alternatives

Chapter 13

To Make of our Lives a Study: Feminist Education as Empowerment for Women[1]

Evelyn Torton Beck

Women's Studies is at the centre of a revolution whose aim is nothing less than the transformation of the university.[2] In the last two decades, Women's Studies in the United States has developed from a loosely conceived interdisciplinary 'field of study' into an emerging academic discipline that is at once highly respected and yet still viewed in some quarters with a degree of suspicion (if not alarm). While such uneasiness may be an understandable response to the newness of its conception, it is true that Women's Studies *by its very existence* threatens the status quo. Moreover, Women's Studies has provided the necessary energy and enthusiasm, intellectual leadership and political expertise that have resulted in the successful implementation of other feminist initiatives within the university. These include feminist trans-formations of scholarship across the disciplines, curriculum-transfor-mation projects, the establishment of women's resource centres and the creation of women's commissions which have been central in pressuring universitites to establish policies on parental leave, childcare, pay equity, sexual harrassment and non-sexist language. Such initiatives are not confined to the United States, but have occurred around the world since the early 1970s.

Forged by feminists and supported by progressive administrators of both sexes, these mutually reinforcing strategies have given much hope to women in institutions of higher learning across the United States. Since women now constitute more than 50 per cent of the student population and 37 per cent of the professors – albeit bunched at the lower levels of the academic hierarchy – the transformative potential of these efforts is substantial. Even when these strategies are implemented only on a limited basis, they create a community of women within the institution which serves to improve the 'chilly climate' of the univer-sity.[3] While I recognize that 'woman' and 'feminist' are not identical, it has been my experience that many women who deny allegiance to feminism nonetheless feel isolated in the university and are willing to acknowledge the existence of gender-based inequities; they can often be moved by the community to further consciousness and even a degree of activism.

Fundamental to these interrelated transformational efforts is the recognition that the exclusion of women from both the profession of higher education and the structure of knowledge was not accidental but intentional. In a 1986 lecture given at the University of Maryland-College Park the feminist philosopher Elizabeth Minnich argued that the exclusion of women (and male slaves) from 'liberal' education in ancient Greek society laid the foundation for their continued exclusion from Western civilization and is responsible for the classical curriculum which informs 'traditional' thinking on these matters even today. Disagreement on this issue led to a debate between 'traditionalists' and those who seek to institute curricular change.

We are engaged in a contemporary 'Battle of the Books'. For the past ten years there has been a major debate within higher education focusing on whether or not to expand (or in any way alter) the traditional curriculum. The recent decision made by Stanford University faculty to change the readings in a required core course in western civilization to include women, people of colour and non-Western classics sent reverberations around the country – some of delight, others of dismay.[4]

It was the recognition of deliberate exclusion of women from the professoriate, the curriculum and from positions of power in the university administration that provided a major impetus for the creation of Women's Studies, conceived as the 'academic arm' of the contemporary movement for women's liberation. This movement itself grew out of the ferment of the late 1960s, when women who were active in a number of liberation movements (such as anti-war efforts, the civil rights and black power movement, students' rights, and gay and lesbian liberation) came to recognize their 'otherness' in patriarchal society. This coming to consciousness closely resembles what Virginia Woolf describes as a *'sudden splitting off of consciousness'* that often overcomes a woman 'say in walking down Whitehall, when from being the natural inheritor of that civilisation, she becomes, on the contrary, *outside of it, alien and critical.*'[5]

Movement activists who were located in the university, either as students or professors, took their newly developed consciousness of oppression (women were expected to make coffee while men built theory), and began to apply these understandings to the curriculum, the classroom and the institution of the university as a whole. If, as feminist theory held, 'the personal was political', then so was the academic. Suddenly the commonplace practices of the university (from discriminatory hiring practices to androcentric curricula) were seen as oppressive to women and these became the focus of student/faculty protests.

In spite of such pressures, most institutions of higher learning remained unresponsive to the call for Women's Studies until massive sit-ins and public demonstrations were organized. Once the battle was won and Women's Studies courses were not only established but produced high enrolments, Women's Studies suddenly became good for university business, especially in institutions that were enrolment-driven, and programmes began to proliferate. The earliest Women's Studies classes were typically taught off-campus by graduate students and untenured professors who were not paid for this work. Only after considerable protest did these classes finally become regularized as legitimate university offerings. By 1971, 20 programmes had been established and 600 courses were being offered across the country; by 1973 those numbers had jumped to 80 programmes and 2000 courses nationwide.[6]

New programmes increased dramatically in the next decade: by 1977, 276 had been established; by 1989, that number had almost doubled to 519 – 54 of which offer an undergraduate Women's Studies major.[7] This count includes only programmes or departments that offer a regular major that is institutionalized within the university. The actual number of Women's Studies majors is probably considerably higher, since many undergraduates at institutions that do not have 'free-standing' majors choose the option of constructing an individual or independent major – a choice which is available at most colleges and universities.

On the graduate level, 55 institutions offer a Women's Studies graduate certificate or master's degree and 26 offer the PhD – though virtually all have a specialized focus in conjunction with another discipline. The National Women's Studies Association (the professional organization of the discipline) publishes an annual directory of Women's Studies programmes as well as a listing of graduate programmes in Women's Studies.[8]

Yet, in spite of high enrolments (or, as I sometimes think in my more cynical moments, *because* of them) some lingering prejudice against Women's Studies remains alive on many campuses. Women's Studies is frequently derided as if it were a woman, the whole enterprise viewed as 'too soft' and 'insufficiently rigorous' in spite of student testimony of its demanding nature. And because Women's Studies necessarily includes both the study of lesbian lives and a critique of institutionalized heterosexuality, it is frequently the focus of homophobic attacks which are meant to discredit the subject altogether and to strike fear in the hearts of all women. The academy is also extremely suspicious of what Women's Studies perceives to be one of its strongest contributions to knowledge – the link between who we are and what we know.

Most Women's Studies programmes have overcome such prejudices by maintaining the highest standards of excellence in research and teaching, and by behaving 'as if we believed the system would work for us'.[9] We have also organized within the university, creating broadly based Women's Studies communities that unite students, faculty and staff from across the campus in the form of large assemblies and smaller study groups focusing on a range of contemporary and historical topics of wide interest. In addition, Women's Studies programmes regularly sponsor research colloquia, lectures and forums that introduce the new scholarship on women and gender to the community at large. Women's Studies has also taken the lead in challenging departmental isolation and forging links and co-sponsoring events with other departments, especially African-American and ethnic studies programmes whose missions parallel that of Women's Studies. One of Women's Studies' major contributions is its commitment to interdisciplinary study.

Though individual Women's Studies courses had been offered across the country since the late 1960s, in 1970 the first official programme was established at San Diego State University (then San Diego State College); later that same academic year a second programme was established at Cornell University. While such programmes tend to function like departments and have their own budgets, only a few have faculty lines of their own (professorships in Women's Studies) and can thus maintain full control of their faculty and their curriculum. Joint appointments between Women's Studies and other departments are far more common, though considerably more stressful since such arrangements demand the fulfilment of two sets of departmental obligations. They also lessen chances for tenure since, with a joint appointment, tenure is usually lodged in a traditional department not necessarily hospitable to feminist research or teaching. In some institutions only the programme director is budgeted in Women's Studies, and teaching faculty are 'borrowed' from other departments to teach Women's Studies courses – an arrangement even less desirable than joint appointments.

There is some debate on this point among practitioners of Women's Studies, some of whom prefer joint appointments because they believe that these strengthen the Women's Studies sphere of influence. Some faculty like to retain the opportunity of directing doctoral dissertations in traditional departments, since most Women's Studies programmes do not offer graduate degrees. But wherever they are located, faculty involved in interdisciplinary Women's Studies tend to prefer to keep some scholarly ties to at least one of the more traditional disciplines.[10] To encourage feminist research across the disciplines, the National Women's Studies Association has in the past few years established a task force in feminist scholarship.

When I compare my experiences working first in a large programme staffed entirely with joint appointments, then in a small programme staffed entirely with Women's Studies faculty, I conclude that departmental autonomy is critical for the full development of the emerging discipline. Most critically, departmental status allows for independence in hiring and tenure decisions. It also confers prestige and the necessary political clout to influence university-wide decisions.

However, because of the interdisciplinary nature of Women's Studies, even at institutions with fully-fledged Women's Studies departments students remain dependent to some extent on disciplinary-based Women's Studies courses located in other departments to fulfil the requirements for the major in Women's Studies. This curricular inter-dependence could be viewed as one of the strengths that Women's Studies brings to a university community in which the disciplines are typically quite sharply divided.

While the initial aim of Women's Studies was to correct the omission and distortions of women in all spheres of knowledge and to encourage new scholarship on women across the disciplines, its effects have been far broader. Interdisciplinary work in Women's Studies has created 'paradigm shifts' in virtually all fields of knowledge, questioning the very assumptions on which the disciplines have been built.[11] The creative energy and excitement generated by the new scholarship on women has led to a complex questioning that goes well beyond the focus on women that was the initial impulse behind feminist explorations. An essential component of the philosophy of Women's Studies has been its insistence that the study of women should not be constructed monolithically to replicate patriarchal thinking by creating a white, middle-class, Christian, heterosexual woman as a replacement for the male norm. Over time, Women's Studies has come to insist that gender identity is always constructed in terms of other specificities such as race, ethnicity, religion, sexuality, class, age and dis/ability, and that gender hierarchies intersect with other structures of dominance. This principle is embedded in the consitution of the National Women's Studies Association and is ideally reflected in the curriculum and pedagogy of the Women's Studies classroom.

However, much early feminist work did not take difference adequately into account and posited a universal 'woman' who, with the exception of her gender, resembled her Euro-American male counter-part in the traditional curriculum. When Third World women and women of colour, lesbian, Jewish, working-class, and disabled women began to challenge this model, the focus shifted from 'woman' to 'differ-ences among women'.

While this attention to 'difference' has generated a good deal of excitement (and an explosion of writings) in the Women's Studies movement, it has also created new debates. Some feminists have objected to the use of the word 'minority' to describe people of colour, arguing that the term is both Eurocentric and demeaning, since it implies a permanent kind of marginality that is geographically circumscribed and not true if we think in global terms. What further complicates the issue in the USA is that in discussion, 'minority' becomes elided with 'people of colour', and 'colour' becomes equated with African-Americans who are in turn equated with poverty. While this conflation may be understandable in the light of US history, it nonetheless causes resentment among Latin, Asian-American and Native-American (and middle-class African-American women) who feel they are being made invisible. It has led to the creation of separate task forces within the National Women's Studies Association (though these do not supplant the still viable Women of Colour Caucus).

In this context, Jewish identity presents yet another set of problems. Because Jews of European origin in the United States are not underrepresented in the professions and have access to 'white skin privilege', they tend not to be viewed as a 'minority' at all, though they still make up less than 3 per cent of the total population and continue to be subject to anti-Semitism (which is rising with alarming rapidity in the USA and Europe).[12]

As a result of the on-going discussions of difference and the critiques of feminist theorizing made by those located outside the dominant culture's 'mythical norm',[13] many Women's Studies programmes are currently reassessing their own courses (and staff) to make certain that they are inclusive of the spectrum of difference at the core of their conceptualizations. To implement and expand this imperative, most US Women's Studies programmes are beginning to develop a range of courses focusing on particular groups of women such as African and African-American, Asian and Asian-American, Jewish, lesbian, Third World, working-class and older women. The exploration of how identities are constructed and how oppressions overlap and intersect is the major focus of current Women's Studies research and feminist theorizing in the United States.

Virtually all Women's Studies programmes offer introductory courses (interdisciplinary in nature) that unmask gender stereotypes and analyse representations of women in (mostly Western) culture, although a more global, less Eurocentric perspective is increasingly being developed. These courses also introduce students to the contributions of women across the spectrum of differences, offer a gynocentric analysis of cultural norms and institutions, and invite students to integrate their personal experiences with theoretical concepts. Such courses are usually required for an undergraduate certificate or degree program in Women's Studies.

On the more advanced undergraduate level, courses are focused around themes or issues, as for example, feminist theory; power, gender and the spectrum of difference; women and work; the politics of sexuality; racism and anti-Semitism; women and the arts; feminism and religion; particular groups of women, and of course feminist research and capstone senior seminars. The subject of motherhood provides a particularly good example of an interdisciplinary theme course since the subject virtually demands an analysis of traditional representations of 'the mother' in literature and the arts as well as in ancient and modern myths. Of necessity, it must also take into consideration contemporary political and legal factors that determine 'the institution and experience of motherhood'[14] for any given woman, which would differ according to sexuality, race, ethnicity, class, religion, marital status, country and culture.

Feminist pedagogy

To match its transformational curricular efforts, Women's Studies has developed a set of teaching practices designed to invite women to place themselves at the centre of their learning and to use their own experiences of the world as valid material for theory building (recognizing too that 'theory' helps us to reinterpret and reconstruct our 'experiences'). Feminist pedagogy empowers the student by abolishing the rigid, impersonal student/teacher hierarchies that mark patriarchal teaching/learning practices. In such an environment the teacher does not remain the impersonal guardian of knowledge, but reveals herself to the class as a living, thinking human being. The degree to which Women's Studies teachers ought to reveal information about their personal lives has been the subject of discussion and has shifted over time.[15] While in practice, feminist pedagogy is not without problems, this experience of creating community in the Women's Studies classroom in which women's perpectives 'ways of knowing' are validated is a transformative and empowering experience for both student and teacher.[16]

Feminist learning is facilitated by small group work in which emotions are allowed to surface and differences not glossed over. Women's Studies professors regularly give students the opportunity to lead discussions, participate in collaborative projects and choose assignments that encourage both creativity and analysis. Taken together, these strategies attempt to create a safe space in which *every* voice can be heard. Women's Studies classes encourage students to be present in a holistic way, and as a result, they often form strong bonds of friendship that extend beyond the classroom environment. Women's Studies also teaches a kind of critical thinking that students take with them to other courses, where the absence of material by and about women begins to be marked as a serious omission, and students start to ask openly, 'Where are the women?' In addition, students develop a complex interdisciplinary perspective that teaches them to question the 'givens' upon which knowledge is based and to analyse the non-conscious ideology of a given culture. Women's Studies classes encourage activism in and out of the classroom and our students often become campus leaders or engage in activist work in the larger community.

Women students and faculty alike assert vigorously that Women's Studies courses change their lives. Women's Studies often presents the first (and possibly only) opportunity for a student to focus on issues of critical importance to the lives of women. Women's Studies may also be the only course in which sexism, racism, anti-Semitism, heterosexism, homophobia, ageism and class bias are named and analysed and their intersection explored; where women's contributions to art, culture and history are taken seriously. For faculty, Women's Studies may provide the first legitimate opportunity to engage in feminist education.

The question most often asked of Women's Studies, 'How many men are enrolled in Women's Studies classes?' is also the question that most clearly reveals the patriarchal bias of the university. The answer, 'A steady 10 per cent which seems to be rising' is both good and bad news for Women's Studies. Although most of the men who enrol in Women's Studies appreciate the experience and take their work seriously, some are so used to being at the centre that they continue to take up far more than their fair share of space; a few take pleasure in deliberately disrupting the class.

When Women's Studies classes become an option to fulfil a general education requirement, the presence of men in our classes rises sharply, and this has generated some controversy in the Women's Studies community. The source of empowerment of Women's Studies *for women* is the fact that they feel stronger and safer when men are in the minority because so many women have been socialized into acquiesence or silence in the presence of men. This problem can be mitigated to some extent by dividing the class into sex-segregated small groups for at least part of some class hours. To the extent that the success of Women's Studies is measured by the number of men who take our classes, we may end up 'succeeding' in the eyes of the university but undermining our mission to empower women.

Gender studies

Because the study of women inevitably leads to a consideration of gender, some universities are establishing gender studies programmes either instead of, or as part of Women's Studies.[17] This trend is also discernible in the creation of new journals like *Genders* and *Gender and Society* which are still feminist in orientation. While there is no question that gender is an appropriate category of feminist analysis, and is a logical extension of feminist scholarship, I feel strongly that we must hold on to the word *women* and keep the focus on the study of women, or real women will once again be obliterated and Women's Studies subsumed. So long as the word 'woman' makes the patriarchy uncomfortable, so long do we need to insist upon its presence.

Feminist scholarship in the other disciplines

In concert with the interdisciplinary emphasis of courses located in Women's Studies programmes (or departments), feminist scholars have developed a range of discipline-based courses which are central to the development of feminist scholarship within these disciplines.[18] In spite of minor variations, there is a clearly discernible parallel development of feminist transformations across the disciplines. These may be summarized in the following categories (here given with examples from literature and art). They are not listed chronologically, because the different stages were occurring and continue to occur simultaneously:

1. The *inclusion* of women whose names were known but whose work had been ignored or trivialized: for example, Gertrude Stein, Virginia Woolf, Georgia O'Keefe, Zora Neale Hurston. Stein's literary theories and technical innovations had been dismissed, and she was known only as a 'muse' to male artists and as a collector of art; Virginia Woolf was known only as a 'lyric' novelist, but not as a feminist theorist – *Room of One's Own* and *Three Guineas* were out of print and unavailable; O'Keefe was dismissed because her flower images were seen as symbols of female sexual organs and therefore trivial; Hurston's works were out of print and she was known not as a contributor to the Harlem Renaissance, but mainly as having lived an unconventional life.

2. The *rediscovery* of 'lost' works that had fallen into oblivion: for example, *The Awakening* by Kate Chopin, *The Yellow Wallpaper* by Charlotte Perkins Gilman, *Bread Givers* by Anzia Yezierska, *Incidents in the Life of a Slave Girl* by Harriet A Jacobs, *Our Nig: Or Sketches from the Life of a Free Black* by Harriet E Wilson, *I am a Woman – and a Jew* by Leah Morton; paintings by Frieda Kahlo (who had only been known as the wife of Diego Rivera), Carrington, Gluck, sculpture by Edmonia Lewis.

3. The *re-evaluations* of women whose work had been misinterpreted from a patriarchal perspective. This category might well be said to include the work of all women. It includes lesbian re-readings of texts by Willa Cather, Emily Dickinson, Toni Morrison, paintings by Romaine Brooks.

4. The *re-evaluations* of the portrayals of women in the works of men. This category is fairly all-inclusive.

5. The *unmasking* of myths and cultural stereotypes about women on which Western civilization and the disciplines are built: for example, Pandora, Eve, Lilith, the Madonna, the whore, Sapphire, woman as witch, bitch, spinster, siren.

6. *Questioning* the validity of research results which were based only on samples of white middle-class presumed-to-be heterosexual Christian males; *challenging* the *objectivity* of their perspectives which claimed to be 'neutral'.

7. A *reconceptualization* of how knowledge is constructed and a questioning of the methodology and the basic assumptions of the disciplines.

Curriculum transformation

Recognizing that in spite of the considerable success of the Women's Studies movement, Women's Studies programmes cannot reach more than a relatively small number of the overall student population, feminist scholars began to urge that a systematic examination of the curriculum in other departments be undertaken and that the works, perspectives and accomplishments of women and minorities be included. With the help of federal funds and private foundations dozens of such curriculum transformation projects were designed and successfully implemented in the USA.[19]

Such transformation projects often bring together interested faculty from across the disciplines in small year-long seminars or intensive summer seminars. In some cases faculty receive summer salary if they participate, in others they receive a small sum to cover books and some release time from teaching. The expertise and energy for such projects usually comes from the Women's Studies programme, though some programmes refuse to become involved in transformation projects because they believe such work drains time and energy from the development of the programme's central mission. I believe that Women's Studies should not become involved in the creation of transformation projects unless the institution is willing to supply the *additional* faculty position, support staff and operating budget. Studies have shown that institutions that have strong Women's Studies programmes *and* a number of feminist scholars in traditional departments have greater success with curriculum transformation.

Transformation projects are of vital importance because they bring feminist education into the intellectual life of the larger university community where it is taken seriously and validated publicly. From this vantage point, it can also have a wider sphere of influence. Like Women's Studies, transformation projects often provide a sustaining 'life-line' for feminist scholars isolated in departments where they may not have much support for their work. They also make it possible for those who have been impressed with the force of feminist scholarship to try to understand it for themselves in an unpressured welcoming environment. It is not easy for someone who has been using a particular perspective and methodology for 20 years suddenly to question it. Transformation is a long and slow process. But if it is to happen at all, it must have a beginning somewhere.

Summary

The Women's Studies movement is part of a revolution that has spawned other revolutions. Feminist transformations of scholarship in the disciplines, curriculum-transformation projects and the curriculum-reform movement, feminist pedagogy and challenges to epistemology, the inclusion of women in affirmative-action pro- grammes, the inclusion of sexual identity as a protected category of employment and the development of gay and lesbian studies as legitimate academic pursuits can all be seen as outgrowths of Women's Studies.

Many forward-looking administrators acknowledge that the best things happening in the university today are coming out of Women's Studies. They understand that Women's Studies provides a model of what is possible in a transformed university and they would like the rest of the university to follow suit. Immodest though it may seem, I cannot help but agree.

Notes

1. The title of this essay alludes to a poem by Adrienne Rich which includes the lines, 'No one ever told us we had to study our lives, make of our lives a study. ... But there come times – perhaps this is one of them – when we have to take ourselves more seriously or die.' 'Transcendental Etude', in *The Dream of a Common Language*, New York: Norton, 1978.

2. For recent overviews of the situation in the United States see 'Women's Studies at twenty', and 'Women's Studies enters the 1990s', *The Women's Review of Books*, VI:5, February 1989 pp 13–22 and VII:5, February 1990, pp 17–31.

3. The concept of a 'chilly climate' was coined by Bernice Sandler and Roberta Hall and developed in a series of publications: *The Classroom Climate: A Chilly One for Women?* (1982); *Out of the Classroom: A Chilly Campus Climate for Women?* (1984); *The Campus Climate Revisited: Chilly for Women Faculty, Administrators, and Graduate Students* (1986). See also Yolanda Moses, *Black Women in Academe: Issues and Strategies* (1989), Project on the Status and Education of Women, Association of American Colleges, 1818 R Street, NW, Washington, DC 20009, USA.

4. This debate is documented in the pages of *The Chronicle of Higher Education* from 1988 on; discussion of the issue has not yet abated.

5. Virginia Woolf, *A Room of One's Own*, New York and Burlingame: Harcourt, Brace and World, 1929, p 101; emphasis mine. Whitehall, of course, is the seat of government in London.

6. Parallel developments in Women's Studies occurred around the world beginning in the 1970s. Eight of the nine countries represented in this volume have some form of Women's Studies programmes and all have centres for research on women.

7. Harriet Andreadis, 'Women's Studies programmes: a brief survey, *NWSAction* I:4, Winter 1988.

8. These *Directories* are available from the National Women's Studies Association, The University of Maryland, Art/Sociology Building, College Park, MD 20742, USA (priced at $5 each).

9. Mary Leonard, Staff Psychologist and Associate Professor of Counseling, University of Maryland-College Park offers this insight as a strategy for women's empowerment.

10. This may become less true as more graduate degrees in Women's Studies become available.

11. The concept of a 'paradigm shift' in the fundamental assumptions upon which a field of research is based is developed by Thomas Kuhn in *The Structure of Scientific Revolutions*: Chicago, IL: University of Chicago Press, 1964.

12. Anti-Semitism plays a part in the exclusion of Jewish material from the majority of Women's Studies classes and is part of the resistance to taking anti-Semitism seriously as a feminist issue. See Evelyn Torton Beck, 'The politics of Jewish invisibility', *NWSA Journal* I:1, Spring 1988, pp 19–29.

13. 'In America, this norm is usually defined as white, thin, male, young, heterosexual, Christian, and financially secure. It is with this mythical norm that the trappings of power reside within this society.' Audre Lorde, 'Age, race, class and sex', *Sister/Outsider*, Freedom: CA, The Crossing Press, 1984, p 116.

14. This phrase originated in Adrienne Rich's groundbreaking study: *Of Woman Born: Motherhood as Institution and Experience*, New York: Norton 1976, reissued with updated preface, 1986.

15. See Evelyn Torton Beck, 'Self-disclosure and the commitment to social change', in *Women's Studies International Forum* VI:2 (1983) pp 159–163; and Charlotte Bunch and Sandra Pollack, *Learning Our Way*, Freedom, CA: The Crossing Press, 1983; for further discussion see also Margo Culley and Cathy Portuges, *Gendered Subjects*, London: Routledge, Kegan Paul, 1985 and *Gender in the Classroom*, Champaign-Urbana: University of Illinois Press, 1990.

16. See Mary Belenky et al, *Women's Ways of Knowing*, New York: Basic Books, 1986 and Carol Gilligan, *In a Different Voice*, Boston: Harvard University Press, 1982.

17. As for example, the Women and Gender Studies Programme at Macalaster College in St Paul, Minnesota, or the Program for the Study of Women and Men in Society at the University of Southern California in Los Angeles.

18. See for example, Julia Sherman and Evelyn Torton Beck *The Prism of Sex*, Madison: University of Wisconsin Press, 1979; Dale Spender *Men's Studies Modified*, Oxford: Pergamon Press, 1981; Carol Ellen DuBois, et al, *Feminist Scholarship*, Champaign-Urbana: University of Illinois Press 1985); Christie Farnham, *The Impact of Feminist Research in the Academy*, Bloomington: University of Indiana Press, 1987.

19. These are sometimes referred to as 'mainstreaming' projects or 'balancing the curriculum'. I reject these terms because they give the impression that the process is additive. You cannot simply 'add women and stir', or, as Elizabeth Minnich put it so elegantly, 'You cannot add the concept that the world is round to the concept that the world is flat'. Such fundamental reconceptualization means transformation.

    For details of how one such recent curriculum-transformation project came to be funded by a major state university see Evelyn Torton Beck et al, 'The feminist transformation of a university: a case study', special issue of the *Women's Studies Quarterly*, Spring 1990 dedicated to curriculum transformation. About 200 such projects are underway at large state institutions and small liberal arts colleges across the United States.

Chapter 14

A Feminist University in Norway

Berit Ås

In 1985 the Feminist University opened in Norway. Ten years in the planning, one woman's radical idea became a reality. Hundreds of women helped, and funds were obtained from around the world. It even had the support of the government. Predicated on the assumption that there now exists a new feminist knowledge-base that is of critical importance in solving the complex political and ecological problems of the planet, the Norwegian Feminist University's intellectual orientation is grounded in the rationality of care. Up until this time, most of the intellectual contributions stemming from this pedagogical orientation have been made by women; great philosophers like Bertha von Suttner, who enhanced our understanding of disarmament; Rachel Carson, who established modern ecology; and Virgnia Woolf and Rosa Luxemburg, who forged a tie between feminism and human rights.

The story of the founding of the Feminist University in Norway is a personal story, one deeply interwoven with my life experiences in academia, politics and family. The story includes the initiatives, thoughts and actions of many other women in Scandinavia and around the world. Without these hundreds of women who served on committees and in work groups the Feminist University would not be a reality today. Neither would it exist if it had not been for all the hundreds of US dollars contributed, along with gifts in many different currencies raised at international conferences around the world. The contributors include women from Tibet to Groeningen, from Haifa to Umeå, and from Spetses to Mexico City and Nairobi. All contributed to a dream that has now come true.

During the ten years of planning it took to establish the Feminist University, our efforts were guided by two principles. The Feminist University was to be directed by a board of women only, and it was to be an educational institution that would teach issues from a feminist perspective, refusing to accept the philosophical orientations of

Aristotle, Descartes and Bacon. The number of students would be small in order to allow for the implementation of a democratic model of administration and a rotating leadership. It was designed to attract and admit students (predominantly women) of different ages and with different educational and religious backgrounds. All of the planning took as a given the possibility that government funding might be withdrawn so that a means of supporting the institution had to be found, preferably by combining the acquisition of knowledge with the production of goods, such as arts and crafts. Finally, it saw its main obligation as the education and rehabilitation of women who were victims of violence and discrimination.

These principles were articulated in the University's by-laws, although in the initial version of the by-laws the term feminist was not used. Now that the university has been in existance for five years, providing the opportunity to teach students the meaning of the concept of feminism, the term has assumed a central place in the institution's mission:

The goals of the feminist university consist of building a centre for education based on feminist values and feminist methods of instruction.

A decade of planning

The history of the founding of the Feminist University spans a period of ten years. In 1975 approximately 150 female social scientists gathered in Norway to discuss their research programmes. A number of feminist scholars had been studying the lost contributions of women through the ages, and shared their findings with us. We were inspired by their stories, but also furious that the contributions of our foremothers had been rendered invisible by the patriarchial educational establishment. I reasoned that, given the history of women's struggle for equal rights, what happended once might very well happen again. I suggested that one way to protect ourselves from being forgotten would be to found a women's university that would at least function as a archive for our work. To my surprise no one supported my idea. On the contrary, I was accused of espousing separatism at a time when women had finally won admittance into almost every field of study in the universities.

Despite this lack of encouragement, I decided to start looking for a building within the borders of Scandinavia in which to house my dream. I did not try to persuade those who did not agree with me, but rather worked with the few who were as worried about preserving our recent gains as I was. Given the changes that have occurred in the attitudes of young women today, I am convinced that I did the right thing.

During the 1980s a new group of young women emerged in our universities. They believe that equality between the sexes has been successfully established. Not only have they accepted the (male) media message that discrimination based on sex is a relic of the past, they have also become convinced that taking an interest in women's issues is old fashioned, even silly.

In the beginning I worked mostly as a 'lone wolf'. I searched for a building everywhere in Scandinavia. During an eight-year period six buildings were seriously considered.

The buildings

The first building I looked at was in the northern part of Finland. It had a dormitory for 40 students. One other woman explored the project with me.

The second attempt was to locate the Feminist University in two buildings in the Swedish town of Umeå. One of these buildings was part of a private school for the continuing education of adult women that had been left to the town on the condition that it continue to be used to meet women's special needs. The second house was the main part of an old farm located in the centre of town close to the university library and the Women's Studies department. The feminists in Umeå felt that the first building comprised too great a financial responsibility for them to handle and it was ultimately purchased by the Pentecostal Church. The second was 'pulled out from under us' by a leader of a study organization when we were about to make the final decision to settle there. In both endeavours a wonderful group of feminist women, many now involved in the peace movement, worked with me.

The third attempt – renting a building in southern Norway for a 5 year period – was halted when I backed away from assuming the full financial responsibility alone. On the day the contract was to be signed none of the three co-signatories appeared. I learned a valuable lesson from this experience. Women cannot be asked to assume great economic responsibility without access to capital or property to back them.

Throughout this period, all the voluntary groups I worked with were very enthusiastic about the project; but enthusiasm was not enough. I initiated a second stage of programme development by constituting a Women's University Foundation, financed soley from the proceeds of my book, *Women Unite: A Handbook for Liberation* (Ås 1981). Although this income was not tax exempt it did amount to about $7,000 – enough to get the foundation up and running.

Five women served on the board of the foundation, which started to support loosely organized women's university groups by paying office rent and hiring part-time help, as well as covering the costs of mailings, telephone bills and travel. The board was responsible for investing the funds raised to support the Feminist University from women around the world while the search for a building continued.

One thing we learned from the first phase of the attempt to find a building was how to utilize volunteer effort effectively. The volunteer group had split up into working groups to address issues of curricular development, public relations with both the local and feminist communities here and abroad, fundraising, budgeting, and organizational tasks like answering the phones and dealing with the mail. This high level of activity was a good means of including large numbers of women in the process and capitalizing on their skills. In the second stage, each group was asked to set their own schedules and define their own tasks. The board served a coordinating function. This organizational structure appears in Figure 14.1

The second phase of the effort to found a Feminist University represented a transition from an informal, voluntary non-hierarchical organizational structure to a more formal one. The board now elected a treasurer, took minutes and spent time on financial matters. Meetings became more formal and business-oriented.

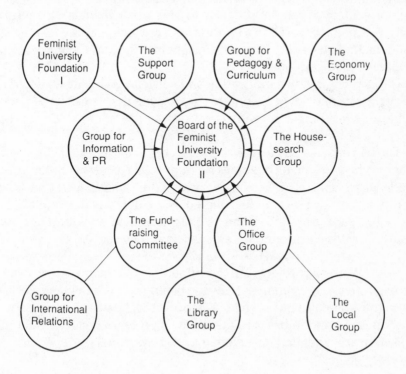

Figure 14.1 *The organizational structure of the Feminist University*

When the investigation of a fifth building became possible, it was the board that assumed responsibility for developing relations with authorities and women's organizations within the community, as well as coordinating the financial arrangements. The building's owners, the Board of the Missionary Association of Norway, became a critical element in the acquisition attempt.

A trip to look at (and temporarily to occupy) the building we were considering was organized, and the need for another organizational unit became apparent. A registered legal body was constituted to represent us. We turned to a feminist attorney at one of the most conservative law firms in Oslo to accomplish this task as the firm's credibility was impeccable.

Unfortunately, we ran into a community problem we had not anticipated. The building was a beautiful hotel built in the last part of the nineteenth century, a favourite of the German Chancellor, and the Norwegian royal family, who liked to fish for salmon in the nearby rivers. On our preliminary visit to the site, the townspeople saw members of our board drinking beer on the veranda. Following this incident, one of Norway's most colourful lay preachers had a dream in which God came to him to warn him about the anti-Christian, communist feminists. He contacted the Missionary Association about his dream and convinced the community to sell the property to him rather than us. Not surprisingly, the media covered this episode with great glee. So we lost the fifth building, though we did gain some insight into the functioning of a small fundamentalist community.

At this point my own motivation and spirit lagged. Friends urged me to get away and let a committee take over the search. I left for a semester's teaching as a visiting professor at the Mount St Vincent University, a former women's college in Halifax, Canada.

When I returned to Norway in December I learned that three communities had offered us buildings for our project. One was Løten, one of the least prosperous places in Norway. Løten had invested in a new facility for the elderly and they offered us the old one. We went to see it on New Year's Day and found it charming. The surroundings were beautiful: fields and mountains as far as one could see. We said we would be happy to rebuild it and use it, but we wanted the council's unanimous support (Women's projects are too vulnerable to become issues in local party politics!). I was impressed by the beauty of this house as I reflected on all the women's houses I had visited around the world, many of them in slum areas and in bad condition. This building's beauty would heal broken hearts and lift depression in a few days' time.

Early days

The day the Feminist University opened in August 1985, the Conservative minister for womens's affairs gave the opening speech. The
Farmer's Party's female representative on the parliamentary committee
who, like me, was a member of the Women's University* Board, spoke
about its cultural significance. The Labour Party leader in Løten thanked
the lay minister for sending us to his home district. The Liberal Party's
woman representative, who had once chaired that party and was now
the ombudsman for the National Committee on Equality Between the
Sexes greeted the crowd. I, a former leader of the Socialist Left,
introduced our curriculum. It was like a scene out of a fairy tale. But I
know that the day might come again when the parties would no longer
allow their members to support feminist causes.

The city government of Løten was not convinced of the unique
character of the new university until they visited China and saw an
article on the front page of the *China Daily* about the Women's
University of Norway, located in a part of Norway about which the
Chinese had never until that day heard.

Opening day was not accomplished without a struggle. That spring we
were unprepared for the news that the building needed extensive
repairs before it was safe for use. An American feminist I had met in New
York responded to my desperate call for help. She had told me that if we
ever got into trouble we could count on her. Well, we were in trouble,
and I picked up the telephone. I told her my name and said, 'I am in
trouble'. After a short silence she asked, 'How much'? A cheque for one
million Norwegian crowns ($137,000) arrived from New York on the very
day the Feminist University opened – a delightful coincidence.

The university gained an unlikely financial credibility from a
journalist for Norway's largest conservative newspaper who misread
the amount of the cheque and reported it to be ten times what it was. A
miracle, perhaps.

There have been many commitments, strategies, yes, miracles over
the last fifteen years. We never told people about the donation except on
opening day because we wanted the support of the government for our
enterprise. We knew that if we could survive the first two or three years
of operation there was a good chance of gaining government endorse-
ment and funds.

Indeed, when the head of the department of education visited us in
1986 he shook his head in amazement and insisted that we had

---

*The official Norwegian title is correctly translated 'The Women's University'.
It is referred to as 'Feminist' because of a 1989 by-law change which includes a
paragraph stating that this is an alternative feminist institution.

accomplished the impossible. 'It is difficult to walk on water', he said. I confided that the first two steps had been the toughest, but that after that it was easy! A radio reporter repeated the story locally and it was picked up by a journalist for the Christian paper where it appeared with the headline, 'Now Berit Ås walks on water!' Another miracle.

Commitments were expressed in donations from 100 community councils around the country. The fundraising committee had requested a donation of one crown for every adult woman in the community if they had not done enough for their women during the UN Decade of Women. Fortunately, the woman on the parliamentary committee for education backed the Feminist University when it was suggested that we could not receive government funds because we did not occupy a line in the state budget. 'Let us construct a category for them', she said.

And they did. In 1987 the Feminist University received 600,000 Norwegian crowns ($100,000) in government support. That was doubled in 1988 and last year we were allocated 2,200,000 crown ($350,000). This year's budget is in excess of 5,000,000 Norwegian crowns ($800,000).

It was critically important to protect the women members of the board from having to assume any personal financial responsibility for the board's collective actions. So, on 23 August 1983, the Women's University Foundation was formally registered. The signing was held in one of the rooms of the Norwegian Parliament.

Our by-laws are of interest because they were constructed to codify our special mission as a university and to specify the composition of our board as exclusively women. Our claim to be a new kind of teaching institution was challenged but when the protests reached the department of administrative affairs and the department of justice the challenges were denied through the efforts of female ministers in both bodies. The specification of a board composed of women only was potentially more controversial as it was contrary to the Norwegian law of equality between the sexes. However, as our attorney pointed out, any move to tamper with the composition of our university's board would have raised parallel questions about the considerable overrepresentation of men on the boards of the traditional universities. The matter was dropped.

Politics of the Feminist University

Historically, research pertinent to the poor, the underprivileged, the weak, the disadvantaged, has been the property of the establishment. Even though there exists a literature relevant to the acquisition and maintenance of power, that literature is not made accessible to those who might use its findings to advance their cause. Needless, to say, those who have the most use for this information (workers, citizens of the Third World, proponents of peace, feminists) are not in the position to fund the studies they need to produce effective change. It is important to make the results of research about weak and oppressed groups available to them so that they can use the knowledge to improve their situations,

For example, it is the responsibility of the Feminist University to help women who have been battered, who have been oppressed, or who have been victims of discrimination in their work and professions, to understand the dynamics of their situations in order to change them. The psychological literature relevant to sex differences in attributions for success and failure is pertinent to understanding why women are less likely than men to see themselves as having great ability, and more likely than men to see themselves as personally responsible for failure. Because women are oppressed regardless of their race or class or socioeconomic status, information such as this is critical to understanding the plight of women from all educational and economic backgrounds.

Given the breadth of the problem and the need to reach women who vary greatly in educational training and experience one might ask why it is necessary to insist on founding a university. Why not just a house, an institute or a foundation? The reason is that only a university is appropriate to the task. The evidence on which the arguments to halt the oppression of women are made is scientific. It is based on methodologically sound research findings. And the educational mission of those who chose to teach in the Feminist University is both rigorous and demanding. Educating a diverse student body is a pedagogical challenge that few traditional universities have accepted. These are elite institutions. The Feminist University is a university for *every* woman. Finally, the status of a university conveys the value with which the work of women scholars must be imbued if we are to be successful in accomplishing our mission.

During the 1970s women's struggle for liberation resulted in a number of initiatives. Refuges for women were established by women. Feminist journals sprang up everywhere. Centres for research on women were established at many traditional universities. However, as time went by, it became clear that these initiatives were vulnerable because they were not interconnected. This raised the question of what kind of comprehensive programme to construct to alleviate this problem. Iceland provided one model. A feminist party had been established there and there was a network of women's crisis centres that extended across national boundaries. But the insufficient funds allocated to these centres, coupled with the relative poverty of both their clients and staffs made it clear that a mechanism to encourage the collaboration of feminist women from all walks of life – including law and politics as well as those involved in grassroots organizations – was required.

It would take the efforts of all these women to plan, fund and build a women's university. It would take architects, planners, economists and educators along with researchers and public-relations specialists. Outreach to grassroots organizations for women would be needed, as would an international network of support. Financial concerns had to be considered and women politicians recruited to help. Finally, a feminist model for finance, administration and education had to be developed. In this regard the work of Jo Freeman, Adrienne Rich and Dale Spender was invaluable. The task was enormous. It was also exciting.

One of the pedagogical challenges was to construct a vocabulary to express the social reality of women: to describe the feminist universe. As Dale Spender had so clearly demonstrated, all educational institutions practise discrimination against women, albeit unconsciously. Separate classes for the victims of discrimination were seen as one way to redress this problem. Male misogyny could not be tolerated in the classroom, conscious or unconscious. Ths history of women in women's colleges in the USA appeared instructive. If women's separate education provided women with a competitive edge in the patriarchal marketplace there, it ought to be equally effective in Norway.

Other pedagogical issues were also seriously considered. To the extent that women's morality (Gilligan 1982) was different from men's this was a factor to take into account, along with differences in women's rationality (Halså 1988). From these feminist concepts grew new paradigms to build theory upon.

Clearly, establishing a feminist university was both a political and an educational necessity. The Feminist University could play a critical role in the process of integrating feminist theory into the scientific disciplines. As Peggy MacIntosh (1986) has suggested, this process has many phases. In the beginning there is often no support for the notion of a feminist perspective on science that is different from the prevailing (objective) one. But gradually the recognition that women's status may give rise to a perspective that is uniquely their own does occur. Often the short-term solution is to add a page or two describing this perspective to standard texts. But recognition is not integration, In fact, it is at this point that real resistance to change begins. Women students may rise up to protest the masculine bias in science, to contest the construction of general theories that do not fit the female experience. Here feminist scholarly analysis poses a threat to conventional knowledge and truth. The fourth step in the process is signalled by the advent of women's studies programmes espousing a comprehensive feminist perspective. Here there is a special place for the feminist university where feminist research and theory can grow and mature unchallenged by patriarchy.

At some future point feminist theory and knowledge will have be compared to conventional patriarchal wisdom. We cannot now know what the outcome of the intellectual confrontation will be.

Commitment and conflict

The story of the development of the Feminist University is not free of conflict. Originally, there were opposing views about the advisability of establishing a feminist university at all. Later, conflicts arose over its mission. Some argued that establishing a university that did not have stringent entrance requirements would discredit women's scholarship. Some Marxist and socialist feminists left the project at an early phase. Conservative (heterosexual) women took for granted that their concerns about sexist treatment would not be relevant. Women in some peace groups did not find the principle of tolerance for differences acceptable when it could, in principle, extend to tolerance for problems of women in the military. Many women became discouraged because the project confronted so many obstacles and was forced to take so many detours.

Although space prohibits a full discussion of conflict resolution, we did rely heavily on the assistance of a feminist minister who was also a member of the board, and had professional training in crisis management. One lesson we learned was that to implement non-hierarchical organizational structures successfully requires clear boundaries and divisions of labour as well as carefully worded mandates for action among subgroups, rendering the assignment of tasks a very complicated endeavour.

The Feminist University today

The Feminist University consists of a main building and three small houses, including a spacious children's house. There is a barn and 150 acres of land, a third of which is good for farming. Twenty-eight overnight guests can be housed on campus and other accommodation is available in the immediate vicinity. The houses have three lecture halls, seminar rooms, a library, common rooms and a pottery shop.

Courses, lectures, seminars and thematic gatherings comprise the curriculum. Some of these have been arranged independently, others in conjunction with the state labour bureau, voluntary study groups, the environmental movement, and the labour movement's study organizations. Seven focal areas represent the perspectives through which all courses are considered:

- ecology;
- power and solidarity;
- female culture and creative activity;
- feminist critiques of technology;
- alternative economics and production; and
- the ethics of care and feminist theology   (Skjønsberg et al 1990).

These focal areas meet a series of challenges provided by the times in which we live. Courses developed to explore these issues last anywhere from one day to one year. Some are offered for credit, others are non-credit. Currently, there are about 100 students on campus every day and plans are underway to increase the student body to 200.

Students come from neighbouring towns and communities as well as from all over the country. A course on administration and leadership from a feminist perspective has proved to be especially attractive. Women refugees, and some men, attend courses. There have been seminars for women politicians and female peace activists from all over Scandinavia. One international course has been offered in construction and gardening. Overall, approximately 2,000 students a year attend the variety of courses offered.

We are working on plans to extend the courses to the graduate level and to start a research centre. During the last year our research foundation achieved tax-free status and the funds are increasing slowly. We hope to restore some rooms in the near future so that we can house visiting scholars to stay with us to do research, teach and renew themselves.

Recently, we were honoured to have Margaret Fulton, the retired president of Mount St Vincent University, spend eight months with us as a visiting scholar. She repeatedly advised us to remain small. We are committed to following her advice. Rather than expanding our facilities in Løten, we are trying to move toward establishing small units around the world. This means we have continued needs for growth and development.

During the original discussions about the Women's University, women from the North of Norway asked why this valuable resource was to be located in the prosperous South, once more excluding their direct involvement. Three years ago the county council of Nordland, an area partly inside the Polar Circle, allocated a large sum of money to start a pilot project. Women from three communities visited Løten, and I have offered to assist them in building a decentralized university structure.

Following two trips to Spain to speak about the Feminist University, we have received requests from Malaga for information about forming a unit there. Another initiative has begun in Mexico City. The former president of the Feminist University in Norway, Ingrid Morken, travelled to Palestine as a United Nations consultant to analyse the educational needs of the adult female population there. She suggested using the Løten model to establish a facility in Palestine.

In January I visited Overtorneå, a town in Sweden, near the Finnish border. The women in the area showed me their beautiful high school, with a dormitory and extensive equipment which are seldom used. I suggested the possibility of establishing an exchange programme between Halifax, Canada and Overtorneå for women of Nordic descent whose ancestors migrated to Canada generations ago. A similar programme might be offered to Finnish and Soviet women from Murmansk and Karelen. The possibilites are virtually endless. The age of the feminist university has just begun.

References

Ås, B (1981), *Kvinner i alle land: Handbok i frigiøring (Women unite: Handbook for liberation)*, Oslo: Aschehoug & Co.

Gilligan, C (1982), *In a Different Voice: Psychological Theory and Women's Development*, Cambridge, MA: Harvard University Press.

Halså, B (1988), A feminist utopia, *Scandinavian Political Studies*, vol 11, no 4.

MacIntosh, P, lecture by the author at the Greek Women's Studies Organization (SPETSES) Conference in Kegmeg, Greece, summer 1986.

Skjønsberg, E (1990), *The Feminist University of Norway: A Demographic Profile of a Feminist University*, Løten: The Feminist University Press.

Chapter 15
Strategies for Change
Virginia E O'Leary and *Suzanne Stiver Lie*

Women scholars, whether or not they consider themselves feminists, need to be cognizant of our place in history. Women's studies courses have sprung up on campuses all over the world, and they have helped to legitimize the study of women, but we have a long way left to go to attain equality and real social change. Indeed, it is important that we understand the process by which change occurs so that more can be encouraged.

It is important that the new knowledge based on feminist re-vision of history, art and science – a revision that spawned intellectual history and challenged the literary canon – be included into the academic curriculum. We need to make salient the issues that should be addressed from a woman's perspective that are not limited to 'women's issues'. The inclusion of case material in the present volume is intended to provide a basis for comparison across the experience of a diverse group of women in a range of cultures; to move readers away from their tendency toward nationalistic myopia. We hope that women actively engaged in creating change in their own lives, at their home institutions and within the borders of their nations will find the book both intellectually interesting and pragmatically useful.

Within the pages of this volume, one can find creative solutions to common problems experienced by academic women. As Jessie Bernard has so provocatively noted we live in the period of 'feminist enlightenment'; a near revolution caused by women writing, discussing and publishing – demonstrating the effect that words can have (Bernard 1989). That revolution was made possible in part by the availability of women role models, although many more are needed if the feminist enlightenment is to be successful in extending its range of influence to extend to the entire academy.

The strategies employed by women intent upon storming the tower and taking their due over the last twenty years can be organized into three categories: personal, institutional and governmental. Numerous examples of these approaches can be found in the case studies included in this volume. In this final chapter we will attempt to summarize some of the strategies that have been most successful at each of these three levels and to provide some additional illustrative material.

Personal strategies

At the individual level, the most common strategy for women who have been denied access to the ivory tower – or promotion once they arrived – is to fight back through the formal grievance mechanisms available to them. Although much has been learned about ways of dealing with the system from the experiences of individual women (for example the importance of asking for agreements and feedback in writing), the personal cost associated with fighting is generally high and most often unsuccessful. For example, in her book, *The Campus Troublemakers: Academic Women in Protest* (1986), Athena Theodore presents a depressing picture of what it was like for women in the heyday of the US women's movement (1970 to the early 1980s), to challenge the sexist practices of universities and colleges. Full of hope, high expectations and confidence in the judicial system women filed internal and external grievances and complaints when they were denied comparable salaries, contract renewal, tenure, or promotion. Few protestors were successful, and the institutions against which they complained remained unchanged. Support was hard to obtain regardless of whether it was social, psychological, legal or financial. Apathy and fear prevented colleagues from coming forward to assist, and unions were hesitant to take up women's causes. Most disturbingly, the protest experience had a 'strong negative impact' on the protesters regardless of whether they won or lost. Theodore concludes that one clear lesson to be learned from the experience of the 470 academic women protesters she interviewed is that the next stage of revolt must be better organized, more unified, and widespread. Alliances with outside political groups are essential.

In West Germany, students and faculty have worked together to effect change collectively by developing a week-long 'summer university' for women. First organized at the Free University of Berlin in 1975, the summer university now attracts some 7500 women from all over the country and is partially subsidized by public funds. Employed women even obtain paid leave to attend. However, the courses are not for credit and many of those who attend are not regular students, so while the effort has assisted women generally it has not addressed the status of academic women directly.

Institutional strategies

Strategies to effect change in the status of women at the institutional level have met with greater success, especially when they have involved the adoption of formal policies for evaluation and promotion in which the criteria are stated explicitly. The Affirmative Action Plan guidelines developed at York University, Toronto, Canada illustrate this point.

At York, each academic unit is required to formulate its own plan to create an adequate pool of women applicants for positions, a prerequisite for increasing the proportion of women faculty in that unit, the overall goal of affirmative action. The university has an implementation committee comprised of three faculty members and three administrators. The committee, established in July 1988, makes a positive or negative recommendation to the president on every hiring and promotion decision in the university. Every unit is required to appoint a representative to the committee. That representative is trained by the committee in the development of affirmative-action plans and is responsible for seeing that a plan is submitted to the committee from that unit for approval.

Each plan calls for the unit to collect background information on its current affirmative-action status, to set goals for the proportion of women faculty to be hired and promoted in that unit and to access this information in the light of the availability of women in the discipline in question in Canada as well as abroad. Each unit is expected to identify ways to increase the pool of women applicants applying for positions through sex-neutral recruiting procedures and to minimize the bias at the level of the search committee. Efforts are made to ensure that women are adequately represented in the interview process and that they are given opportunities to be evaluated fully and fairly. A unit's failure to comply with its own affirmative-action procedures can result in the committee making a negative recommendation to the president on their preferred candidate – an incentive for them to adhere to their guidelines carefully. The fact that the committee was mandated as part of the faculty's most recent collective-bargaining agreement explains, at least in part, the ability of the women faculty to wield this much power. The strong support of several women full professors is another critical component of the strategy's success.

Another example of an institutional strategy comes from the University of Tennessee at Chattanooga, where a 'Grow Your Own Program' has been established to encourage ethnic-minority students to obtain graduate degrees at other institutions and then return as faculty members. One such student, a Black woman currently working on a PhD in developmental psychology, will join the UT, Chattanooga faculty as an assistant professor once she receives her degree at the University of Virginia.

Institutional change in higher education can be most effectively accomplished through well-presented and documented arguments. Here, access to data is critical. It can be used to assess the status of women and to monitor their progress. Interestingly, Women's Studies programmes backed by administrators as a means of isolating 'the woman problem', have been particularly skilled at collecting and using data to transform the institutions the administrators were trying to protect. This has been true despite the vulnerability of Women's Studies programmes to arbitrary budget cuts.

In 1982, West German activists in Women's Studies issued a memorandum to the ministry of education urging that the proportion of women faculty in the universities be increased to 50 per cent. This memorandum was based on their analysis of the inequitable distribution of women and men throughout the university system nationwide. In 1987, Israel created a coordinator of the status of women in universities to analyse issues related to the status of female students and faculty in the universities, and in order to propose solutions to existing problems. One solution involved providing women faculty with the option of holding a part-time appointment during the year in which they have borne a child. Those who chose this alternative are assured that it will not adversely affect their status or their tenure decision.

Appointing a person or a group to monitor women's progress, generate data and plan programmes to assist women in achieving their rightful place within institutions appears to be a critical element in all the strategies that have been successful at the institutional level. Of course, these strategies have the potential to be even more effective if they are implemented as government policies.

Political strategies

Despite women's frequent involvement in the political process as grassroots organizers, they have until recently been less assertive than men in using the political system to lobby for their causes. This is true even in those countries where equality between the sexes is constitutionally guaranteed such as India and the United States.

Norway provides an example of a country where women have been particularly effective in using the governmental apparatus to advance their cause within the nation's universities. The Norwegian Research Council for Science and the Humanities represents the success of a carefully planned initiative aimed at increasing the number of Norwegian women engaged in research as well as coordinating and promoting research on women.

Since the late 1960s there has been a gradual and unobtrusive incorporation of feminist values into the institutional structure of the Norwegian state, a phenomenon Hernes (1987) refers to as state feminism. This has been possible because of the value Norwegian society places on equality. Today, Norway is often likened to a 'modern matriarchy' because of women's success in the realm of politics. It set a world record in politics in 1986 with a female head of state and eight women out of 18 Cabinet members. Although this record was set under the Social Democrats' regime, the coalition government of non-social-democratic parties now in power has been pressured to follow suit, guaranteeing an almost equal representation of women in their government in order to be elected. Today, 36 per cent of the members of the national assembly are women. Equally impressive are the figures at the county and municipal levels.

The brainchild of feminist researchers, the Secretariat for Women and Research of the Norwegian National Research Council owes its existence to the efforts of women both inside and outside the university. In 1974, the research council adopted a policy to strengthen women's research. The secretariat, which has national status, was instituted on a trial basis in 1977. Its mission was to support and facilitate research on women in the social sciences. In 1982 the council's equal-opportunity committee recommended that the secretariat become interdisciplinary and that its mandate be broadened to include women in the humanities, the natural sciences and technology. When the trial period of three years expired and the secretariat was in danger of being disbanded in 1985, women's groups all over the country mobilized their forces to save it. Due in large measure to the support of women in the political parties, female members of parliament and women union members, the secretariat was not only saved, but at its recent evaluation early this year was established as a permanent body. Not surprisingly, features of the secretariat's model have been adopted in other Scandinavian countries.

In 1986, the government set aside funds for the appointment of qualified women to the position of full professor at the universities. Since 1986, several women have been appointed as full professors and their appointments have been the primary reason for the increase in the percentage of women full professors in the country from 4 per cent in 1985 to 6 per cent in 1987. Other policy changes are in the making. The *Government Report to the Parliament on Research 1988/89* (p 54), recommends that:

1) women's perspective must to a greater extent be incorporated into Norwegian research; 2) 40 per cent of research scholarships should be reserved for members of the under-represented sex; 3) selection committees for faculty posts must include at least one woman when there are female applicants; 4) female researchers with extra workloads because they are women should be given priority when research leave and funds are distributed.*

Conclusion

Although success stories such as the Norwegian are encouraging, it is important to keep in mind that there continues to exist a great disparity between the rhetoric and reality of equality in higher education. It is essential that the disparity be made salient to the general public both because real social change depends on broad-based societal support, and because so many young women have blindly accepted the myth of equality and must be convinced of the importance of supporting feminist initiatives.

In order to take the tower we must rely on persistence, negotiation and publicity. We must work at the individual, institutional and governmental levels simultaneously. The strategies offered here will be more or less successful depending on the sociopolitical context in which they are applied. Those who wish to use one or more of them to change the system in which they operate should be mindful of the need to modify them to fit their specific situations.

The assault on the tower has met a modicum of success to date and will not be turned back as long as we remember that we are not alone: we have sisters around the world ready to support us, consult with us and cheer us on.

References

Bernard, Jessie (1989), Educating the majority: the feminist enlightenment, in Carol S Pearson, Donna L Shavlik and Judith G Touchton (eds), *Educating the Majority: Women Challenge Tradition in Higher Education*, London: American Council on Education, Macmillan Publishing Company.

Hernes, Helga M (1987), *Welfare State and Woman Power: Essays in State Feminism*, Oslo: Norwegian University Press.

Norway, Ministry of Cultural and Scientific Affairs (1990), *Report No 28 to the Norwegian 'Storting' (1988–89): On Research*, Oslo: Ministry of Education and Research.

Theodore, Athena (1986), *The Campus Troublemakers: Academic Women in Protest*, Houston, TX: Cap and Gown.

*These recommendations were praised in a later parliamentary treatment of the government report. Only point 3 was regarded as difficult to implement because of the extra burden this proposal might cause female faculty members in some disciplines. Nevertheless, they recommended that this proposal should be carried out as far as possible.

Index